How to Set Up
Information Systems

How to Set Up Information Systems

A non-specialist's guide to the Multiview approach

Simon Bell and Trevor Wood-Harper

Earthscan Publications Ltd
London • Sterling, VA

First published in the UK and USA in 2003
by Earthscan Publications Ltd

Copyright © Simon Bell and Trevor Wood-Harper, 2003

All rights reserved

Previous edition (*Rapid Information Systems Development*) published in 1998 by
McGraw-Hill, Maidenhead

ISBN: 1 85383 958 2 paperback
       1 85383 957 4 hardback

Typesetting by MapSet Ltd, Gateshead, UK
Printed and bound in the UK by Scotprint, Haddington, Scotland
Cover design by Danny Gillespie

For a full list of publications please contact:

Earthscan Publications Ltd
120 Pentonville Road, London, N1 9JN, UK
Tel: +44 (0)20 7278 0433
Fax: +44 (0)20 7278 1142
Email: earthinfo@earthscan.co.uk
Web: **www.earthscan.co.uk**

22883 Quicksilver Drive, Sterling, VA 20166-2012, USA

Earthscan is an editorially independent subsidiary of Kogan Page Ltd and publishes in
association with WWF-UK and the International Institute for Environment and
Development

A catalogue record for this book is available from the British Library

Library of Congress Cataloging-in-Publication Data

Bell, Simon, 1957-.
   How to set up information systems : a non-specialist's guide to the Multiview
   approach / Simon Bell and Trevor Wood-Harper.
      p. cm.
   Includes bibliographical references and index.
   ISBN 1-85383-958-2 (paperback) — ISBN 1-85383-957-4 (hardback)
   1. System design—Amateurs' manuals. 2. System analysis—Amateurs' manuals.
   3. Electronic digital computers—Amateurs' manuals. I. Wood-Harper, A. T. II. Title

QA76.9.S88B416 2003
004.2'1—dc21

                                                              2003008346

This book is printed on elemental-chlorine-free paper

CONTENTS

LIST OF FIGURES AND TABLES

Figures

Tables

PREFACE

This book is intended as a practitioner's guide for those users who are intending to plan and develop information systems, that is: become involved with the process of systems analysis and systems design (SA&SD). Our key focus is 'sustainable' information systems. Sustainability here is taken to mean not cheating on the future but building systems with a view to the needs of tomorrow. The tendency to build systems for yesterday's needs is an ever present tension.

The authors recognize that many other approaches are possible in this complex and evolving field and that greater depth of understanding than that which arises from reading one book will be required before exponents could be said to have achieved mastery of all the techniques included here. Nevertheless the authors believe that, as when they first engaged with the contents of this book in 1992, there is a lack of understanding in the information system planning profession of the need for planning tools for non-IT specialists (sometimes referred to as 'high end users') and that these tools do exist and can be understood and applied by non-specialists relatively quickly. This book should be seen as an introduction to the information systems development process and as a guide to one particular method. It is to be hoped that this may encourage more professionals working in this field to write valuable materials for non-specialists.

Our sincere hope is to encourage managers and users to grasp the initiative and take an active part in the information systems which affect – and at times afflict – them.

The authors welcome any constructive comments and observations arising from the application of principles contained in this text, especially from users working in situations of rapid change and minimal time for long drawn out development procedures. This book is written in recognition of the need to draw together 'clean' theory and what is often 'dirty' practice in one view.

The examples used in this book are amalgams brought together from field experience, theory, teaching and anecdote. They do not represent any one single context. Any resemblance to any real organization is coincidental.

Simon Bell (s.g.bell@open.ac.uk)
Trevor Wood-Harper (a.t.wood-harper@salford.ac.uk)
April 2003

ACKNOWLEDGEMENTS

The authors wish to express their gratitude to many collaborators and friends from both the developing and industrial worlds. Fellow-travellers, often struggling with information systems concepts of formidable complexity, are the silent collaborators who made this book possible. As well as all the postgraduate students and hardworking professionals who have used and commented on the methods included here, special thanks should be extended to Guo, Yong Hong and Mingzhe in China, Angus and Yusaf in Pakistan, Iqbal and Shahjahan in Bangladesh, Adewole and Efiong in Nigeria as well as Gilroy, Hugh, Martin and Ian in the UK who worked with us, provided us with much support in the application of this approach in developing countries and were always willing to share comments and insights.

Words fail to express the gratitude which the authors owe their families for their support and patience since 1992 as this book has taken form and evolved.

Special thanks are due to Rachel Furze for much of the artwork in this edition.

LIST OF ACRONYMS AND ABBREVIATIONS

DA	data analysis
DOS	disk operating system
DSS	decision support system
ETHICS	effective technical and human implementation of computer-based systems
FD	flow diagram
GIS	geographic information system
GST	general systems theory
HAS	human activity system
HCI	human–computer interface
IS	information system
ISAC	information systems and analysis of change
IT	information technology
JSD	Jackson system development
KADS	an expert systems development methodology
LAN	local area network
LEA	local education authority
M&E	monitoring and evaluation
MIS	management information system
NGO	non-governmental organization
OOP	object orientated programming
PC	personal computer
RAD	rapid applications development
SA&SD	systems analysis and systems design
SSA	structured systems analysis
SSADM	structured systems analysis and design methodology
SSM	soft systems methodology
STRADIS	structured analysis, design and implementation of information systems
STS	socio-technical system
SWOT	strengths, weaknesses, opportunities, threats
TS	technical specification
WAN	wide area network
WWW	World Wide Web
YSM	Yourdon systems method

INTRODUCTION TO THE BOOK

Purpose

It was not the authors' intention to produce a work of pure systems analysis and systems design (SA&SD) theory. If this is what the reader is hoping to find then he or she will be disappointed. Nor was it our intention to provide readers with an idealized analysis and design procedure. This book is about doing systems analysis and systems design under conditions where the only alternative to rule of thumb methods is to not use any methods at all. This book is intended for those whom the information systems profession would refer to as amateurs but we prefer to label as non-specialists. It is aimed at assisting non-specialists in doing the preparatory work (called systems analysis and systems design or SA&SD) which should occur before an information system is purchased, developed and installed. We wish to assist those involved in doing this work because, to date, there has been very little support for them in their travail unless they proposed undertaking a three-year university degree or expensive professional training courses, sometimes of dubious value.

Tools and methodology

This book does not contain pure examples of applied methodology. Almost all the examples discussed here are drawn from work undertaken in the challenging environment of developing countries where computer awareness and computer systems development remain in their infancy and where the 'digital divide' ensures that minimal resources are wickedly linked to massive need. Therefore the analysis and design tools discussed here have had to be adopted and adapted rapidly when there has been little time and in low support environments (low support in terms of poor climatic conditions, poor infrastructure and low awareness among stakeholders in the IT systems). Nevertheless, we believe that an adapt and adopt approach used in imperfect conditions is better than no approach to planning at all and it is with this in mind that the following is offered. We further believe that from the use of these tools can arise systems of real value and of enduring, sustainable productivity.

The main method set out in this book is a variant of Multiview (Avison and Wood-Harper 1990), builds on a learning process with this approach (Bell 1996) and following this the previous work of Bell and Wood-Harper (1998). However, it also contains a number of other analysis and design approaches which have been adapted from their original state to meet the needs of variable situations. The approaches have been adapted in the light of participatory and thoughtful consideration with the stakeholders in information systems (IS). If the adaptations made here are offensive to the authors of these approaches we offer our apologies but also invite their consideration of our central point:

In learning how to provide an analysis and design tool for non-specialists, the authors believe that it is necessary first to understand the perspective of the stakeholders in the proposed IS, second to agree with them what they can usefully achieve and third to adapt analysis and design tools in the light of this learning.

Structure

This book attempts to provide the user with an understandable set of rules of thumb for planning an information system without there being 'experts' available to fall back on. As a 'user's guide' this text does not go into great detail concerning the theoretical context of the planning tools we apply. A list of suggested reading for further study is included.

The book is organized so as to reduce the amount of time which the reader has to spend on areas which may not be of immediate interest. Implicit in the approach we are adopting here is the understanding that in many situations where information systems are required there is not always a lot of time to carry out in-depth planning. Because of this, a focus on sustainable information system planning or development techniques is required to enable organizations in developing effective information systems. With this in mind we will briefly outline the structure of the book.

Chapters

The chapters are organized so as to cover the sequence of activities involved in planning any potential information system. Each chapter is structured as follows:

- **Keywords:** a listing of the major keywords and expressions dealt with in the body of the chapter.
- **Summary:** a brief summary of the topics and issues dealt with in the chapter.
- **Main text:** Chapter 1 provides an introduction to information systems while Chapter 2 describes systems analysis and systems design in more detail and Chapter 3 considers the role of the systems planner or systems analyst. Chapters 4–9 contain a step-by-step explanation of the working of our analysis and design methodology and contain examples of each stage. In Chapter 10 everything is brought together at the final stage and training, software and hardware selection, and implementation are considered. A case study of a government department dealing with roads in a developing country is used an an example.
- **Systems analysis schedule:** a schedule of the progress of the planning process is provided as we go through. This is not intended to be absolute but should provide the reader with a rough guide as to the amount of time to be devoted to each activity in the planning process.
- **Exercise:** Chapters 1–9, which deal with the fivefold aspects of the Multiview methodology we use, each conclude with a tutorial or sequence of exercises. These are intended to be of value if the book is to be used directly as a stimulus to the planning process in an organization or set as an introductory text in analysis and design teaching. Suggested answers to the exercises are given in Appendix 3.

Appendices

Since we are dealing chiefly with the *practical details* of planning, unnecessary theory which may be of interest but is not central to this theme is located in *theory appendices* (Appendices 1 and 2) at the back of the book. Each provides the reader with further insights into the subject.

Appendix 3 sets out one particular approach to answering the exercises in the tutorials.

Glossary of buzzwords

Much of the vocabulary used in information systems and information technology (IT) related areas consists of jargon. Some jargon is useful and some is unavoidable. In order to assist the non-specialist all major jargon and abbreviations used in the text are covered in the glossary.

Suggested reading and references

Suggestions for further reading dealing with specific topics in each chapter and in the technical appendices are given, with full details of these and other publications in the alphabetical list of references.

CHAPTER 1

INFORMATION SYSTEMS AND ORGANIZATIONS

KEYWORDS: sustainability, planning, change, risk, failure, learning organization, methods

SUMMARY: Information as a commodity is briefly discussed. The sustainability of information systems is introduced and the need for information systems planning is introduced and described. Incidental virtues of information systems planning (eg, learning about and with your organization, developing an understanding of the stakeholders, assumptions and mindsets of colleagues) are discussed. Common problems with information systems are reviewed.

Introduction

It may appear to be obvious but information systems (IS) are supposed to inform people. In the process of planning or development it is advisable never to lose sight of this primary objective. By informing, the information system assists people or 'users' to make intelligent decisions based upon good information derived in turn from reliable data. Therefore, if the information to be used is:

- poorly gathered and sorted;
- inadequately edited;
- incorrectly analysed or analysed under the wrong assumptions;
- analysed for the wrong things; or
- badly presented;

The information system will probably fail in its primary function. This in turn has a knock-on effect on decision-making, the results of which feed through to the effectiveness of the organization as a whole. Therefore any information system needs to be carefully planned in terms of:

- The data to be gathered.
- The information products being derived from the data.
- The ultimate knowledge which is thought by the planner to be the final requirement of the system (this can be a very difficult thing to define).

In our experience, it is all too often the case that an information system will be designed prior to anyone having asked what question(s) it is intended to answer. Thus, incorrect data is gathered, inappropriate information products are generated and insufficient knowledge is derived for effective decision-making.

Organizations of all kinds, be they small private companies, non-governmental agencies or large government departments, are primarily users and producers of information. Information is a most versatile and pliable commodity. Literally anything which leads to any form of action could be seen as being information. A kick in the rear, an impact or sustainability indicator or a bank statement are informative and could lead to action, maybe immediate or delayed, possibly positive or negative, experienced as brief or sustained.

It is worth briefly describing some of the major attributes of information systems:

- They deal with endlessly changing commodities – the need for knowledge and the proliferation of data.
- They are required to facilitate decision-making.
- They exist in all organizations.
- They are vital to an organization's function.
- They are increasingly thought of primarily as computer-based applications.
- They are frequently badly planned.

An information system, particularly a computer-based information system, can appear to be efficient and yet be experienced by end users as being unhelpful or even hostile. There can be many reasons for this, some of which we look at in the second section of this chapter, 'Information systems: A catalogue of failures?'. At this point we need to make clear that an information system is rarely isolated but is an integral and integrated part of the wider organizational system.

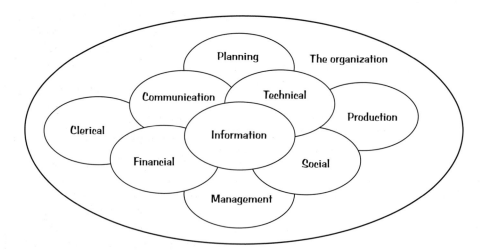

Figure 1.1 *Linked aspects*

The way in which an organization functions is very often experienced by those within and those outside as being highly complex. Information systems impinge upon most of the features of organizations. Therefore, as well as being established on technically sound principles, the planning process needs to be both diligent and sensitive to organizational needs and user thinking.

When we refer to 'organizational needs and user thinking' we mean such common issues as:

- Lack of experience of the planning or systems analysis and systems design (SA&SD) process in the recipient community.
- Senior management reluctance to adopt suggested change.
- Staff reluctance to adopt new practices and procedures.
- Absence of local, reliable support for incoming systems.
- Sense of risk and uncertainty in a new endeavour.
- Staff too stretched to accommodate changes gladly or to be able to provide time and effort to working with the development of a new technology.
- Distrust of change processes.

This book is designed to introduce one means for effective information systems planning for organizations whilst taking into account this range of issues.

Whilst not wishing to give the impression that information systems in use today are generally unfriendly and inappropriate, it is our experience that there are a large number of such systems which fail because they do not take into account the views and worries of the end users. A glance through just about any edition of *Computer Weekly* would confirm this statement, the litany of disasters relating to information technology (IT) are numerous (see Suggested Reading). The headlines themselves are instructive:

- *Lack of systems back-up causes hospital chaos.*
- *Bank chief learns from computer failure.*
- *GPs' network buckles under huge workload.*

AUTHORS' NOTE: There is a great deal written about organizations and their capacity to deal with change including the changes which IT brings with it (see Suggested Reading and References at the end of the book). This book focuses on analysis and design but we would particularly like to flag the work of Morgan (1997). In his book he indicates a range of metaphors which can be used to help us in describing organization (eg, organization as machine, as brain, as prison). In Chapter 3 we make use of metaphors to describe the systems analyst. Metaphor is a useful device to develop insights into a complex context. To think of an organization as being 'like' a brain is to raise questions like:

- 'Is this organization behaving rationally?'
- 'Is this organization learning?'

These types of question are provoking and can be really helpful in the early stages of systems thinking when we are trying to understand problems. We will return to this approach in Chapter 5.

- *How British Gas took the blame and still managed to survive.*
- *Why British Gas jumped out of the frying pan...*
- *The politics of risk: Trials and tribulations of the Taurus project.*
- *Bug delays £25m court case system.*

Both private and public sectors are prone to massive IT project failure (£80 million in the case of the City of London computerization 'Taurus' project) and the big headlines tend to dominate the news on this topic. This disguises the massive amount of time and energy lost in irritating errors, localized failures in information delivery and frustration in non-working technologies.

One of the problems which often arises with new computer-based information systems is that users feel that the new information system is being imposed upon them with little or no discussion. It is our observation that, generally speaking, the end users of information systems do not have enough say in the analysis and design process.

AUTHORS' NOTE: There are a number of approaches to information systems building which are intended to develop the users' input to the system, eg rapid applications development (RAD) and prototyping. However, these approaches require that the user be given technical support in developing new information systems making use of software tools. In this book we wish to focus on empowering the user to think about and plan his or her information system and not on the approaches designed by technical facilitators.

Lack of input to processes can often result in a lack of sense of ownership amongst the end users of the system supposedly being implemented to improve 'user efficiency'. Further, the information systems analysis and design process is suffering from a dose of 'expert imposition'. To explain what we mean by 'expert imposition' we have to look no further than the types of problem which have been confronting architects in recent years.

After years of quiescence the end user (in this case the householder or office worker) is asking architects questions like: 'would *you* live in one of your buildings?'. Anecdotally, in the UK, architects are thought to tend to prefer Georgian detached homes in quiet mews not the tower block habitations which they are often designing for 'others' to live in. The question being asked of information systems planners is:

- Would *you* like to work with one of your information systems?

Simply stated, one of the major problems implicit in information systems design appears to be that if information systems are planned at all they tend to be planned *by* computer experts *for* users.

Our observation is that information systems often suffer from a highly technocratic, project-based approach derived from experts of the computer profession. Those that use this approach tend to be large companies and/or government departments and agencies which have access to the necessary financial resources required to purchase the professional skills for systems analysis and systems design. Generally speaking, the type of information systems project planning engaged with is characterized by the information system being designed in isolation from the end user in most stages. *Systems for smaller organizations usually develop on an evolutionary, piecemeal basis with little or no overall project planning.* The problem can be broken down as follows:

- Between the computer profession and the general user there is still a considerable knowledge gap. This gap is partly incidental because of the newness of the computer profession but might be argued to be partly contrived by the computer profession due to a tendency to obscure simple or obvious ideas in confusing jargon.
- The knowledge gap is a convenient means for information systems analysts and designers to keep away the uninitiated and the eventual user of the system under design.
- This tendency can be seen as professional conceit on the one hand and user mistrust on the other.
- Users participate in information systems project planning other than in a consultative capacity.
- Yet, returning to our initial problem, users do require working information systems and they often require them rapidly and to offer sustainable service.

For the majority of organizations without access to professional skills, how are the information systems to be planned? What features of an organization need to be analysed? How is the final information system to be implemented?

If computer experts are not available, are too busy, too intimidating or cost too much, users will often tend to fall back on their own means and muddle along. This situation can lead to considerable difficulty and cost but it is an increasingly apparent tendency. Unplanned or poorly planned systems are on the increase because:

- There are literally millions of PCs globally which are not run by experts from the computer profession.
- Contrary to the opinion of some computer experts ten to fifteen years ago, PCs, far from being a 'blip' are becoming increasingly sophisticated and undertake an immense range of tasks.
- Powerful hardware and software often require exceptional and new skills from users.
- User training has tended to be badly organized and under-subscribed to.
- Output is required rapidly.
- This has resulted in lack of method in planning information systems and to massively under-utilized technology (eg powerful PCs, intended for sophisticated accounting operations, being used for word processing).

The purpose of this book is to demonstrate an easy-to-use method for identifying what the information systems planner (that is you) needs to know. Following this we:

- Demonstrate ways to model the range of technical, economic, social, cultural, political, and other issues which may be critical to the running of the information system.
- Produce a definition of the proposed new information system.
- Identify key technical and social combinations which will achieve the new system requirements at a given cost.
- Plan for the interface between users and technology.
- Outline the major technical processes and facilities which may be needed to be in place for the system to work effectively.

Finally we set out software and hardware selection procedures and the implementation process.

We need to make clear several major features of this book:

- You do not need to be a system engineer or even know much about computers to be able to make effective use of the book. Ideally you should have an information system which you would like to plan.
- The book deals with information systems design. The end product probably will be automated but *may be semi-automated or even manual.*

THINK POINT: Before going on with the chapter, think about the following questions. In this chapter we have set out reasons why planning at the stakeholder (rather than IT expert) level is important:

- Are you aware of planning in your organization's adoption of IT?
- Does your organization involve a wide range of stakeholders in its IT planning?
- Can you think of five problems which might arise from the exclusion of stakeholders who are not IT specialists in the IT planning process?
- Can you think of reasons why including people in decision-making and planning could be seen as a problem?

- Many people put in charge of new information systems have little previous experience. Therefore the book is aimed at managers who need a simple-to-use, non-technocratic analysis and design tool.
- Existing workers in the profession sometimes doubt the value of current technical analysis and design tools and sometimes have very limited time to come up with an end product. Therefore, we also intend the book for information systems analysts and designers who need a rapid-use tool.
- Many disciplines make use of information systems but do not always have specialist computer professionals on call to deal with planning. Hence we have made provision for the book to be useful to both a wide range of professionals working in their own disciplines and lecturers and students interested in bringing some design skills into their specialist area (eg, management, business, economics, planning).

For all the end users of the book, we hope that they find in it a technically sound but rapidly applicable and socially sensitive planning tool.

Information systems: A catalogue of failures?

A central theme for this book is the problem of devising a clear and user sensitive approach to determining exactly what is the problem for which an information system is perceived as being the answer. How do we plan this system and offer a reasonable chance of successful use? With this in mind it is useful to look at some of the standard problems which we have encountered in previous systems planning exercises. The types of problem which are in some ways typical of IT adoption include:

- Patchy understanding of the computing involved by the potential users.
- Very wide range of requirements by the user.
- Awkward environmental factors involved in the placement of proposed systems.
- High cost training and staffing implications.

These points led us to an observation concerning the impact of information systems in organizations where situations of risk and uncertainty prevail: *Users appear generally to believe that little can be understood about an information system prior to installation. Further, it is often believed that IT will probably lead to negative rather than positive work experiences.*

Taking this as our lead point, our approach is to reassure the user on these counts. But why are users apparently so wary of information systems? Some examples may help to explain.

Our first example in Figure 1.2 shows that the problem for the analyst is not the data to be prepared or the staff to be trained. It consists of senior management intransigence. If management is left out of the decision-making process and is not included in discussions or consulted then systems can fail.

This demonstrates that it is vital to get the support of major stakeholders in the system. In this case the failure results in continuation with existing manual practices which could be easily, technically improved upon.

The first learning point would seem to be: **Always draw management into the analysis and design stage – do not make the technology appear threatening (or any more threatening than it is already!).**

Figure 1.3 demonstrates our second problem situation. Here the problem is the planner or system analyst her (or him) self.

In this example the planner devises and suggests a new system but this is quite different from that which the major stakeholder in the organization requires. Problems arise when an analyst's enthusiasm to create systems which are theoretically sound (in terms of the personal preferences of the analyst) rather than contextually appropriate (what stakeholders want) predominates. The result is that the analyst is at odds with the preference of the end users or clients and ends up creating conflict and ultimate failure. This situation can be resolved in two ways. Either the stakeholders tell the analyst to think again, or as in this case, the analyst imposes the system. This example will generally be restricted to cases where either the planner has been given *carte blanche* to impose his or her will or if a larger, parent or funding body outside the organization which is being studied and which is possibly commissioning the study, backs the analyst's judgement.

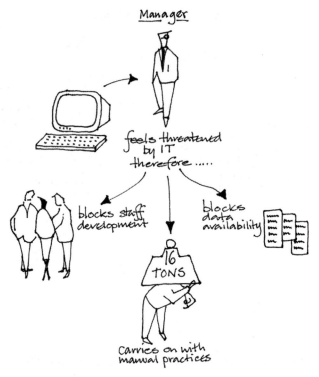

Manager

feels threatened
by IT
therefore .....

blocks staff
development

blocks
data
availability

16
TONS

Carries on with
manual practices

Figure 1.2 *Problems with IS 1: Senior management intransigence*

The result is fairly predictable – a conflict of objectives and outcomes between planner and client and ultimately failure. The learning point is: **Irrespective of professionalism, the planner/analyst must have the humility and common sense to see the client/customer/stakeholder perspective as central to a working system.**

Our third example is shown in Figure 1.4 and can be seen as a problem of over ambition and the price of initial success. Information systems like any other systems have to provide their utility to the end user for some considerable time – this is a question of sustainability. If they do not provide this utility they can end up being more disruptive in their effect than continuing with outmoded and outdated manual practices. In Figure 1.4 the organization is left with a potentially catastrophic situation where the information system ultimately fails but the confidence during the first few years has been so high as to lead to the dismantling of all previous information systems which could act as back-up. The learning point is again quite stark: **Short-term success can lead to long-term failure unless real long-term sustainability is built into projects. This is a danger for all information systems projects.**

Our fourth example demonstrates again the problems of short-term successes. The problem in this case is the over-adoption of a computer system. This type of problem can manifest itself in many ways. Examples include PC systems running for over 20 hours a day, 7 days a week and printers outputting day and night. In Figure

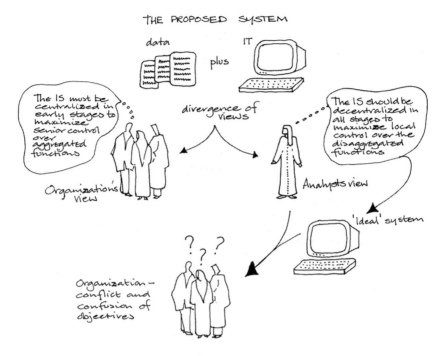

THE PROPOSED SYSTEM

data

IT

plus

The IS must be centralized in early stages to maximize Senior control over aggregated functions

divergence of views

The IS should be decentralized in all stages to maximize local control over the disaggregated functions

Organization's view

Analysts view

'Ideal' system

Organization – conflict and confusion of objectives

? ? ?

Figure 1.3 *Problems with IS 2: Poor analysis perspective*

1.5 the computer-based information product produces such a positive response from the organization that it encourages a massive increase in use. The learning point from this is again predictable: ***A system should be designed to meet the needs of today and tomorrow and the next day so far as we can predict it.***

Our fifth and final example depicts what might be thought of as the usual problems which a computer-based information system might have to deal with.

The key to almost all the problems depicted in Figure 1.6 is poor security. The requirements for security are directly related to the specific factors at work in the potential information systems context (that word context again!). Generally there is a trade-off between ease of access to information systems and security. The higher the security the more difficult the system is to use. Conversely the more open the system is the easier it is for computer hackers to gain access, for computer viruses to be imported into the system and for software to be pirated. All of these problems tend to be symptomatic of a less than adequate approach to information systems design. Related issues include insufficient attention being devoted to training of staff and the resulting lack of confidence and morale of these staff members. Finally, we must recognize that information systems are often being installed in high risk contexts. Risk varies with situation but can refer to:

• Organizational problems such as lack of training.
• Local infrastructure factors such as intermittent or fluctuating power supply.
• Climatic factors such as heat or humidity.

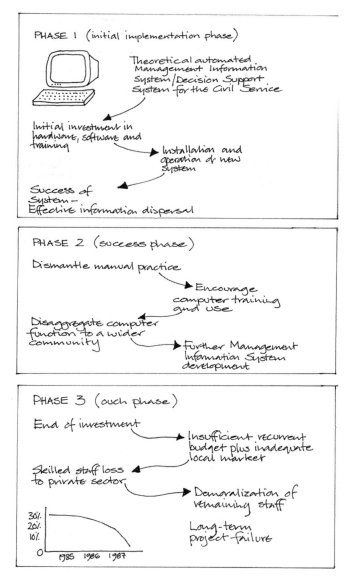

Figure 1.4 *Problems with IS 3: Over-ambition*

- Financial risks such as insufficient recurrent budget for computer support.
- Social and political risk such as antipathy to the incoming system.

The learning point we draw from this is: *It is good practice always to assume that an information system is going into an environment which is hostile to some degree. Modest systems planned for difficult situations can always be built upon and extended later. Technically sound, ambitious systems may suffer teething problems which take years to recover from (if ever!).*

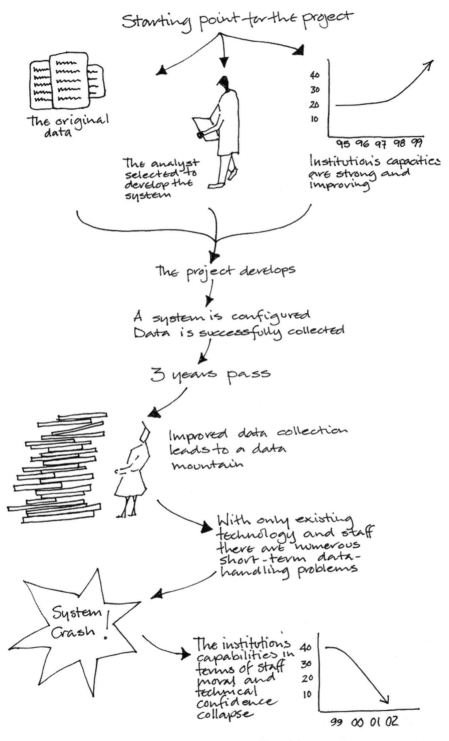

Figure 1.5 *Problems with IS 4: Task/machine development mismatch*

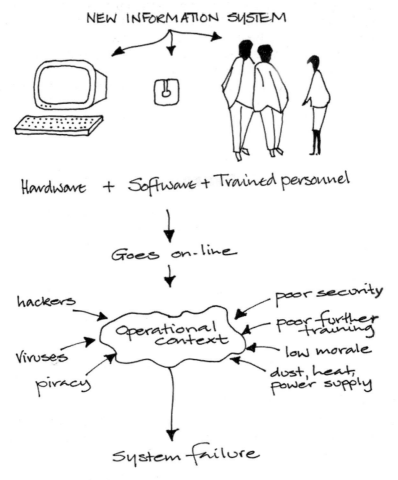

Figure 1.6 *Problems with IS 5: Technical management breakdown*

Conclusions

From the foregoing we would like to draw out some conclusions:

- All information systems exist to support some form of decision-making.
- Effective decision-making is vital for personal and organizational well-being.
- Therefore information systems have to be properly planned with the decision-making end point in mind.
- Poorly planned or unplanned systems can (and do) lead to catastrophe.
- Many planned systems are too technocratic and also lead to problems for the end users.
- Therefore: a key requirement is for a readily applicable method for planning information systems.

The usual term used to describe information system planning is 'systems analysis and systems design' or SA&SD. This is rather a mouthful and can appear to be quite an off-putting expression to the non-specialist. However, in order for us to make sense of the planning process we need to understand analysis and design in outline at least – much of it is proceduralized common sense (although, as someone once said, sense is not always common). Later on we will be using tools drawn from various types of analysis and design to plan for our own information systems but first it is useful to know a little more about what we are referring to as analysis and design.

Exercise

Read through the following article and consider the following question: do the problems evident in the context relate closely to the problems for information systems set out in the second section of this chapter, 'Information systems: A catalogue of failures?'?

'GPs' network buckles under huge workload'

by Tony Collins. *Computer Weekly*, 28 November, 1996

'A National Health Service network used by four out of five GPs has buckled under high workloads, losing messages, delaying patient's test results and throwing surgeries into confusion.

Many of the 7,500 GPs on the network have invoked paper and clerical back-up procedures in an attempt to restore normality and to trace messages that have not reached their destinations.

The problems have delayed test reports, including breast screening and cervical smear results.

They have been caused by an unexpected surge in demand for the Healthlink service, from an average of 40,000 to 75,000 messages a day between January and October. The system allows GPs and health authorities to swap information on practice patients lists, treatments carried out and laboratory results.

Racal Managed Services, the network supplier, said there has been a strain on the central systems controlling the Healthlink X.400 (84) network. To cope with demand – 90,000 messages a day – Racal has boosted the system's processing power, disc capacity and disc cache.

Racal said it has accelerated the testing of a major upgrade to the X.400 (88) standard, expected to go live early next year.

The problems have led to GP surgeries spending thousands of hours over several weeks trying to resolve the difficulties.

Health authorities and doctors claimed this week that difficulties are continuing. Dr Grant Kelly, a GP, chairman of the General Medical Services Committee's IT sub-committee and head of the Joint Computing Group of the Royal College of General Practitioners, said test results were taking longer to arrive than by post. "You have to see a gain from these systems and we haven't yet", he said.

Linked to Healthlink
7,500 GP practices
500 hospitals
17,500 NHS users
51 breast clinics
increasing by 200 users per month
sending 90,000 messages per day

The problems have particularly hit GPs who sent "items of service" invoices to health authorities for registering and treating patients.

This has led health authorities to consider giving GPs emergency "hardship" payments based on previous records to maintain surgeries' cash flow.

In a statement to Computer Weekly, *Racal said that with BT now operating in the same market "the message throughput on Healthlink is very much against expectations. It was anticipated that the growth would be shared between the two service suppliers. However the market has voted with its feet and continued to support Healthlink".'*

One answer to this tricky context is provided to this exercise in Appendix 3.

CHAPTER 2

WHAT IS SYSTEMS ANALYSIS AND SYSTEMS DESIGN?

KEYWORDS: systems analysis, systems design, learning organization, exploration/research approach, systemic, reductionist, methodologies, tools

SUMMARY: How does a stakeholder or stakeholder community begin to plan an information system with systems analysis and systems design? The experts have produced a vast range of methodologies for the planner with a bewildering array of approaches. The incomprehensible language often used and the belief that analysis and design takes months rather than days often invokes the question from the non-specialist: 'how is any of it of use to us?'. In this chapter we look briefly at the range of methodologies and focus in on some major, useful themes.

Introduction

Systems analysis and systems design (SA&SD) is the term used to describe the means used to plan an information system. Usually SA&SD is set out within the context of an exploration into a problem of some sort. The exploration (or research approach) will contain a methodology of some form. Generally the methodology will tend to have the range of elements set out below.

Basics of a systems analysis and systems design methodology

- Discover what the information problem/s is/are.
- Discover what is the setting for the problem/s.
- What resources and constraints are evident?
- What are the major information components of the problem/s?
- Structure the problem/s into a model.
- Design model solutions to the problem/s.
- Test and cost the model.
- Implement the model as appropriate.
- Monitor and evaluate the results.

The virtues of the 'learning organization' as described by Peter Senge and colleagues (Senge et al 1994) relate to a number of practices carried out within the organization. Senge sets these out as five disciplines which are:

AUTHORS' NOTE: At this point we would like to make a major aside. This list of activities for analysis and design raises an issue which we consider to be of the highest significance: the opportunity for SA&SD to provide organizations with a learning opportunity.

1 Systems thinking.
2 Personal mastery.
3 Mental models.
4 Shared vision.
5 Team learning.

The five are set out in more detail in Table 2.1. The overriding virtue of the five disciplines is that together they constitute a shortcut to organizational learning. By team learning, the organization shares learning allowing the knowledge which arises from information and data (as set out in Chapter 1) to be widely shared and known around the organization. Systems thinking provides a tool for thinking about the organization as a wholeness. Mental models provide teams with the ability to step back from the reality of their work lives and question assumptions about what 'is'. Shared vision is a powerful tool to building a consensus within the organization and personal mastery is the outcome of a deep understanding of issues and tasks within organizational settings. Together they can lead organizations to move from relative self-ignorance to relative self-understanding – self-understanding both of how the organization works and of how it is reacting and integrating with its environment.

In the following example we show how the general stages of SA&SD can be seen as relating to the five disciplines and how these in turn can be seen as leading to a rich learning experience.

Table 2.1 What are the five disciplines?

Discipline	Definition	Where applied?	Outcome?
Systems thinking	Links and loops – loops can be re-enforcing (small changes become big changes) or balancing (pushing stability, resistance and limits).	Contexts where cause and effect are unclear.	Description and insight.
Personal mastery	Numerous variations but one threefold view is: articulating a personal vision, seeing reality clearly and making a commitment to the results you want.	Contexts where individuals are in transition.	Empower-ment.
Mental models	Based on reflection and inquiry but also the recognition that we all make up unconscious mental models all the time.	Any action learning situation.	Clear self-analysis.
Shared vision	Built around six core ideas: organization has a destiny, deep purpose is in the founders' aspirations, not all visions are equal, collective purpose, forums for people to speak from the heart, creative tension.	In contexts of dramatic change.	Organization-wide clarity of purpose.
Team learning	Learning through conversation, dialogue and skilful discussion – the aim is to achieve 'collective mindfulness'.	In contexts of team development.	Group consensus.

Example of a systems analysis and systems design methodology in action

1 Discover what the information problem/s is/are. In this stage systems thinking and team learning are used to discover that there is an unacceptable lag between the preparation of departmental budgets and the presentation of these budgets to central financial committee for approval.

2 Discover what is the setting for the problem/s. Again system thinking and team learning combine here with mental models to arrive at the shared vision that three major departments are the main offenders – Planning, Design and Maintenance – but all departments are occasionally late with their presentations. Rather than seeing this as a problem for ascribing blame, the issue is seen as an opportunity to develop new and improved practice.

3 What resources and constraints are evident? Personal mastery is the lead of the five disciplines here. Central management have indicated a budget of several thousand pounds on a feasibility study into the problem, and procurement of IT and related staff. There is evidence that young, junior staff would be keen to see changes. One important learning point is that in the past there has been senior staff intransigence to change and to the perceived whittling down of responsibility and power implicit in a computer-based solution.

4 What are the major information components of the problem/s? System thinking and mental models are useful in drawing out the information components (such as departmental projections and agreed performance criteria).

5 Structure the problem/s into a model. This requires the production of an overall plan encompassing an organizational chart of some kind giving key departments, stakeholders in the proposed system and identifying where the existing blockages and delays are with regard to setting projections and performance criteria. The development of a shared vision of the context is important at this stage.

6 Design model solutions to the problem/s. Team learning, systems thinking and mental models are used at this point to identify issues in terms of blockages and delays. When these have been identified, model solutions can be designed which focus initially on the main centres of concern.

7 Test and cost the model. Depending upon the resources available a thorough examination of any new model is required. The examination would normally take the form of a pilot study developing the shared vision and involving the team and wider organization with the suggested improved system, with key information indicators being monitored for comparison with existing practices, eg how long did it take to get manager reports assessed on the new information system as opposed to the original system?

8 Implement the model as appropriate. Implementation will build upon the shared vision and personal mastery developed so far and will normally follow a successful pilot study and can take a wide variety of forms – eg parallel systems, a continued pilot approach or simple switch over (these and other implementation strategies are described in Chapter 10).

9 Monitor and evaluate the results. All five disciplines are involved in the monthly and/or six-monthly reporting upon criteria which measure the processes and impact of the project (this topic is covered in much greater depth in Chapter 9).

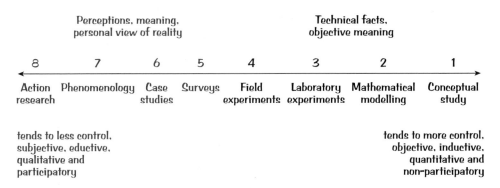

Note: Brief résumés of the eight approaches are provided in the Glossary of Buzzwords.
Source: Adapted from Wood-Harper 1989

Figure 2.1 *Problem exploration approaches continuum*

The purpose of the example set out above is to show how the SA&SD process is a rich opportunity for organizations to learn from an examination of information process and development within the organization. If treated in a learning organization fashion then the explicit learning of the exercise (eg technologies and techniques to improve information systems) can be linked to a range of implicit learning (eg senior manager intransigence to change) to lead to improved efficiencies in the organization as a whole. As well as the learning organization approach, a vast array of different methods are available for fulfilling this sequence of nine tasks. The approaches all have their own benefits and weaknesses. Generally they vary from each other along the lines of the different experiential and research backgrounds and training of the individuals who designed them. One way of understanding what is meant by 'research background' can be seen in terms of an axis which shows a range of approaches to problem exploration or research (see Figure 2.1).

Do not panic about this. A few words of explanation may be required! The axis (called a continuum) is shown here with eight points on it. There may be many more points which we could add but the eight shown here should be sufficient for our example.

To the left are what we refer to as the 'soft' or generally social sciences, people focused approaches to exploring problems; to the right are some of the technocratic, 'hard' science approaches. All eight of the approaches briefly shown here have salient features making one different from all the others. Each has its own assumptions or worldview. This is an important point.

The assumptions of the methods to the right of the continuum are derived from sciences akin to engineering and are focused on a controlled and controllable universe in which science knows or can know all that is needful to know. In contrast the assumptions of the approaches on the left are based upon the difficulty of saying one 'knows' anything with regard to the vagaries of human nature. They assume that there are very few fixed points upon which the analyst can depend and often assume that nothing can be absolutely known.

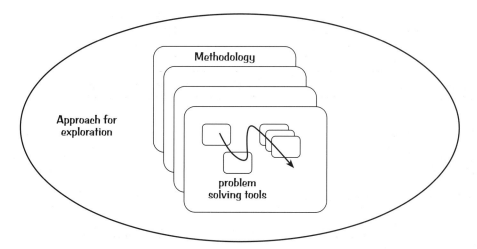

Figure 2.2 *Exploration, methodology and problem solving tools*

Before we go any further we need to make it clear that understanding and applying techniques of exploration is important for our main task – namely making working information systems. Setting up an information system requires the user to undertake research, to explore the context. To understand problems, deduce the strengths and weaknesses of the environment, plan a new system and test it prior to implementation requires some skills in exploration. The main point which needs to be understood is that most people are quite able to undertake research, indeed we explore difficult new contexts most days of our lives. All that is required is for the potential researcher to see research in the context of the problem.

For our purposes we use the word 'exploration' instead of research and in this text it refers to the adoption of an overall framework for the application of a methodology and the tools which comprise a methodology. The tools are then applied in a sequential and logical manner in order to arrive at an understanding of the problem, some suggestions for improvement, and means for producing the improved situation (see Figure 2.2).

How does the exploration, methodology, tools sequence work? In one example, a management systems planner wants to know if a series of measures aimed at supporting decision-making at middle management level will be accepted by staff. Because she is working for a large, multinational company she cannot ask every single member of middle management if they agree with the proposed system. So, the first priority is to specify means to begin exploration. In this example a case study (point 6 on our axis in Figure 2.1) approach is used. Certain representative departments are checked. The methodology applied is called participative interaction which requires the problem solving tool of questionnaires to be applied.

In another example an agronomist is employed to discover the most appropriate of six seed varieties for the production of maize. He applies the mathematical modelling research technique (point 2 on the axis), uses a sampling methodology and makes use of tools for measuring leaf growth and seed production among the six varieties.

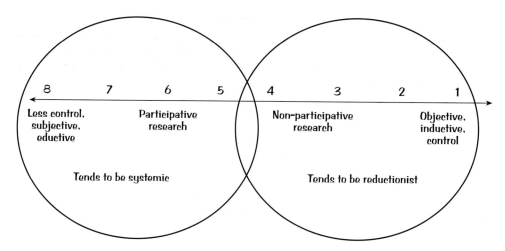

Figure 2.3 *Systemic and reductionist tendencies and the continuum*

As planners of information systems we need to be sure that we are aware of and reflect upon our approach to exploration, the methodology to be used and the range of tools which that methodology makes use of. Before we get to this point it is useful to first explain a little more of what the continuum means to us as planners. How do the eight approaches affect us?

The eightfold division is not definitive and could be added to. However, this range of backgrounds indicates two basic approaches to thought or systems of analysis and design (see Figure 2.3). These are known as the rationalist, science school which is often argued to be reductionist, and the inclusive and holistic approach which is called the systemic. Although we go into some greater detail concerning various methodologies in Appendix 1, it is useful to get an overview of the two main traditions of thinking behind methodologies of all sorts here.

The reductionist

We argue that reductionism is the worldview which lies behind most of the 'hard' sciences. Reductionism is in turn based on the philosophical teaching of positivism.

> *'All genuine human knowledge is contained within the boundaries of science. That is, the systematic study of phenomena and the explication of the laws embodied therein. Philosophy may still perform a useful function in explaining the scope and methods of science, pointing out the more general principles underlying specific scientific findings, and exploring the implications of science for human life. But it must abandon the claim to have any means of attaining knowledge not available to science.'*
>
> Flew (1979)

With a reductionist approach, out go ideas about the reality and importance of 'unscientific' aspects of life (hunches, guesswork, instincts for rightness and even in certain circumstances illogical activity – ie activity which is not consistent with a narrow definition of efficiency). To this worldview the universe is fixed, knowable, measurable and, therefore, predictable. If it is not these things, then it is not worth knowing. Of course this is a stereotypical definition of positivism/reductionism but we would argue that this is the underlying structure of thinking behind three common analysis and design methods influencing analysis and design today, ie:

1 Structured systems analysis (SSA).
2 Technical specification (TS).
3 Data analysis (DA).

The systemic

This is not yet a term to be found readily in dictionaries of philosophy but the approach arises from the systems thinking and therefore is embraced by the term holism:

> 'The contention that wholes, or some wholes, are greater than the sum of their parts ... A theory that claims that society may, or should, be studied in terms of social wholes.'

Flew (1979)

Systemisists are involved in the necessarily subjective world of real human activity. Central to the systemic approach to information systems is the belief that social and political forces will and must interfere with any technocratic information system – they are elements of the whole. Further, it is understood and accepted that the information system planner will impose opinions and beliefs upon logical and objective new systems which are being planned – as will all other stakeholders in the context. The systemic view of reality is characterized by an inter- and trans-disciplinarian approach, ie linking together various sciences and approaches and not compartmentalizing the world into exclusive boxes. Again we have three approaches to SA&SD which we might use to illustrate its working in practice:

1 General systems theory (GST).
2 Soft systems methodology (SSM).
3 Socio-technical systems (STS).

Appendix 1 contains a discussion concerning approaches to analysis and design.

> THINK POINT: If you were asked to set out the single, major difference between systemisism and reductionism what would it be?

What is the research approach and methodology of this book?

This is the most subjective question to ask. Implicit in the continuum shown in Figure 2.1 is the observation that all methodologies have their strengths and weaknesses. It is not a question of selecting the 'right' methodology, rather we believe that a better approach is to select the *appropriate combination of methodological tools for the particular situation* in which you are working.

Before going on to this however we should define the form of exploration or research approach of this book. Generally speaking we assume that you, the planner/analyst and designer, are a member of the organization for which an information system is scheduled. In this case you will figure in your own analysis; you are part of the problem context.

We argue that in most contexts which we have experience of – situations which are common – irrespective of any reductionist, 'hard', objective planning tools which we might use later on, an overall systemic, 'action research' (point 8 on the axis in Figure 2.1) approach is of great value.

Figure 2.4 demonstrates the major components of an action research approach as set against the situation which can prevail if the approach is wrongly applied or not applied (anti-action research).

ACTION RESEARCH MODEL

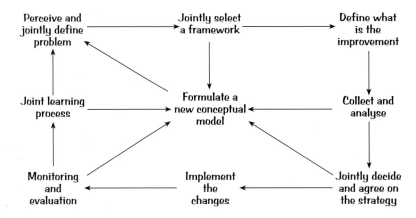

ANTI-ACTION RESEARCH MODEL

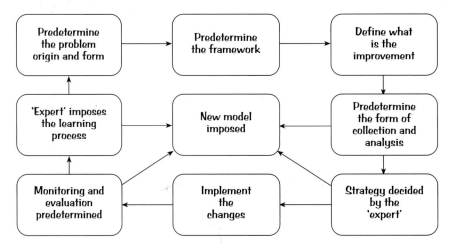

Source: Adapted from Warmington (1980)

Figure 2.4 *(a) Action research model (b) Anti-action research*

The action research approach (Figure 2.4a) shows several important and useful themes:

- The analyst and the client for whom the system is being designed work together as a team (an important point from a learning organization point of view).
- Strategy is jointly agreed on.
- Final policy is jointly undertaken.

Whilst not wishing to imply that any other approach would be fatally flawed, the anti-action research model (Figure 2.4b) shows some of the range of problems which can arise if less emphasis is paid to the major stakeholders in the context.

The methodology which we will be using in the book will be based upon the themes of the action research approach. By this means we intend to encourage planners to draw in interested parties to the work which they are involved in thereby reducing the possibilities of alienating stakeholders and/or missing vital organizational constraints which lie outside the narrow confines of the proposed information system. Further, the approach will allow us to see the way in which we as planners fit into the system which we are devising.

The second question is that relating to methodology. The methodology we use here goes by the rather grand title of a *multiperspective*, eclectic *methodology* evolved from field work based upon 'Multiview' (see Suggested Reading). If you think that this sounds off-putting perhaps we should explain that the approach is difficult to define without the use of terms like these but is much easier to understand and apply. What the title means is that the methodology makes use of a wide range of tools (it is eclectic) and attempts to perceive the problem which an information system confronts from a number of different directions (it is multiperspective). The methodology consists of five components. Four of these relate to methodologies which we have already discussed. Figure 2.5 shows one way in which these four relate to each other and to wider issues already discussed in this chapter:

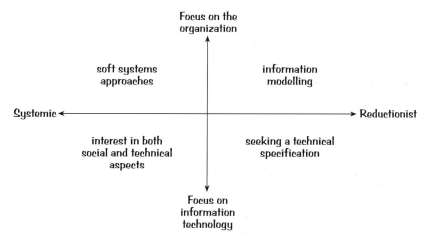

Figure 2.5 *Multiview and its constituent parts*

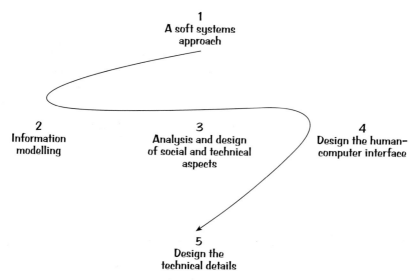

Figure 2.6 *A rapid planning methodology for information systems implementation*

The diagram shows that two of the approaches are largely systemic and two broadly reductionist. Also, two tend to be more concerned with the needs and demands of the organization whilst two have more focus on the technology. The fifth component of our methodology is that which deals with the interface between the user and the computer itself, human–computer interaction or interface (HCI).

We will go into greater depth concerning the specific details of the methodology in Chapter 4, but it is useful to see the overall layout now, and this is shown in Figure 2.6. Before we discuss this methodology in more practical detail we can usefully define the role of the analyst, the person who is the central actor in the exploration (ie you).

Conclusion

In this chapter we have identified the approach to information systems planning that we are going to adopt and have demonstrated our reasons for selecting this approach in particular. Key points to remember are:

- Our approach will involve the active assistance of the recipient community – we look upon them as participants in the exploration.
- The approach is not intended to be confrontational to any other but adopts:
  - key ideas from methods designed to improve the social significance of information systems and IT; and
  - key ideas from technically rigorous methods which produce well designed, technologically sound systems.
- We can therefore state our approach to have the characteristics shown in Figure 2.7.

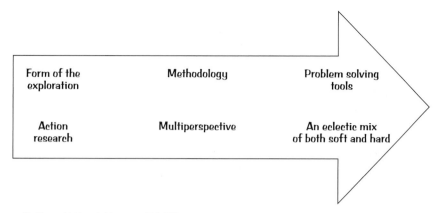

| Form of the exploration | Methodology | Problem solving tools |
| Action research | Multiperspective | An eclectic mix of both soft and hard |

Source: Bell and Wood-Harper (1998)

Figure 2.7 *Systems analysis and systems design approach of this book*

Exercise

Read the article below. Would you think a systemic or reductionist approach to this project would be most effective?

'Bug delays £25m court case system'

by Karl Schneider, *Computer Weekly*, 20 February, 1997

'Technical problems have stalled a £25m project to computerize all 250 county courts in England and Wales.

Roll out of the Caseman system has ground to a halt just five months into the contract, which EDS won with a bid believed to have been 50% lower than those from rivals such as Sema.

The system manages the progress of cases through the courts. But a key part of it, the printing of documents such as bailiff's reports, is still not working.

EDS has developed software to tackle some of the problems but says there is a bug in the Unix version of the Wordperfect word processor package.

... The system was due to go live in the first batch of courts next Monday. EDS says it now has a fix for the bug and will ask for roll out to start in early March.

But the Court Service want two trouble-free days of printing at the proving courts before it starts the programme. Senior staff were due to meet EDS this week to review progress.

The delay has disrupted a massive training programme to familiarize 3,000 court staff with the system...'

An answer to this question is provided in Appendix 3.

CHAPTER 3

THE ROLE OF THE SYSTEMS PLANNER OR SYSTEMS ANALYST

KEYWORDS/EXPRESSIONS: The function of the analyst, past experience, methodology, area of use, self analysis, reflective practice

SUMMARY: The role of the analyst is to help the end users of information systems to clarify their information processing requirements and choose the most suitable systems design to meet these requirements. The analyst must perform the detailed analysis and work with programmers and others to help to build and implement a working system. This role, or some parts of it, may be carried out from different positions within the organization, or from outside it. The analyst is part of the context. The analyst brings along his or her own ideas, baggage, agendas and preferences. It is our contention that these personal issues are best addressed at the outset of analysis in order to clarify commitments and surface personal issues which, if left, might jeopardize the information system development process. A little self-knowledge is a powerful thing. This chapter looks at how the analyst can arrive at a clear idea of his or her own background.

You the analyst: First thoughts

All analysis must start from the basis that *reality is very often experienced as being complex and the analyst is part of this complexity*. Information systems, intimately linked to so many elements of the social, technical, political and cultural aspects of our lives are also experienced as being very complex. What we often fail to fully recognize is that we, as analysts, are also part of the overall context within which our information system will work. As our action research approach recognizes, we are within the research frame and we will influence what goes on. Our own personal preferences will have an impact upon our planning and we will, consciously or unconsciously, attempt to influence stakeholders towards our own pre-set ideas about what is 'right' (as we saw in problem 2 in Chapter 1). We cannot guarantee to avoid this kind of trap and therefore it is best understood at the outset.

It is not the purpose of this book to set out the complex and often confusing aspects of behavioural psychology and self analysis. In this chapter we wish to make clear that our perceptions change over time, that these changes can be monitored and that the understanding of our own personal bias will help us to understand the decisions which we make.

First of all, what is it that we, as analysts and designers, are trying to do? Our initial task is to attempt to understand local context, to make generalized models of the existing situation in order to go on to create an information system. By formulating generalizations about current practices in organizations we can develop models of reality which we can then test for adequacy in hypothetical situations (eg 'will this model payroll system cope with 23 new staff being re-employed following dismissal notices being sent out accidentally?'). If our model is proved by experience to be adequate then we can, with humility (that is, recognizing that the system will always contain some faults and thus can always be improved upon), plan the working automated (or non-automated) system.

Understanding the complexity of reality is the nub of the analyst's dilemma with regards to making a reasonable model. Before going on to look at the tools the analyst employs we need to consider the role which the systems analyst plays in an organization. Let us start with a very general definition:

> 'The systems analyst works with the user within his or her socio-political and economic context to specify the information system requirements of an organization. The system is modelled according to terms of reference and the final outline plans are produced for hardware, software and necessary processing.'

This conveys the intermediary, 'go-between', aspect as well as the architectural aspect of the job.

The title Systems Analysis and System Design is often used to convey the creative aspect of the role. There is a sense in which the analyst is like an architect producing designs to the client's specification, or for their approval, which can then be turned into an actual construction by the implementing agency although this view minimizes the importance of the final system user in the analysis and design process. Our focus here is to set out:

- How different types of individual will conform to different types of analysis and design stereotypes.

Our stereotypes of analysts form a similar function in aiding our understanding to the organizational metaphors of Gareth Morgan's, referred to in Chapter 1. The stereotype does not represent an actual person but provides a metaphor which we can use as a means to understand our own strengths and weaknesses. This is described in more detail shortly. Building on this reflection we see:

- How the recent history of analysis and design indicates how these stereotypes arose.
- How a quick review of one's own intellectual background, methodologies and work environment helps in assessing how our current approach has arisen.

First, and generally speaking, we identify four types or categories of analyst. These four are not definitive and more could be added but, we believe, they represent a

Figure 3.1 *The technocratic analyst*

cross-section of the major tendencies among the professionals working in the area. The technocratic analyst (Figure 3.1) 'fixes' problems. He or she is best thought of as a technical expert like a doctor. The tendency of this approach is to take over the situation and impose one's 'expert advice'.

In our second example the radical analyst (Figure 3.2) seeks to overthrow existing wrongs and bring in new and improved systems. The metaphor of a warrior might appear to be a bit strong but the underlying tendency of wishing radically to alter what currently exists is a fundamental aspect of the resulting approach. Here the analyst will attempt to assert the radical reform of current practices.

Figure 3.2 *The radical analyst*

The third image (Figure 3.3) is the one which most would probably wish to be associated with. It is a benign metaphor and has close associations with the learning organization approach which we have already discussed in Chapter 2. In the case of the facilitator and teacher the analyst seeks meaning and attempts to assist clients by facilitating their own problem solving efforts. The analyst attempts to draw the clients into the problem solving process and encourages them to become involved in all stages. Analyst and stakeholders are drawn into a learning process.

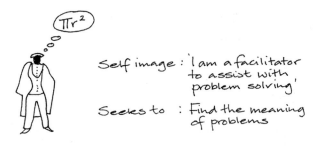

Figure 3.3 *The facilitator/teacher analyst*

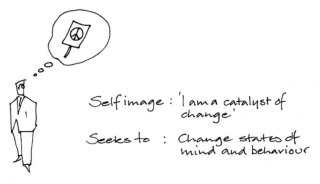

Figure 3.4 *The emancipator analyst*

In our fourth example (Figure 3.4) the analyst is an agent of change again but now in the sense of an emancipator – a catalyst assisting others to change their own lives. The difference between this analyst and the facilitator is that here change and confrontation are inevitable. Therefore, the approach is 'hands-on' and can be highly assertive.

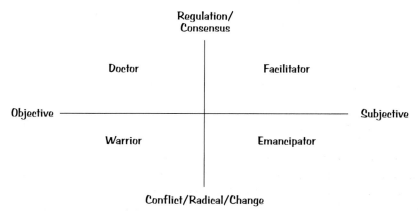

Adapted from Burrell and Morgan (1979)

Figure 3.5 *Four metaphors of the analyst*

THINK POINT: At this point it is useful to ask yourself some questions:

- 'In developing information systems am I seeking change or meaning?'
- 'Am I planning a technical fix to the problem in hand or am I assisting others to recognize existing problems and develop internal solutions?'
- 'What is my self-perception – what kind of person am I?'
- 'How will this affect the way in which I carry out my analysis and design?'

What are the answers you come up with? What type of metaphor best describes you in your analysis and design context? Maybe skilfully thinking ahead and acting with caution – a snooker player? Maybe you see yourself as drawing out the stakeholders but at the same time keeping a degree of order in a discordant context – a facilitator with 'attitude'? Whatever the metaphor that comes to mind what does it tell you about the way you get on with others in the context. What about the metaphor which best sums up your main stakeholders? If you are a facilitator type but working in a 'thrusting' new dot com agency, surrounded on all fronts by emancipator and warrior types does this inform the way in which you will go about your business?

All four of our examples of analysts can be represented as elements of continua on two axes:

The self image of the analyst is very important. The four options we see here are derived from four very different perspectives, consensus seeking at the top and radical at the bottom. Similarly the analyst can be seen as moving between the points of objective, 'scientific' behaviour (tending to the reductionist) and that of subjective preference and possibly more holistic.

The review of types of people we and our stakeholders are is a useful precursor to undertaking our exploration of the analysis and design context. Of course, any action arising from answering such questions is largely dependent upon ourselves and how we interpret what we discover. But it may well be that if one approach to analysis and design does not seem to be working, a different one can be tried which fits in better with the mood of the organization and the stakeholders within it. Of course other types of metaphor might be employed in the understanding of the actors in the context. In our own practice we have employed a range of such tools from the formal to the highly informal. Morgan's approach to considering organizations as metaphors can provide valuable insights (Morgan 1997). The Myers Briggs personality index is a useful tool for getting stakeholders to see themselves in a powerful positive light. Astrological signs can be used as a means to open up stakeholder groups to views of themselves in a light-hearted fashion. We have even made use of the Winnie the Pooh characters for people to identify with! (see Suggested Reading). What ever the tool used, self-reflection is a powerful aid to understanding the analyst in the context.

The answer to the questions set out in the think point above will largely depend upon where we see our own point of origin in the development of the present situation. To understand this it is useful briefly to look at the history of the analyst and designer in the wider history of the development of IT.

The history of the analyst

Others (for example Awad 1988) have attempted to break down the recent history of computer development into distinct periods or epochs. Here we take an adaptation of such a model and apply the salient features of the epoch as they concern the planner/analyst.

In the early days of isolated computing (1975 and earlier) the hardware system was all important. The main use of computing systems was cost reduction accounting. The salient features of the period were:

- Mainframe orientated.
- Computer experts were extremely remote (in terms of physical location and general attitude) from users.
- The analyst was invisible in the system and dealt with technical matters.

Then followed the second period of consolidated computing (approximately 1975–1980) This was a period which was dominated by programmers and poor documentation! The salient features were:

- Mainframe and minicomputer orientated.
- Programmers – no user interface!
- Analysts or, more properly, programmer-analysts, were still buried in the system. They were mainly involved with designing systems for computers not systems for people.

When the power of technical systems began to be appreciated by a wider managerial audience, faults arising from systems orientated to the wishes of programmers were recognized. This was the third period when management controls and restraints were imposed (1980–1985). The key to this process was the enforcement of standards in terms of programming, new systems development and system functions. The key features were:

- Mainframe, minicomputer and microcomputer orientated systems. (The 'micros' were disliked by some professionals and were considered to be not serious, a 'blip'!)
- Computer experts worked directly under business management control.
- There were the beginnings of crude user interfaces.
- At this time the analyst became a management aid. The beginning of the 'humanization' of many of these individuals began. Problems became organizational and less machine based – not 'what can the machine do?' but 'what can the machine do for me?'.

This approach still did not allow easy access to computer power. The development of microcomputers (the 'PC') has ushered in the (much celebrated) role of the user (1985–1990) – focusing on applications software (eg packages), distributed computing to remote officers (via the desktop PCs), far from the computer department. Key features included:

- The advent of microcomputer networks.
- The expert operating as a *facilitator* of user needs.
- The emplacement of strict control of the computer function by the organization.
- The analyst becomes central to understanding the needs of the user.

Most recently, but still beginning around 1990, following the trend above, we have seen the focus on the user/machine interface, making users and computers more equal to the struggle of communication. Key notes for this process have been the development of user focused approaches.

- Networked IT becomes the norm in all parts of the organization: most recently this can be seen in the form of the internet and the intranet. The rise of the World Wide Web.
- Invisible technology: 'I don't want to understand it, I just want to use it'.
- Invisible experts: 'Don't get in my way, just make the system easy to use'.
- The era of 'We are all users now'.

The theme here is that information systems are generally becoming more available to the user and they are losing their technical/programming appearance. The analyst is now concerned with understanding users and making information systems dovetail into their needs. The movement from isolated computing to the user machine interface (which has taken a mere 25 years) can be summed up by two statements which convey the focus of epoch 1 and epoch 5.

Epoch 1
'The computer expert is the centre of the system. The computer expert is given the necessary support to indicate priorities and to control the process of providing automated procedures to alleviate problems. The user is peripheral to the needs of the data processing department and acts as a problem object to the computer expert.'

Epoch 5
'The user is the centre of the system. The user is given the necessary support to indicate priorities and to begin the process of providing automated procedures to alleviate problems. The computer expert is peripheral and acts as counsel and support to the user.'

Perhaps the most striking point which arises from the two statements is the movement between two metaphors – from the hard, technocratic view to one which focuses on facilitating the needs of the often despised user. In a sense the five periods can be seen as being not just representative of periods of history but also of states of mind. In this sense and in our experience, there are still plenty of epoch 1 people around!

You the analyst: Second thoughts

Because background determines the approach for our exploration into information systems needs of organizations and this in turn influences our selection of methodology which then goes on to determine the problem solving tools applied, it is quite useful (although still largely not practised by analysts and designers) to review and reflect on one's own background and assumptions with regard to the particular situation in which you are going to work. The analyst is as human as anyone else and if you intend to carry out your own analysis it is useful to have a system to recognize, before beginning the process of analysis, where your own ideas and concepts arise and possibly how likely they are to influence the task in hand.

Present reflection and self analysis

One means for such self analysis is shown in Figure 3.6 The figure demonstrates a fairly simple and easy to use tool for identifying the pre-dispositions of the analyst with regard to background, immediate problem context and methodology being used.

If you have never undertaken analysis and design before, you should still be able to express a methodology preference from the information given in Chapter 2.

The first task is to identify background. On the scale provided here this ranges from organizational interest to technical interest, from largely soft to largely hard, from generally systemic to generally reductionist. The second question – with regard to methodology – similarly sets the task of identifying a preference to a soft or hard approach. The third question indicates the technological sophistication of the area being worked in (eg a computer-wise city bank or a naive farmers cooperative – or a naive city bank or a computer-wise farmers cooperative!), and the fourth question asks for an indication of risk and uncertainty for IT in that environment (eg is it well understood, financed and supported: low risk – or the reverse of these: high risk?). The result will be a mark between 1 and 10 for questions 1 and 2 and 3 and 4. For questions 1 and 2 marks tending to 1 indicate a soft, people focused background while marks tending to 10 indicate hard and technological. For questions 3 and 4, marks tending to 1 indicate high risk and low sophistication while marks tending to 10 indicate low risk, high sophistication.

A useful rule of thumb for understanding this type of exercise is shown in Figure 3.7. The tool can be used as a rapid way of assessing the value and appropriateness of the analyst's approach in the given situation.

> THINK POINT: Try the criteria on yourself and the organization you are working in. What are your initial thoughts on the omens for information systems development?

Reflecting on the development of the analyst

This is another approach which can be used in conjunction with that set out in Figures 3.6 and 3.7 – it is developed more fully elsewhere (Bell 1996a). The method is intended for those who have undertaken systems analysis and systems design before and consists in reviewing personal development over several years. This can be undertaken focusing on three key areas (see Figure 3.8).

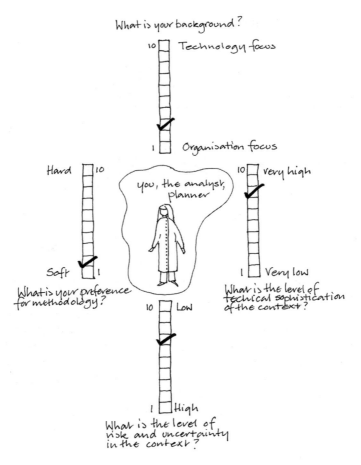

What is your background?

10 ☐ Technology focus

1 ☐ Organisation focus

Hard ☐ 10

you, the analyst, planner

10 ☐ very high

Soft ☐ 1

1 ☐ Very low

What is your preference for methodology?

What is the level of technical sophistication of the context?

10 ☐ Low

1 ☐ High

What is the level of risk and uncertainty in the context?

Figure 3.6 *Self analysis: Analyst 'know thyself'*

1 What is my intellectual framework – the set of ideas and principles which underlie the way I work?
2 What methodologies have I applied? If you have not undertaken systems analysis and systems design before what is your manner or style of working?
3 What were the situations in which I worked?

In Figure 3.8 the analyst can be seen as developing and learning from past to present to the next context for intervention. In each case the intellectual background develops, the methodology may well change and the area of application of that methodology will also change. The process is dynamic with many opportunities for learning.

Look at your own intellectual framework as thoughtfully and impartially as possible. It will tell you a lot about how you will approach the subject of the analysis (warrior or doctor?) and may also indicate whether you will tend towards technical solutions or soft measures to make systems work. 'Man know thyself' is as relevant to the systems analyst as it is to the mystic. One example of such an analysis is

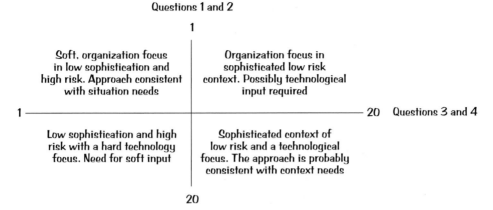

Questions 1 and 2

Figure 3.7 *Assessing the four questions*

shown in Table 3.1. The table shows five major shifts in the intellectual background, methodology and area of application of an analyst. It generally indicates a movement from hard to soft approaches. Table 3.1 shows five 'snapshots' in an individual's development. The example is academic but gives some general themes which are of interest. The snapshot shows five frames over five years. Intellectually the analyst moves from his university concentration on 'development studies' (the study of third world development) through technocratic school of analysis and design to approaches which make use of soft systems thinking and practice like Multiview. His methodological development mirrors this movement, from hard technical specification to soft multiperspective. Areas of application range from East and West Africa to Asia.

Table 3.1 *The chronological development of an analyst*

Frame	Intellectual framework	Methodology in use	Area of application/ problem context
Frame 1	Development studies literature	Technical specification type approaches (TS)	North East Africa
Frame 2	Hard systems, operations research literature	Increasing focus on mathematical and quantitative methods	West Africa
Frame 3	Critical of reductionism, 'muddling along', a time of drift	Amended TS	West Africa
Frame 4	Web modelling, soft systems approaches	Multiview	Asia
Frame 5	Soft systems and other qualitative approaches	Multiperspective methodologies	Several areas of Africa

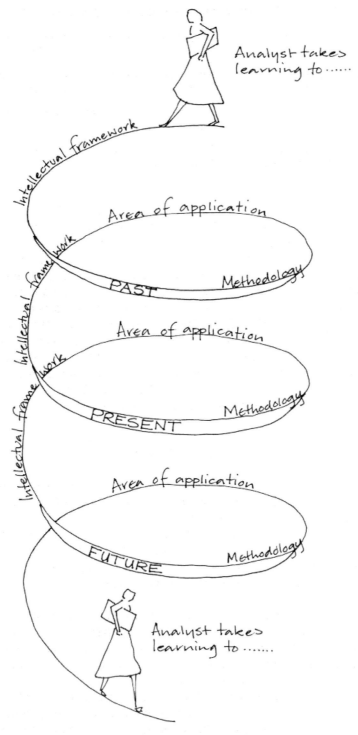

Analyst takes learning to.......

Intellectual framework

Area of application

PAST

Methodology

Intellectual framework

Area of application

PRESENT

Methodology

Intellectual framework

Area of application

FUTURE

Methodology

Analyst takes learning to.......

Figure 3.8 *The developing analyst*

Table 3.2 *The chronological development of an accountant*

Frame	Intellectual framework	Methodology in use	Area of application/ problem context
Frame 1	Financial record keeping and accounts	Workaholic, work as a grind	Small electronics business
Frame 2	Corporate mentality	Team approach and team responsibility	Local government
Frame 3	Leaner and fitter, a predatory approach	Competitive edge to the team dynamics	Local government

A more conventional, business orientated approach is shown in Table 3.2. The second model, which does not relate directly to information systems design, shows the key snapshots in the development of an accountant. She begins work in a small electronics company and works to the book of her accountancy training. The second frame shows her movement to local government. A team approach is important in a large organization and with this comes what we call a corporate mentality. The mentality requires the accountant to concentrate on the aspect of the local government body she is working for and not the total situation – her experience when working for the electronics company. The third frame shows a switch in the direction of local government (such as that which occurred in the UK in the 1990s and beyond). Accounting thinking becomes much more 'predatory'. Costs are being cut and fiddles are being sought out – value for money rules. This in turn brings a competitive edge to team work and also introduces a 'dynamic' edge to the team concept.

Conclusions

As we have seen in Chapter 2, systems analysis and systems design is a highly complex subject incorporating many different 'flavours' – from the hard and scientific to the soft and holistically focused.

Along with the analysis of problem contexts we have to recognize that we, the analysts and designers, also come into the frame. We affect what we work upon. In order to be fully aware of the impact which we are having upon the work in hand it is quite useful to gain knowledge on two major areas of concern:

- First, where our own strengths and weaknesses are in the problem context. We can get this information from a present-self analysis. The task in hand may require a shift in our present approach to analysis and design and may lead to further shifts in the light of the findings. This indicates a positive switch towards reflective practice and to a learning culture.
- Second, what our path has been to the present situation and therefore what our overall tendencies have been in terms of intellectual development and work methodology. We can ascertain this information from the chronology of self-development. Our current area of application may require a substantial change in intellectual framework or methodology.

All self analysis procedures provide the analyst with an overview of his or her current state. This can be vital if problems arise with the analysis and design procedure and there is a need to rethink the approach. For example, there may be a situation in which the analyst favours the soft approaches, tending to focus on client/user self-help and workshops to discuss problems. The client, however, requires more leadership and drive from the analyst ('why ask us to think it out? that's what we are paying you to do'). Although other reactions might be preferable, the analyst may feel that it is appropriate to shift focus to the hard tools in the methodology and to adopt a more managerial style. More challengingly, the analyst may seek to switch focus to a still more facilitating role thus involving the client in the planning process by illustrating for the client the potency of participation in the information systems analysis and design process. In either case, knowing what you are doing and self-consciously knowing why you are changing direction is important in understanding your relationship with stakeholders.

As we shall see in Chapter 4, the methodology we apply here allows the analyst a certain amount of freedom in the selection of tools in the problem context. If problems arise due to the analyst's approach the analyst can substitute soft for hard tools (or vice versa) or can reschedule their use.

Exercise

Imagine you are the project manager, being paid by a major publisher in the following scenario. Read the scenario and decide what qualities you would require from a systems analyst.

Non-governmental organization (NGO) in London UK

The NGO is involved in the provision of educational books to developing countries. Although quite a small concern the agency is well connected to major publishing concerns and gains substantial quantities of text books at no cost. The main work of the organization is to react to demand from other educational trusts and agencies working in the field. When a request for books come through the NGO tries to meet demand.

The NGO has been convinced by the main publisher it works with to place all its contacts, projects and stocks onto a central computer. The computer, analysis and design and staff training budget are all being donated by the publisher. The idea is being enthusiastically taken up by the NGO's Director who is charismatic but who has no grasp for or interest in the details of the project. The Senior Administrator is hostile to the project because she does not have enough time or assistance to maintain manual systems – the organization is very busy and seems to lurch from crisis to crisis. There are three clerical staff who work part-time.

An answer to this question is provided in Appendix 3.

CHAPTER 4

TERMS OF REFERENCE AND SELECTING OUR PLANNING/DEVELOPMENT TOOLS: SEQUENCE AND SCHEDULE

KEYWORDS/EXPRESSIONS: project cycle, terms of reference, human activity system, rich picture, root definition, conceptual model, information modelling, social and technical systems, human–computer interface, technical aspects, tool selection, context

SUMMARY: All planning or analysis and design begins with a set of terms of reference. Following these the analyst will have some idea as to what specific work is expected, under what conditions and with what resources. Following on from this, the analyst can select the tools which are appropriate within the context of the problem being reviewed and set out their sequence and schedule.

The reality of analysis: Terms of reference

It would be pleasing to the ego and satisfying to the power hungry to believe that the analyst can be all-powerful in the problem context. Like Julius Caesar, to cry 'Veni, Vidi, Vici' (I came, I saw, I conquered) would be a rather satisfactory way of concluding the analysis. This will not happen to you very often if at all if our experience is anything to go by!

Many systems analysis and systems design books set out as though the analyst's word were law and the specified logic of the analysis were always carried out to the letter. This is rarely the case and possibly especially so in situations of rapid change and risk. Financing agencies, be they banks, international donors or accounting departments, putting up the cash for analysis and design, tend to impose very strict guidelines or *terms of reference* upon the analyst, which will mean that a certain amount of prejudging of the situation will have taken place (sometimes by individuals carrying out feasibility studies with little knowledge of information systems, sometimes by decision-makers who think that they already know the answer to the problem – before they know what the problem is or even if there is a problem!).

It is no good the analyst specifying a new, multi-user PC-based management information system and intranet for an organization if the terms of reference restrict all further development to standard office software running on a PC local area network (LAN). Sometimes you may feel disheartened when your analysis tells you very different things from the guidelines you have received.

The ability of the analyst to move freely within the context of his or her terms of reference and the associated budget and manpower limits will depend very much upon:

- the ability of the analyst to convince the funding body that more or less may be required (the latter is easier!) and
- the willingness of the funding body to be flexible.

The golden rule is never to exceed the boundaries of the system as seen by the funding body without first convincing all the major stakeholders in the system that such a course is both right and necessary. This introduces a larger issue, the position of the analysis and design procedure in what is called the project cycle (see Figure 4.1). In this figure analysis and design is one element (item 6) of the cycle and depends for its integration on self analysis and methodology selection and testing as described in Chapters 2 and 3. In this figure the terms of reference are the guiding principles which guide the pre-analysis (item 1). In this figure we have included the 'learning cycle' of Kolb (Kolb 1984) in which all activity is based upon reflecting on what has gone before (eg terms of reference, previous analysis and design experience). This is followed by connecting (eg seeing what is relevant from other approaches and experiences). The deciding aspect is the final selection of the methodological tools and techniques and the doing is the analysis and design itself followed by implementation of the project. The learning cycle means that lessons from experience are gathered by the team and, as we saw in Chapter 1 in the Senge model (Senge et al 1994), by making use of systems thinking and mental models (in items 6 and 7) driven by shared vision achieved during the first four items of the cycle, various benefits arise including the development of team learning and enhanced personal mastery in analysis and design procedures as well as understanding the organization (identifiable in item 8).

Understanding the information environment: Information audit

Organizations are very often unaware of their own information footprint – their own information context and use. If knowledge is power then information is the basis of power. If the information base of an organization is unclear – or merely assumed – it is hard for an organization to plan effectively its knowledge needs or improve its information systems.

One way to gain insight into the information base of an organization is to use a method known as information audit. Others have covered this area in far greater depth but working from some of the ideas from Orna (Orna 1999; Orna and Stevens 1995) it is possible to set out some preliminary assessments which can be usefully undertaken in anticipation of analysis and design.

In an information audit of an organization the essential information needs of stakeholders in the project in view are understood and the existing information structure is mapped. The keyword is 'information' – not data. For our purposes information can be defined as:

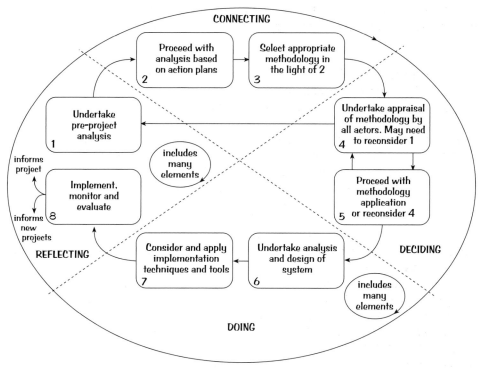

Source: Adapted from Bell (1996)

Figure 4.1 *A view of the project cycle*

'data which has been brought together by some agency, analysed and/or abstracted in some manner in order to provide a decision-maker with the basis for intelligent action'.

A good example of information is the GDP figure for a nation. It is an indicator (this is often the kind of information that stakeholders need) which tells us how a country compares across a common set of data with other countries.

In an information audit a process with a number of steps can be observed:

- Be clear on the limits of the audit. Who are stakeholders and who are not? What information are you interested in and what is non-essential?
- Be clear on who is leading the audit. Usually one person takes overall responsibility for reporting back and also for negotiating times to talk to key stakeholders.
- Identify key stakeholders and list all those who you are going to interview over the audit.
- Devise a common interview format for the interviews: the key question is 'what information does the stakeholder use and what problems do they experience in this use?' The underlying question is 'what works well and what does not work so well from the stakeholder's perspective?'

- For a full information audit we need to know all the major pieces of information that users make use of to do their job.
- Another way of doing this is to have a workshop or series of workshops with stakeholders and get them to work together on tasks and issues to outline their information context (we will be dealing with the way in which tasks and issues can be developed more fully in Chapter 5).
- Be sure to get details of the information problems – or tasks and issues.
- Be sure to focus on information problems which we can do something about. There are often political issues behind information problems and although these may be major issues they are often beyond our power to change. Strictly they are beyond the remit of most information audits in the real world.
- Undertake the interviews or the workshop. They need to cover the full range of stakeholders.
- Document all interviews/workshops.
- Compile the results and make a list of the problem issues and the areas of agreement that things work well.
- Be sure all problems and issues as well as areas where things work well are related to data sources – this is our concern – we need to link these up to the data sources.
- Look out for:
  - common problem areas;
  - common data set problems;
  - problems of data not information being presented to users;
  - unclear information;
  - data swamping;
  - inconsistent data and information storage formats;
  - badly worked out formats leading to ambiguous information;
  - bottlenecks; and
  - blockages.
- Look for the flows of information from supplier to user and for the transformation agents who transform data to information.
- Be aware that your sample stakeholders will represent different aspects of the organizational system, different parts of the organization – so they will probably see the same information or data differently. Also, different stakeholders will see data and information differently.
- One way to represent all findings is an information audit 'map', as in Table 4.1.
- Following this we identify all data sources noted and compare this to the data analysis findings (to be described in Chapter 6).

As we noted at the outset of this section, an information audit can be undertaken in a far more rigorous manner than that advocated here. However, as a means to get grounded in the organization and as a means to let local stakeholders know that an information systems process is being initiated, it is a powerful means to gain attention and get focused on problems and issues.

Table 4.1 *An information audit map*

Stake-holder id	Date of interview or used workshop	Nature of stake	Main information	Associated problems ?	Associated benefits ?	Key areas of concern	Main action points to follow up
1							
2							
3 etc							

The context of an analysis methodology: Selecting the right tools

Thinking back to Chapter 3 and the need to select appropriate analysis and design tools, the next activity within our analysis, and building off the audit outcomes, is to select the analysis and design tools which are appropriate to the situation under study, those that conform to:

- the conditions set out in the terms of reference; and
- the personal preferences set out in our self analysis (outlined in Chapter 3 and highlighted in item 1 in Figure 4.1).

We have already introduced, in outline only, the methodology tools which we are going to set out in this text. These are shown in Figure 4.2. In the next section we will flesh out what these tools actually do.

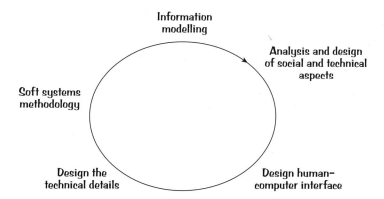

Figure 4.2 *The basics of Multiview*

The soft systems approach

Soft systems comprises the analysis of what Checkland has defined as the human activity system (HAS). The HAS is the main element of our approach to soft systems methodology (SSM) and is, for the purposes of this book, in turn composed of three core items:

- The rich picture, which in our approach is devised to show the principal human, social and cultural activities at work in the perceived environment. The rich picture usually includes the structures and processes at work in an organization.
- The root definition, which by identifying the key clients, actors, transformation expected, assumptions, problem owners and environments, attempts to structure the results of the rich picture analysis into a mutual (analyst and stakeholders) perception of 'what can we do about the problem?'.
- The conceptual model/activity model. This model may be used in two distinct ways in our approach. Firstly as a means to set out the key systems and subsystems involved in the new improved information system. The conceptual model in this sense is an outline of what we are going to attempt to design. In the second sense, the activity model may be a series of key activities to be engaged upon in order to generate the transformation first depicted in the root definition. The use of these two variations is described in more detail in Chapter 5.

Information modelling

The second phase of the analysis is information modelling. In this phase we adopt a more quantitative and technical approach. At this stage we want to develop the conceptual model, which by definition is an idea requiring structuring into a workable information system. In information modelling, building off any information audit we may already have undertaken, we attempt to draw together:

- the major entities;
- the functions of these entities;
- the events which trigger these functions to occur; and
- the attributes, or discrete elements of the entities.

In applying information modelling we are able to generalize the key systems identified in the conceptual model down to a set of data objects and information processing functions which can be the basic design of a new information system. Figure 4.3 shows an outline example of an information model.

Social and technical requirements

The third phase requires that the analyst bring together the right mix of social (human resources) and technical (IT, other technology) aspects. Here the key hardware and identified human alternatives, costs, availability and constraints are integrated to make the appropriate mix. This stage produces a combination of technology and personnel to implement the system outlined in phase 2. The theme of this phase is that the system to be devised it both feasible and sustainable.

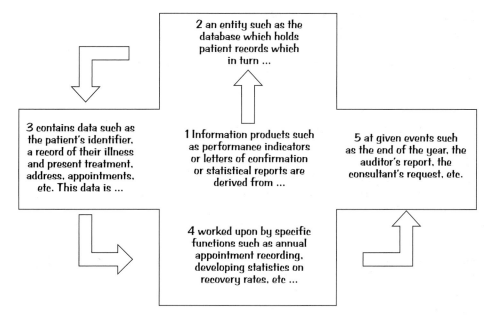

Figure 4.3 *An example of an information model*

Human–computer interface

The fourth phase deals with the human–computer interface (HCI). This involves thinking about the means by which the two aspects of the proposed information system (human beings and technology) can best communicate with each other.

Technical aspects

The fifth and last aspect involves the design of the necessary technical aspects which combine to produce the overall technical solution. The major technical aspects are shown in Figure 4.4.

The six major systems shown are arguably the core of any information system:

1 The *application* deals with transactions within the computer (updating records, gathering data elements for output in digital or paper format).
2 *Retrieval* deals with the output from the information system.
3 The *database* is the core structure containing entities and attributes.
4 *Maintenance* includes both preventative and corrective.
5 *Management* controls the overall information systems process within the organization context.
6 *Monitoring and evaluation* deals with the effective performance of the system and ensuring that learning occurs when and if problems occur.

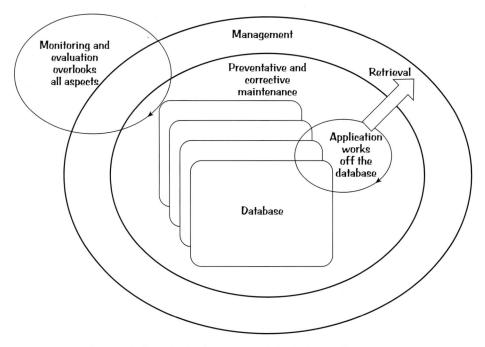

Figure 4.4 *Technical aspects of the information system*

Ways of using Multiview

The current task is to select which, if not all, of the aspects of Multiview to use. Multiview as a whole is set out in Figure 4.5.

Again, do not panic about the complexity of this picture. Figure 4.5 gives us some more detail. First it is worth noting that the first stage of the analysis involves an iterative loop, or period of discussion and feedback between the analyst and the stakeholder group in the context. The second point to note is that the second stage of the analysis, information modelling, may throw up inconsistencies which may lead to a rethink. This type of eventuality is impossible to foresee. For example if the conceptual model requires two departments to share one common information product such as salary details but this idea is strongly objected to by staff. This would require a reworking of the model and most certainly the rich picture. The third point to note is that following the fifth stage of the process comes software selection, hardware selection and implementation strategy – a new sixth stage dealing with software and hardware selection, training and implementation. These issues are not strictly part of the analysis and design but are general issues which will be dealt with in Chapter 10.

The major constraint on the use of analysis and design approaches is cost and time. With analysis and design this simplifies down to time. If we return to the overall picture of our methodology we can identify three separate ways in which the approach can be adapted and adopted.

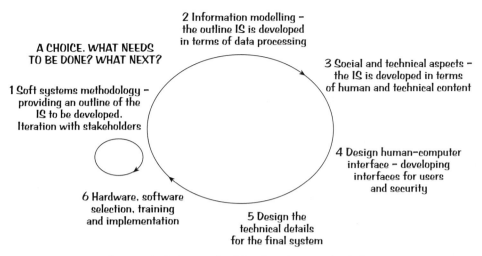

Figure 4.5 *A sustainable planning methodology*

The three 'paths' shown in Figure 4.6 offer three different levels of analysis. They each contain strengths and weaknesses, opportunities and threats (SWOT). SWOT analysis is a useful technique for thinking about an issue. We provide a SWOT for each path below.

- Path 1, the six stage path. Its strength is that it contains the complete methodology and we estimate that this can be completed in six weeks or 30 working days although this is only a guide figure (organizational size and complexity are major factors). However, the weakness is that it requires that you become competent in a number of new skills and does take time to learn. But the value of analysis and design within the organization as an opportunity to learn about organizational processes is enhanced. The threat is that you may discover that there are deeper problems around than you originally thought of. This may mean that the analysis and design is extended.
- Path 2, five stages, as a guide can be completed in 25 working days. A major strength here is the ability to cover ground more quickly; however, the weakness and loss is the design of the human–computer interface. The threat is that the analysis as a whole may be deficient in planning the manner in which the computer interfaces

AUTHORS' NOTE: This book is about sustainable information systems design and we include the word 'non-specialist' in the title. The approach we set out here is based upon the fundamental beliefs that:

- Non-specialists can and do undertake analysis and design.

- A little analysis and design is better than no analysis and design at all.

- That analysis and design approaches often have to be cut to meet the constraints of the context (but as we have already said, a little is better than none).

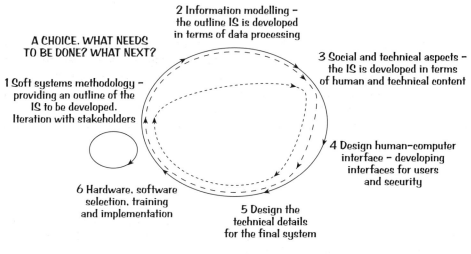

A CHOICE. WHAT NEEDS TO BE DONE? WHAT NEXT?

2 Information modelling – the outline IS is developed in terms of data processing

1 Soft systems methodology – providing an outline of the IS to be developed. Iteration with stakeholders

3 Social and technical aspects – the IS is developed in terms of human and technical content

4 Design human–computer interface – developing interfaces for users and security

6 Hardware, software selection, training and implementation

5 Design the technical details for the final system

PATHWAYS:
1 ——— Steps 1, 2, 3, 4, 5, 6 – guideline of approximately 30 days to do
2 - - - Steps 1, 2, 3, 5, 6 – guideline of approximately 25 days to do
3 - - - - - Steps 1, 3, 5, 6 – guideline of approximately 18 days to do

Figure 4.6 *Which path do I take?*

to the user. However, there is an opportunity in that much IT comes with highly developed built-in graphic interfaces (eg Windows and related software) and sometimes there is little need to consider additional items – the needs of your context will help you understand if this stage is necessary.

- Path 3, four stages, as a guide can be completed in 18 days. Again the strength is the further cutting of time on the analysis and, the weakness is the loss of elements in this case the human–computer interface (as with Path 2) and also information modelling. As a threat, this loss is quite a serious omission and it will result in there being no clear planning of data holding and retrieving structures (the core of most information systems) and the related programmes. Even so, our opportunity is that information modelling is most specifically important where the client is concerned with writing software for a specific and unique purpose. Very often this will not be the case and the end of the analysis will be to propose the client purchase software off the shelf. In this case information modelling is not essential.

AUTHORS' NOTE: A strength of all three approaches is that the review of the human activity system occurs first with each – we are approaching the context from the point of view of the people in the organization and not the data. This means we can build confederacies of interest and develop participation as a major feature of the analysis and design.

Chapters 5–9 outline each of the stages given above. Your current task is to select the best path for your specific analysis. Your choice needs to be based upon the constraints of budget and time and the needs for a detailed analysis and design.

Conclusion

Following on from the review of the approach we are adopting set out in Chapter 2 and the self analysis set out in Chapter 3, Chapter 4 requires us to select the tools which we have the resources to use in our analysis and design. Before going on to the analysis and design proper, be sure in your own mind that you know which of the three paths you think you are going to adopt (you may change your mind in the light of reflection on learning but you need to have an idea of the right path at this point).

Exercise

Read through the scenario set out below and think about it in terms of its strengths, weaknesses, opportunities and threats as an information systems project. Which of the three paths do you think would be most appropriate?

Local education authority management information system

A local education authority (LEA) is attempting to link up a number of schools to a central management information system (MIS) to share information on student and staff records. This is a pilot project which may well lead to extension to all schools if it works. The LEA has pre-selected an MIS package imported from software developers in the United States. The project has a proposed six month cycle and the pilot schools are already selected for the pilot. Schools do not need more bureaucratic intervention at present and the attitude of heads of schools is antagonistic. However, staff are well trained in the use of computers and some of the outputs from the system could help schools in applying for additional resources (eg the identification of children with special needs).

An answer to this question is provided in Appendix 3.

CHAPTER 5

WHAT IS THE PROBLEM? THE HUMAN ACTIVITY SYSTEM: MAKING A MODEL

KEYWORDS/EXPRESSIONS: human activity system, rich picture, context of the user, root definition, new systems model

SUMMARY: To improve the chances of producing a useful analysis and design the analyst needs to clearly define the key elements of the situation and relate these to the terms of reference. This chapter makes this connection and develops the analysis within the context of the rich picture, the prime means for understanding the context for the information system in terms of issues and tasks. Having agreed the rich picture the major factors of the proposed information system environment are developed in terms of the root definition (who is doing what for whom and in what context?) and agreed with the major stakeholders. Finally a systems model is produced which gives the outline of the proposed new system; this can then form the basis for the next stage of the analysis.

Introduction to the human activity system

It should be noted that the development of the human activity system (HAS), as set out in this chapter, is the result of practice in a wide variety of contexts (eg developing countries, newly industrializing countries and industrialized countries). The version we give here is a reflection of our need to adapt methodology for context. If the reader is seeking the definitive text on the conventional form the book by Checkland and Scholes (Checkland and Scholes 1990) is recommended.

In most contexts of information systems development there is a need and a problem – at least one of each! The perception of the problem situation and the resulting definition of the need for information is the nexus of this stage of analysis. Our job is to alleviate the problem by improving the information processing capacity of the organization.

With the key ideas of information need and problem situation in mind we can say that the problem as such will be expressed within the context of the HAS. The HAS can be seen as a view on the social/cultural/ethical/technical (etc) situation of the organization. In outline we can see the process of HAS analysis as shown in Figure 5.1.

Figure 5.1 begins from the standpoint of perceiving the new information problem situation. From this arises the use of our first tool, the creation of the structures and processes of the rich picture. This should define for us the major tasks and issues involved in the problem context. The next stage of the analysis, and the next tool to be used, is the root definition in which we make use of the CATWOE criteria (more on this later, but it can be abbreviated to mean who is doing what for whom, under what assumptions and in what environment) which sets out the fundamental features of the problem context. From this definition we can create a new model of the improved situation as we see it. This model is called a conceptual model in most of the literature. In the examples we develop here we tend to make use of the systems model.

Do not worry about these phrases here. For a definition of each see the Glossary of Buzzwords. Each will be developed in the next 30 pages or so. Like most specialized language and phrases you will find them quite simple concepts in themselves.

AUTHORS' NOTE: We should not confuse the concept of the information system with the more specific *computerized information system*. Quite often the situation requiring analysis will already contain an information system and the result of all the analysis and design may be to prescribe a revised manual system. On the other hand, computerized information systems are very common and the outcome of analysis and design is usually to advocate an improved technologically based facility. The important point is that the analyst should not prejudge the context or the result of the analysis and design process.

Source: Adapted from Avison and Wood-Harper (1990)

Figure 5.1 *Overview of the soft systems approach*

For now, let's return to our problem context, the organization. This organization may be a research institute, a government department, a training centre, a single office within some large organization or a non-governmental organization. It may even be just one person, a sole researcher wanting to keep research records, or a teacher recording student progress.

The purpose of this phase is to assist the analyst because he or she needs to understand the HAS in order to study the information flows involved in the organization.

If an information audit such as that described in the previous chapter has already been undertaken then you will have some idea of the flows, sources and sinks of information and also the attitude and feelings of the stakeholders in the system. If no audit has taken place then you will be fresh to the context. Either way the HAS will improve your understanding of the information context.

With this in mind the first job of the analyst is to help the major stakeholders in the organization define the situation and analyse what the problem is so that they can set about solving it. The analysis of the situation as viewed as a human activity system as shown in Figure 5.1 consists of:

- Perceiving the organization's problem situation as defined in the terms of reference.
- By means of the rich picture identifying the tasks and issues.
- Identifying and noting key conflicts of interest.
- Coming to an agreed definition of the problem that is to be tackled.
- Setting out the outline of the improved system themes in the systems model.

The following sections will develop upon these themes.

The rich picture

Preparation

Often professional analysts will have very little knowledge or understanding about the range of issues as understood by the range of stakeholders involved in the host organization's information processing work. This book is intended for non-professionals and for those planning information systems for their own organization, so we do not assume that you will necessarily be new to the problem context. It can be an advantage to have little knowledge of the organization in which you are working! An outside analyst will have terms of reference, timescale and budget and an outline job to do. As an outsider the analyst will not have problems with existing staff relationships or subjective preferences concerning the way the organization is run. The analyst often needs to understand the problem context rapidly and in this process of understanding has a chance to bring a degree of *impartial and uncommitted* analysis. If on the other hand you are a member of the organization in which your analysis and design is taking place, you probably will have developed your own ideas, which will often be unstated and sometimes not consciously recognized. This can cause problems. For example, an analyst working in a hospital has a strongly held belief that the Accident and Emergency Department is a better candidate for a new information system rather than Gynaecology. This may sound silly but it may arise from a personal belief based upon close familiarity with the one department and comparative ignorance of the other. New systems which in turn reflect this view may cause problems for the user community and ultimately for the analyst. Outsider analysts may also have problems, for example, imposing their expert opinion on situations of which they have little understanding. To reduce the likely problems which may arise from this type of subjective preference we have a series of analysis and design application tools which we will use throughout the following analysis:

- User/client (or more generally – stakeholder) participation is usually essential if the analysis is to be useful. The problem is not the analyst's property – it belongs to the organization and for this reason the individuals in the organization must be brought into partnership with the analyst designer as part of the problem solving team. Some useful tools for doing this include:
  - A preliminary meeting with all those concerned with the analysis and design; this can include:
  - setting out and discussion of the terms of reference. The stakeholders can be encouraged to comment on the task and to make any observations on the way in which the analysis and design might develop. A SWOT analysis by all those present can be very useful.
  - Regular workshops throughout the analysis and design for briefing and sharing of views.
- Rigorous application of the agreed terms of reference. Many forms of systems analysis and systems design tend to spill over into areas which are not contained in the original problem. This form of 'mission creep' is quite a regular feature of systems work. Nevertheless practical analysis which is results focused needs to be focused on the issues which are of primary concern to the stakeholder community. This does not mean that other areas are to be ignored. If the new system impinges upon a larger area of concern then recommendations can be made for a wider study at a later date.
- Reporting. All stages of analysis need to be adequately reported, primarily for the analyst's own benefit (it is frighteningly easy to forget the outcomes of previous work) and also as an aid for the stakeholders. Information systems professionals are renowned for providing poor or no documentation.
- The use of interview techniques. Much has been written on the various elements of the art of interviews (see Suggested Reading). Key points for the analyst are:
  - Initial contact: dress and manner should be appropriate to the problem setting. It is surprising how many analysts 'lose' their object of study by appearing too glib, off-hand or conceited.
  - Sequence: it's a good idea to lead in your interview with some light and non-threatening conversation (especially with those who seem most uncomfortable with the idea of information systems). More detailed questioning can then follow.
  - Questions must be understandable. This may appear obvious but quite often information systems related questions are far from obvious to those being asked.

- Caution is required when pushing into areas which are sensitive (eg internal audit, inter-departmental competition, budget). A lack of tact can cause an interviewee to dry up.
- Always be neutral/sympathetic in your style.
- Again a basic point: be sure to document the interview, you *will* forget much of the detail otherwise. If you intend to record interviews be sure to tell your interviewee and ask his/her permission.

• Basic observation of site and behaviour. Many key factors for a successful analysis taking place in limited time are literally eye catching. By keeping eyes and ears open we do not neglect the vital clues (eg staff aggression, resentment, poor filing, shabby record keeping).

Quite often the analyst will discover that there has never been a prior analysis or review of the organization's information processing problems and capacities and there may be a fair degree of surprise at some of the findings of the rich picture. In terms of learning and the Senge five disciplines (Senge et al 1994), this stage of the analysis hits a number of major targets (see Table 5.1).

The primary components of the rich picture: Structures

Rich pictures, as used in this book, are composed of two elements: structure and process. These are divided into two key areas: technical 'facts' ('hard', formal areas) and social/ethical/cultural realities ('soft', informal areas). Throughout this book we will be working on one key example and several minor ones to explain the way in which Multiview works. Our first information will be a set of terms of reference. For the purpose of the example we are working out in this book these are as follows:

If you are using this book as an aid to your own analysis and design, then you will need to consider your own terms of reference before proceeding. Our example is selected intentionally to show how systems analysis and systems design tools can be used in situations where resources are limited and conditions are not ideal (eg maybe in terms of cross-cultural analysis or a hostile climate or low access to expert skills) and still produce useful information systems and organizational (and personal) learning.

The conventional way to begin is to produce a map or cartoon of the major structures to be involved in the picture (Hall 1997). These may be departmental boundaries, system boundaries, national borders, etc, as they are applicable to the problem in view.

In our view the best way to undertake this form of analysis is to just get drawing. Usually we get stakeholders involved, get some large sheets of paper, share out the pens and

THINK POINT: How would you use these techniques in an analysis in your organization? Most particularly how might you make use of a general observation of site behaviour? In participatory approaches (Chambers 1997) a technique called *transect walks* which are systematic walks with local stakeholders through the context. The walk through is accompanied with conversation about what we are seeing. The discipline is to note, remember and write up what is seen and experienced.

Table 5.1 *Learning organization and HAS*

Discipline	Value in HAS thinking	Outcome?
Systems thinking	Essential, provides a view of the wholeness which is the context.	Insight beyond what may be the presenting problem.
Personal mastery	In the HAS stage there is the opportunity for the vision which drives the terms of reference to be questioned in context, and this in turn can be an opportunity for the team to develop their mastery of both the task in hand and the realities of the context.	Ownership and control over the problem.
Mental models	In the HAS stage the team gain a number of mental models of the problem context. The models range from an unstructured group perception, a focus on what transformation is needful and a vision of activities to bring about useful change.	Clear, risk-free analysis.
Shared vision	The HAS is the main tool for developing this in the process of developing a view of the problem context.	Improving clarity of purpose.
Team learning	The 'team' should begin to form in the participatory approach at this time.	Consensus on the way forward.

encourage people to set out their context as best they can. Any initial nerves and embarrassment are soon lost in laughter as drawing skills (or lack of them!) of the participants are shown, especially when drawing self-portraits.

However, if you are nervous about getting going on this 'cold' so to speak, then the picture can be developed gradually by process.

Working towards the eventual picture, the exercise can be begun by setting out the 'hard' or formal and uncontested structures in the context. In terms of the government department which is the basis for our analysis Figure 5.2 shows our first stab at these.

Terms of reference as received from the project funding agency:

'Develop the design and present a proposal for an information system containing the non-specialist functions (eg general office processes) of a small government department in a developing country. The design should be focused on the need to improve efficiency and timeliness in terms of day-to-day operations.'

Resources – 1 analyst.

Time allocation – 30 days.

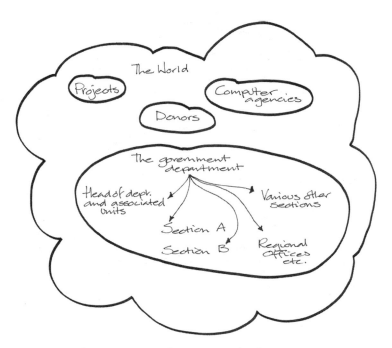

Figure 5.2 *Hard structures in the context*

Immensely simplified as this view is, it shows that the analyst is aware of various agencies at work both within and outside the focus of the analysis – the governmental department. Our hard structure tells us that the department is composed of several discrete sections or areas of activity and that there are three key structures operational outside the boundary of the department, in the world cloud, which may well impinge upon the eventual system to be set up. Note: there will be quite a number of other agencies and groups at work within the context of the department. This initial portrayal of the major areas of interest already shows that we are beginning to focus down on to what the analyst believes to be the key areas of concern as expressed in the terms of reference – departmental management.

Our next task is to set out the less formal or contested and soft structures active within the overall problem context. The important feature of this stage is to set out structures which, although we identify them as being essential for the eventual working of the system, are related more to cultural and ethical than technical points. Because of the sensitivity of some structures, it may not always be possible to show these soft structures in workshops with stakeholders and the final report. In our case the types of structure are shown in Figure 5.3.

THINK POINT: When is a structure 'hard' or 'soft'? (We provide one idea of the answer in the next think point.)

In the soft picture we identify a range of structures: some more formal (the promotions committee), some more informal (language and cultural groups) and some political (faction and interest groups). The reason all these structures are

Figure 5.3 *The soft structures*

termed 'soft' may not be immediately obvious but is because they are identified in our analysis to date as having subjective and therefore to some extent unguessable effects. For example, the promotions committee in most normal circumstances would be seen as having a hard, objective identity in the department. In this case we are not interested in the committee's function and purpose; we are interested in one of its informal functions which is to move staff around for political reasons. This could have a major impact on an embryonic information system or data processing unit. Another soft structure is the externally funded donor unit within the department. Again it is a physical unit with a task to accomplish not directly related to the work in hand. However, its presence is felt by most major actors in the department and for this reason it has a subjective (true or untrue) watchdog function. Most obviously soft are the cultural and language groupings in the department. Any incoming system has to work with the dominant theme in terms of culture and will have to reach an accommodation with other interests. Almost subliminal to the outside, short-term consultant analyst but vital to note are the interest groups and factions within the senior staff groupings. These may not have a direct impact on the project as a whole but they do need to be understood and planned around. In the outside world we have a Ministerial watchdog, problems of power supply failure and fluctuation and the lack of infrastructural support (hardware and software support).

As already noted, it will not always be advisable to identify all structures in reports and workshops. There are often good working reasons why an analyst wishes to keep clear of unnecessary controversy. This is part of the reality of understanding analysis and design in context. The result of the construction of a

Structures in the world		Processes
Projects	⇨	Construct and maintain road network and produce regular reports
Donors	⇨	Liaise with department and control projects
Computer agencies	⇨	Support local companies and governmental departments
Structures in the department		
Central management	⇨	Keep staff records, keep project records, control local management, liaise with donor, liaise with Ministry
Regional offices	⇨	Update central records, manage local projects
Sections	⇨	Control and mechanical good store (A) Control mechanical training (A) Design of projects (B) Computing (B) Planning and liaison (C) Accounts (D)

Figure 5.4 *Hard processes and their structures*

rich picture should be the identification by the analyst of what is possible within the problem context. What is and is not said and made explicit is a decision left to the discretion of the individual analyst.

The primary components of the rich picture: Processes

Our next task is to identify hard and soft processes operating upon structures in terms of the overall work of the department. As above, we can develop our thinking with two separate models. Figure 5.4 demonstrates the relationship

Structures in the world		Processes
Ministry	⇨	Watching brief over department. Coordinate and liaise with department
Power supply	⇨	Intermittent fluctuation and failure
Infrastructure and support	⇨	Breakdown in supplies of consumables and spares
Structures in the department		
Factions and interest groups	⇨	Selective support of projects, selective support of key personnel, obstruction
Language and culture	⇨	Forms for information flow presented in two languages
Promotions committee	⇨	Achieve staff mobility
Donor unit	⇨	Act as a watchdog on developments within the department

Figure 5.5 *Soft processes and structures*

between the structures and processes in the hard context.

The processes which we set against each function are only part of the whole range of activities performed. This demonstrates again the subjective nature of the analysis (there is never a 'right' rich picture in this sense as there will always be something missing) and the attempt of the analyst to stay as close to the terms of reference as possible. Figure 5.5 shows the parallel development of the 'soft' structures and processes model.

With the completion of the soft process and structure diagram we have completed the collection of information necessary for the final composition of the rich picture.

Putting together the rich picture

In one sense this might be thought to be no longer necessary. The foregoing demonstrates that the analyst has got a reasonable grasp of the various areas of the problem context and has sifted out technical from other issues. However, one of the major reasons for producing a rich picture is to visualize the problem situation at a glance. This cannot be achieved if the various elements of the analysis are kept as discrete diagrams. Another major consideration in the development of the rich picture is the value of putting all items together – showing links and

THINK POINT: One way to think about the question: When is a structure 'hard' or 'soft'? is as follows:

- The analyst is the final judge. What is hard to one person is soft to another although this is not always the case.
- Generally hard are fixed and formal, soft are variable and informal.
- Hard tend to be uncontested 'facts'. Soft tend to be contested beliefs and values.
- Hard items tend to be known and of lower risk than soft, which are often denied and therefore a greater risk.
- Hard items tend to relate to the dominant mindset and the world as defined by the powerful. Soft tend to be items relating to alternative mindsets and observations about power.

As you see, arriving at a judgement is more a craft skill than a scientific process.

contrasts. An outcome of this can be new insight and the awareness of emergent issues and tasks not realized before.

Rich picturing first requires us to simplify reality whilst not ignoring or trivializing experienced complexity. One method for doing this is to set out all the processes and structures, the most important characteristics of the major individuals involved and the terms of reference – see Figure 5.6.

In Figure 5.6 the terms of reference, structures and processes are mapped onto one diagram. First the material is divided up into what is happening in the organization and what is happening outside the organization. This draws a boundary but does not inhibit the flow of information, power and resources through the boundary. Our next task is to set out the major groupings within these two components – see Figure 5.7.

In this process the analysis is beginning to bring together all the aspects of the situation into one frame. This in turn provides us with a core concept or mindset

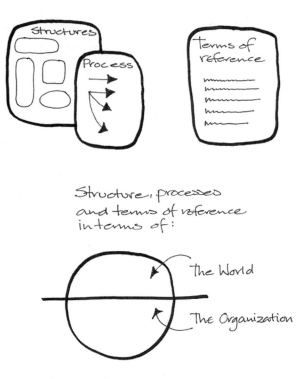

Figure 5.6 *Developing the rich picture*

of the problem. One of the most common complaints that practitioners make at this stage is that they cannot draw, or they do not have a clever computer package to produce quality diagrams. Do not worry about this for now. What follows are various examples of rich pictures, almost all drawn without computers. It is of course useful if a rich picture can be attractive and pleasing to the eye – but this is useless if it

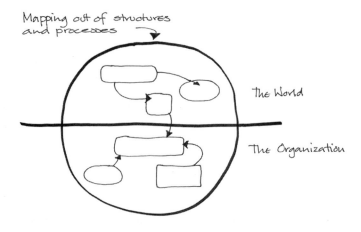

Figure 5.7 *Mapping out structure and process*

does not represent the thinking of those involved. What is most important is gaining an understanding of the meaning of the context which produced the rich picture.

To make even hand drawn pictures useful for overhead transparency use it is of value to use a set of symbols which have a readily comprehensible meaning. In short, to make the final drawings more understandable it is useful to adopt some form of a grammar of symbols.

The symbols which we show in Figure 5.8 are some that we use and like – you might think of more for your own situation.

The resulting rich picture, in this case for the government department, is shown in Figure 5.9.

It may be useful to go back to the beginning of this section to be clear in your mind how this picture follows on from the process set out there. All the pictures on the following pages are simplistic and to some extent are superficial in their scope, leaving out some of the more contentious details of the group thinking processes which formed them. Without the rich picture there is little chance that we could structure into the analysis the type of personal and organizational problems which fall outside the scope of more objective, formal forms of analysis.

> AUTHORS' NOTE: The use of rich pictures is not terribly revolutionary as a way of capturing thoughts. Thinking back to ancient Egypt and the use of hieroglyphics it is evident that the writing of stories by means of diagrams was once dominant. Diagrams still form an important aspect of many cultures. In understanding the hieroglyphs the important thing to remember is that each image is *symbolic*, it represent an idea or a concern. Egyptian hieroglyphs are beautiful and, for those who can read the story, are dense with meaning, allowing Egyptologists to say a great deal about the nature of a society several thousand years dead. Our task is not so sublime, we are attempting to tell the story of a current organization.

It should be noted that the rich pictures developed here and the further analysis which follows are case studies drawn from experiences in various developing countries. They do not represent any particular department and do not reflect the experiences of any similar institutions.

Remember, the vital ingredient and assumption about the rich picture (and many of the phases which follow) is that they are worked through in collaboration and with the consent of the major stakeholders in the situation, in so far as this is possible, and that the information being gathered is not deleterious to the ultimate success of the project. The means by which collaboration and feedback are achieved are:

• developing a state of trust based on:
• workshops and
• regular reporting and
• regular (daily) discussions and feedback as you work through your thinking.

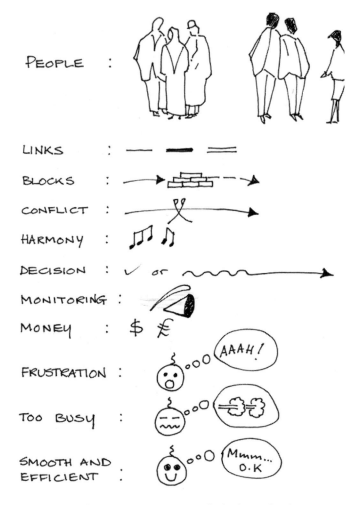

Figure 5.8 *Some symbols for rich pictures*

The examples shown here (Figures 5.9, 5.10 and 5.11) illustrate what is required in the rich picture.

The crosses on lines indicate conflicts of interest or conflicts of some kind between major aspects of the current situation.

For example, in the department of roads (Figure 5.9), the regional offices require rapid rebriefing on details of roads work from the projects. At the same time the Administration at central office also requires regular reports from the regional offices to ensure that records are kept up to date and the annual Ministerial reporting procedure can occur smoothly. Poor communications infrastructure as well as different perceptions of priorities ensures that there is a constant level of friction. The thought bubbles show the main concerns of the major stakeholders involved. You can also see the way in which conflict and competition operate in organizations.

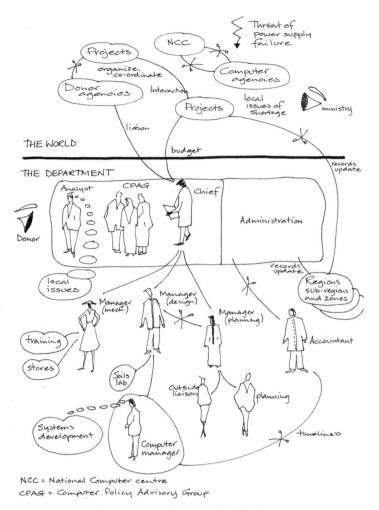

NCC = National Computer centre
CPAG = Computer Policy Advisory Group

Figure 5.9 *The initial rich picture*

It may take many discussions, workshops and papers before the picture is agreed. However, this is time well spent because all further analysis work can be more surely directed towards the agreed problem. In this book we are concerned with sustainable information systems design but we recognize that this stage will need to be accomplished in the matter of a few days. Nevertheless, this time can be packed with interaction and discourse between the various stakeholders and yourself.

Several new points arise from the rich picture shown in Figure 5.9:

- The importance of the power supply issue is re-emphasized.
- The centralized nature of the department around one key personality is drawn out.
- The internal conflict between two major sections is emphasized.
- The peripheral nature of existing IT is expressed.

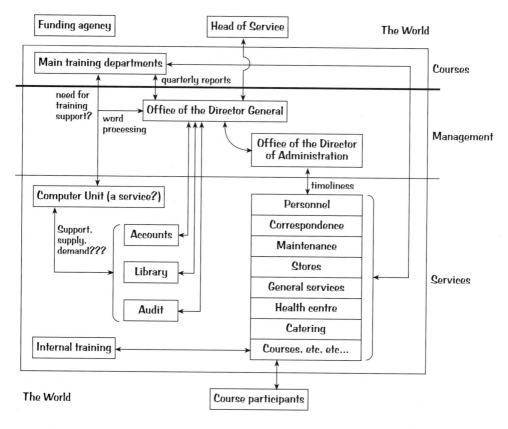

Figure 5.10 *An organogram-style rich picture*

Figures 5.10 and 5.11 show a couple of examples of the variety of ways in which a rich picture can be displayed.

Figure 5.10 shows a training college. The main point made by the picture is the existence of an existing computer unit and the question of its value and relevance. This style of picture can be very helpful for display purposes for senior management. Because the picture is rigidly ordered and very 'neat' this may well have appeal. One word of caution. This type of presentation is often favoured by some stakeholders because of its neatness. However, it fails to represent much of the soft, personality-based complexity which a true rich picture can encapsulate. We argue that even a badly drawn traditional rich picture offers the analyst more in terms of depicting problems in the situation being studied.

Our final example (Figure 5.11) builds on this last point, it is a working copy of a student's rich picture. This may look chaotic and incomprehensible but, to the individual who produced it, it contains the essence of his view of his problem context. We show this rich picture in order to demonstrate that presentation is not the item of key importance. It is much more important to get the context and the meaning of the problem agreed to.

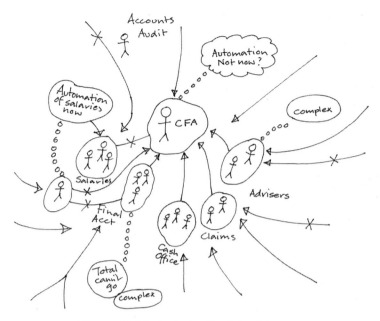

Figure 5.11 *A student's rich picture*

The rich picture when drawn up and agreed should be informative of *primary tasks*, and major *issues*. What is meant by this?

Primary tasks should reflect the most central tasks which need to be accomplished within the problem context. Any incoming information system is usually intended to support, develop and execute primary tasks.

Issues are matters of dispute which can have a deleterious effect upon organizations achieving their purpose. In terms of the information system, the issues are often much more important than the tasks.

In the rich picture of the government department we could say that primary tasks are:

- Review the capacity and use of the existing computer unit and related staff.
- Understand the nature of the relationship of the chief with senior staff.
- Review the capacity of the context to support the management information system (MIS).

The issue might be:

- Internal feuding.
- Poor track record regarding IT.
- Communications problems.

It is usually not possible to resolve all issues and for this reason they should always be understood and recognized. In learning about

> THINK POINT: Try drawing a rich picture now. Maybe produce one of your family or of your organization. Be sure to think in terms of soft and hard structures and processes.

issues and reflecting upon their causality we often discover important factors which we need to be conscious of in developing the information system. Issues are vital in making our analysis and design a learning process for the organization as a whole. Reality really is complex and the analyst should never approach a problem context with a conceited or inflated view of his or her own capacity. Not all problems can be mapped, discussed and designed away. Often the analyst will be required to develop a form of 'wait and see' towards certain problems which are either *imponderable* at the time of the analysis (give time constraints), or *too political*, in terms of the organization's capacity to express them openly and become involved in discussions about them. This does raise an ethical question for the analyst.

Situations can develop in which large numbers of insurmountable problems arise with issues that, in your opinion, are going to cause lasting impediments to the ultimate systems design. In cases of this type only you can decide which course to take:

- Design the system as best you can within these constraints.
- Say unpalatable things to the problem owners and set conditions for further work to be carried out.
- Ignore the problems and design the information system as if they did not exist (we would never recommend this course).
- Refuse to continue the analysis until the issue is settled.

AUTHORS' NOTE: Throughout this book we will keep a tally of the number of days which we think each element of the analysis can be accomplished in. Of course the tally we give is nominal and will vary with your context but we do feel that analysis can be made, in many situations, to fit a schedule.

Each of these courses has quite serious implications. Only the analyst can make the decision concerning which is most appropriate within his or her own context.

The bottom line for the rich picture is to provide the analyst with a means to move from *thinking about the problem to thinking about what can be done about the problem.*

Amount of time devoted to analysis so far:
Total for this stage (rich picture) = 3 days
Cumulative total = 3 days

In most cases we feel that this stage of the analysis can be completed in less than three days, although we may need to recognize that rich picturing should not be artificially curtailed. In the minds of many people, this is the most important part of the systems analysis and sometimes considerably more time is required. If this is so in your case you may need to adopt either path 2 or 3 as set out in Chapter 4.

Keeping in mind the primary tasks and issues arising from the rich picture, we can now go on to look at the specific views of the major stakeholders as they are concerned with the new systems definition (what it is supposed to do). This should result in our tightening up the context of the job which we are to do and harmonizing the view of this job between stakeholders. The mechanism we use for this is called the root definition.

The root definition

Introduction

The assumption of the root definition is that the different stakeholders in the system will have different opinions about it. If you were to ask some of the members of a government department questions like: 'what is the main purpose of your department?', you might get different answers, such as:

- 'to carry out an efficient operation';
- 'to keep people employed';
- 'to provide a service for the national community'.

These are all valid statements of aims, but they may have conflicting implications for the organization and the original terms of reference for the analysis and design into a new information system. Also they are much too vague to help the analyst produce a system which will help the organization in furthering its aims.

It is useful if a point of reference exists whereby the main tasks (in the light of the issues) discovered in the rich picture and produced by the analyst and stakeholders in the context can be tested to make sure that the perception of the elements of the terms of reference are being fulfilled. Therefore, at an early stage a careful definition of the required system (and therefore the change or transformation within the organization) is essential. Of course this is going to be very general but in terms of our approach in this book the root definition contains six ingredients. In terms of the current issue: who is doing what for whom and to what end? In what environment is the new system to be implemented? To whom is the final system going to be answerable? In terms of the HAS these are known respectively as:

- *Customer:* the systems beneficiary or victim;
- *Actor:* the individual(s) involved in the system development;
- *Transformation:* the change which the project is intended to achieve;
- *Worldview:* the fundamental assumptions that affect the proposed information system;
- *Owner:* the eventual system owner; and
- *Environment:* the situation in which the system will be developed – this may also relate to the constraints which that environment imposes upon any new information system.

This leads to the acronym *CATWOE*.

The definition of each of the elements, and the construction of a definition which encapsulates them all, is a matter for negotiation between the stakeholders in the situation, the analyst and the context of the terms of reference for the project. The forms of communication created during the rich picture stage of the analysis should be very helpful now. Depending upon the time available and the complexity of the situation you will need to carry out a *CATWOE* analysis of the major stakeholders. Again, you are the final decision maker in terms of setting out who needs to be questioned.

In our example the definition for the government roads department is shown, from the perspective of:

- The analyst.
- The donor.
- The chief of department.

From the amalgamation of these with agreement on key items we can try to arrive at a consensus view:

- The learning team representing both departmental and non-departmental stakeholders (a consensus view).

The analyst is in the frame because it is very important to be sure that we are working on the same basic assumptions as the organization. There are cases where the analyst has undertaken systems analysis only to find at the end that the organization was under the impression that the research was being undertaken for very different reasons!

Three examples of CATWOE

The definition of each point of the CATWOE can be as drawn out or as brief as you feel necessary. Generally a few words on each item will draw out the main features of each stakeholder's views. In our example sometimes only one word is used.

The analyst CATWOE

Customer: the donor, and the department
Actors: the analyst, potential computer staff, actual computer staff
Transformation: an automated MIS
Worldview: departmental automation is an essential requirement for organizational development
Owner: the department
Environment: the department and regional offices – this includes features of climatic turbulence, very limited infrastructure and negligible technical support

The donor CATWOE

Customer: the department and also the ministry
Actors: the analyst and local staff
Transformation: automated MIS in place for organizational development and increasing efficiency
Worldview: effective automation for management
Owner: the department
Environment: the department is the environment for the MIS

The chief of department's CATWOE

Customer: the department
Actors: staff and external consultants

Transformation: automation of major administrative functions
Worldview: to improve the efficiency of departmental operations
Owner: the chief
Environment: the department is its own environment for the MIS

These views were supplied during interview as were most of the details of the rich picture. They offer us a fair degree of agreement within the problem context. In the analysis and design developed in this book it is the analyst's job to assess the degree of differences between root definitions and to harmonize an overall view which all stakeholders can agree to. This will mean that differences in interpretation will not occur (or are less reasonably likely to occur!) later on. In some cases the root definitions can be seen as fixing together to form a cone focusing on the problem situation at the root of the exercise, as shown in Figure 5.12.

In this case the three levels of root definition can be seen as being focused on one agreed problem context and the transformation of that. The graphic presentation seen in Figure 5.12 indicates that differences in CATWOE relate more to the position of each party (remote or close to the problem context) in terms of local understanding and sympathy rather than marked differences in opinion about the nature of the transformation sought. From this we can produce a consensus view such as that shown below.

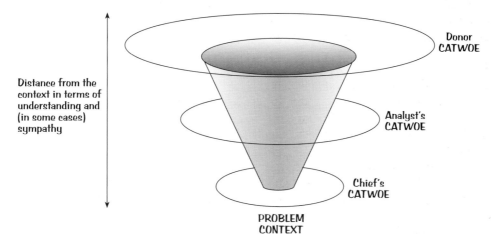

Figure 5.12 *Overlapping root definitions of the problem context*

The learning team of stakeholders (a consensus view)
Customer: the government generally and the department specifically
Actors: the analyst and local staff
Transformation: to improve departmental efficiency by use of an MIS
Worldview: the operation of an MIS in the department would substantially enhance the productivity and efficiency of the department
Owner: the donor (as the remote owner) and the department (as the immediate owner)

Environment: the department as both a central office and (later) as the regional offices – the constraints will relate to power supply, climate and geography

This consensus view needs to be agreed to by all major stakeholders involved. Agreement may require a certain amount of flexibility by all parties and achieving this can be a matter of considerable skill arising from craft knowledge. In developing the vision of the consensus root definition, team learning is enhanced, the vision is shared and boundaries of agreement are being set out. The analysis and design is improving the internal learning of the organization.

> THINK POINT: take a good long look at Figure 5.13. Would you think the outlook for the project is good, bad or average?

> THINK POINT: In this case there is very little agreement among the various stakeholders as to what should be done. The various views could be brought together into a rough consensus as shown in Figure 5.14. This example would appear to be doomed to failure. If this were so then the root definition has served us well, showing up major structural weaknesses in the new information system plan and stopping us from investing in a system which is so frail.

The consensus root definition is firmed up immeasurably if the CATWOE criteria are subsequently developed into a single 'vision' or statement following the lines:

'A *title* project developed by the *actors* for the *customers* and with the *owners* having ultimate responsibility, intended to achieve the *transformation*, assuming the *worldview* and within the *environmental constraints*.'

Such a statement or true root definition provides the information systems project with an unambiguous declaration of intent and purpose which can be literally signed off by all stakeholders.

The establishment of an agreed root definition takes us to the point where, within the context of the situation as set out in the rich picture and the agreed perspective of the root definition, we can begin to design our new, improved information systems outline. This outline is set out in the systems model.

Amount of time devoted to analysis so far:
Total for this stage (root definition) = 1 day
Cumulative total = 4 days

In many cases the root definition can be arrived at in as little as 1 day to as many as 5 days (depending on the complexity of gaining consensus). There can be exceptions to this. Figure 5.13 depicts a very different view of a root definition.

Director of a research organization (RO)

Client – Self and RO
Actor – Key staff in RO
Transformation – Composite data translated into information, quickly
Worldview – 'We have the data not the information'
Owner – Self
Environment – RO

Head of the research department in the RO

Client – 'Him' (the Director) – 'one of his whims'
Actor – 'All too likely to be me!'
Transformation – 'Create more bloody work when we cannot cope now!'
Worldview – 'I have data and information but no time'
Owner – 'Him' (the Director)
Environment – 'As far away as is possible!'

Funding agency for the GIS

Client – RO
Actor – Key staff in RO monitored by United Nations
Transformation – Improve effectiveness to forecast and act against drought
Worldview – We have the technology
Owner – RO
Environment – RO

The analyst

Client – 'Him' (the Director), the United Nations and all departments
Actor – Initially me – to be all departments focused on IT unit
Transformation – Create more work and improve effectiveness
Worldview – Questionable technology – a 'test case'
Owner – The Director
Environment – The RO and Sub-Sahel Africa

Figure 5.13 CATWOE for a geographic information system

The new system (in concept)

Introduction

The rich picture is intended to be 'rich' in terms of people, processes, ideas, conflicts, etc. Once one has a feel for the problem context we can begin the process of drawing out the aspects on which we now know we have to concentrate. The intention of this phase is to build a model of the system which is recognized as being a reasonable basis for the new information system.

Two items to be aware of are:

1 The desire to take elements of this methodology out of context. It is not our purpose here to specify exactly what the system must do, who will do it and how long it will take. This process might more usefully be thought of as arising in the

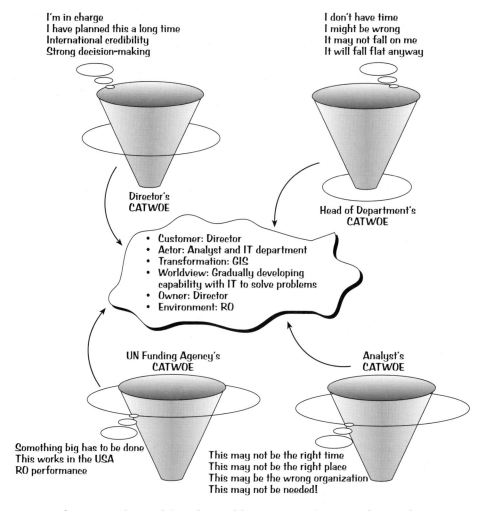

I'm in charge
I have planned this a long time
International credibility
Strong decision-making

I don't have time
I might be wrong
It may not fall on me
It will fall flat anyway

Director's
CATWOE

Head of Department's
CATWOE

- Customer: Director
- Actor: Analyst and IT department
- Transformation: GIS
- Worldview: Gradually developing capability with IT to solve problems
- Owner: Director
- Environment: RO

UN Funding Agency's
CATWOE

Analyst's
CATWOE

Something big has to be done
This works in the USA
RO performance

This may not be the right time
This may not be the right place
This may be the wrong organization
This may not be needed!

Figure 5.14 *Resolving the problem or papering over the cracks?*

second and third phases of the methodology which deals with information modelling. At this stage we are only concerned in separating out the main components of the system and to show how they relate to each other.

2 Beware of the tendency to assume that we are modelling reality. All models are symbols of reality and represent the assumptions of individuals and groups. In this case the model will represent the shared perception of the activities of the ultimate information system as focused and presented by the analyst in collaboration with the major stakeholders. This is quite a different thing from saying that we are modelling reality. This work remains 'conceptual'.

Back to the modelling exercise. Ideally, and according to all the text books, we should remove personalities, though not their roles, from the picture, because we do not want to create a system around particular personalities. Frankly, this is not always possible. Many organizations are so designed around key personnel that to design any incoming system without taking them into account would be a nonsense (you will probably have identified whether this is so in your case during the phase of the rich picture). At best it can be said therefore that at this stage those undertaking the process should, so far as is possible and useful, sideline personalities from the systems design. In phase three of the methodology we will be looking to integrate the information system into the lives of the people who will be using it.

In the creation of conceptual and systems models it is useful to recognize two key issues:

- It is not the job of the models to align existing sub-departments/units with tasks. At present the intention is to set out the incoming system tasks irrespective of units and sections. The new system may well require the substantial reworking of such groupings.
- The models have to comply with the results of our *root definition* and our original *terms of reference*. It is quite easy to get carried away at this point and lose sight of what was originally specified!

Conceptual model/systems model

The information systems project now needs to be defined in an unambiguous manner. For the purposes of this analysis two different views of the emerging system are needed:

1 The activities necessary to make the information system.
2 The systems which the information system will comprise.

The first of these, usually referred to as the conceptual (or activity) model, provides – with the root definition – the outline of the information system development project. The latter provides the outline view of the systems which will be involved with the new information system and makes a good bridge to the next stage of the analysis, the information model.

Conceptual model: Main activities for the information system project

The root definition – if set out as an unambiguous statement and accepted by all stakeholders – is a fine basis for the information system project to proceed. The project needs to be well understood in terms of the activities which will develop it, the outputs which it is expected to produce and the purpose which it is expected to finally achieve. In the root definition we have a clear statement of purpose. The conceptual model provides the opportunity to set out the minimum set of activities which will accomplish the transformation.

Three distinct stages will produce the conceptual model:

1 Brainstorming activities necessary to produce the root definition.
2 Clustering like activities into families.
3 Organizing these families in terms of time and priority.

For the brainstorming stage the stakeholder team are encouraged to take it in turns to write down on adhesive Post-it® notes the activities which will be necessary to achieve the root definition of the information system project. The rule is that each activity needs to begin with a verb or doing word. Activities need to cover all elements of the project from inception to final evaluation. Activities normally include such generic types as 'gather data', 'train staff', 'undertake information audit', 'produce performance indicators', 'monitor and supervise data analysis', etc. The Post-it notes can be placed at random on the wall so all stakeholders can see what is being suggested – although at this brainstorming stage everything is accepted as being valid and there should be no veto on certain types of activity. When 30–40 activities are set out the team can go on to the next stage.

With the brainstorming element completed the stakeholders engage with clustering the activities into families. It is worth noting that these families can be placed under key or headline activities representing major aspects of the project (eg, 'initiate data collection', 'produce main information system application', 'monitor main processes').

With seven or eight main families containing the 30 or so activities set out, these can in turn be organized in terms of time (eg 'initiate data gathering' would come before 'produce main information system applications') and priority – with the most important activities being at the top and the least at the bottom. You should end up with a table of activities, from left to right (time) and from top to bottom (priority). This set would be the basis for the information system project which could subsequently be developed in (for example) a project logical framework (see Appendix 2).

Systems model: Main systems involved in the information system

The conceptual model deals with the main activities of the information system project. The systems model deals with the main elements to be included.

If you are having trouble assessing the dynamics of the new systems design we recommend that you carry out a two-stage systems modelling phase:

1 produce a model which depicts the existing system (or context); then
2 produce the model which demonstrates the transformed situation.

Note that this can only be carried out successfully if you are given the necessary time to do the work (you will know your own constraints) but if this is not possible go straight onto the second activity. The development of our systems model takes six stages.

1 Reassess the consensus root definition to form an impression of the type of system which will be necessary to carry out the transformation generally agreed to.
2 List the likely information systems aspects (eg finance, administration, archive) and for each one associate it with verbs which describe the most fundamental activities of the defined systems (eg record, liaison, purchasing, reporting, inform).

3 Thinking in terms of a simple system (input, process and output), consider how each system relates and links to other systems. Try to describe the input and output where appropriate (see Figure 5.15).

This is a simple idea of a system. Usually systems are developed with regard to the emergence of new properties as items are combined and the hierarchy by which these items are related. For our purposes in setting up information systems practically and rapidly we simplify the issue.

4 Structure similar information system components and their related activities into groups (eg day-to-day accounts, long-term budgets, short-term budgets could be grouped in a financial system). See Figure 5.16.

5 Use lines or lines with arrows to join the activities/systems together. The arrows symbolize information or energy or material or some other form of dependency. It is quite useful to use the arrows as representing the main flows of information between systems. The information output from one system is usually the information input for another (see Figure 5.17). It is not so important at this stage to be too detailed. The important outcome of this stage is the overall concept of the planned information system.

6 Verify the model with the users of the existing system. This is very important. The relationships and major inputs and outputs need to be agreed with all major stakeholders in the system.

Figure 5.15 *A simple input, process, output system*

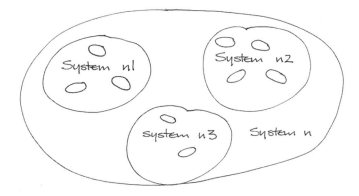

Figure 5.16 *Grouping the systems*

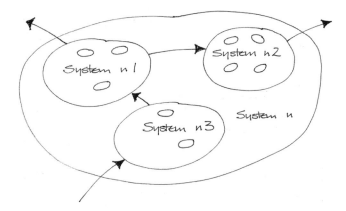

Figure 5.17 *Systems and flows*

Figure 5.18 shows a system model of the government roads department. Note how it has been derived from the corresponding rich picture in Figure 5.9. The boundaries show the various subsystems within the overall organizational system.

In particularly complicated or large organizations (ie in most cases where an analyst is being used in the first place!) there is often the need to produce various

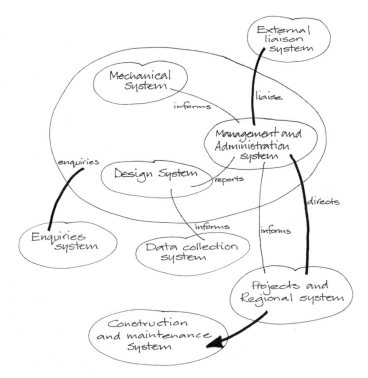

Figure 5.18 *Level 1 systems model arising from the rich picture of the department of roads*

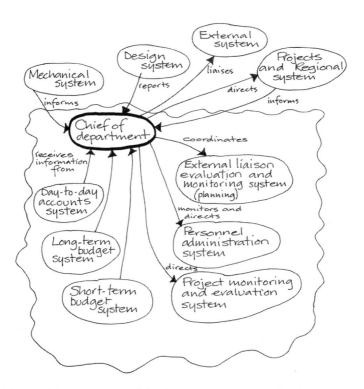

Figure 5.19 *Level 2 systems model: The management and administrative system*

levels of model. Figure 5.19 is a level 2 model showing more of the details involved with the management and administrative system as shown within the level 1 model.

The level 2 model shows the central role of the chief of department and the immediate subsystems which serve that office. Each of these would ultimately need to be further developed in a similar manner to provide the actual workings of each unit. The system model gives us a point of agreement on the information system from which the detailed information modelling exercise can follow.

Amount of time devoted to analysis so far:
Total for this stage (system model) = 3 days
Cumulative total = 7 days

Before the information model can be started, however, it is useful to identify the items arising within the system model which have priority in the development of the initial terms of reference. It is unlikely that it will initially be possible to carry out all the tasks that would be required to set up a total information system. For this process to be effective it is valuable to identify key priorities

The time schedule for the exercise can vary but *if no more is required in the early stages of a project than an understanding of the major systems*, a period of between two and five days should be sufficient.

for the information system in plan, where the analysis has come from and what should be the outcomes at the end of the first stage of the analysis. Through the participation and stakeholder representation stage of the rich picture, the analysis builds up an idea of what is/are the problem/s. The root definition further focuses on an agreed perception of the major components of the work in hand, most importantly the transformation. Finally (at this stage) an overall model system is specified in outline which stakeholders agree they wish to develop.

Final considerations

The terms of reference will make you very selective in your initial problem context identification. Thus, in terms of the CATWOE, the first person who has a say in this may not be the problem owner in the immediate sense but the more remote owner (if there is one in the case which you are dealing with) who is funding the overall operation.

The first job will be to define the boundary between the activities to be included in the analysis and design and those which are pertinent, may well be candidates for further phases within further projects, but which are outside the short-term priorities of the terms of reference. The exact position of the boundary must be a matter for discussion between the analyst and the stakeholders. Often, however, the analyst will be asked to advise on areas of the organization's operations where a new information system could produce the greatest benefits. The area that the analyst selects may be the only one to be tackled, or it may be the first part of a phased study of information processing throughout the organization. However, it can be kept in mind before going into technical detail about what should and should not be in the information system that sometimes political and social interests will preclude the analyst from dealing with the real area of concern at all. All examples of management interference with the analyst's area of study, specifying certain areas out of bounds, demarcating 'priorities', etc, can be seen as political acts but as has already been noted these often have to be accepted as facts of life to the analyst.

Conclusions

By the end of this stage of the analysis you will have moved from a position of seeking to identify the problem situation to having an organizationally shared view of the potential model of a solution. The rich picture gave the overview, the root definition defined the key issues and identified the primary task, and the systems model has outlined the next step. We can now enter on a harder (in the sense of objective and quantitative) phase of the Multiview methodology and look at the process of information modelling. In this stage we will seek to indicate the major components of the proposed system in a manner which can be transposed into a working system.

Exercise

This is the first exercise in a series aiming at building an overall analysis and design. We are assuming that you have an existing organizational problem and would benefit from an exercise, set out in sequence of how to go about the process of analysis and design as set out in this book. Similarly, if this book is being used as a class text the following tutorial can be used for the core of an assessed exercise.

Part 1: The human activity system phase

You are a consultant reviewing the capability of a construction company in one of the poorer countries of southern Europe to make effective use of IT. Here are some details.

Personnel

Managing Director – M R Ario
Director – D F Badro
Director – A F Ario
Departmental Head (A, Policy) – G T Galio
Departmental Head (B, Works) – G V Ario
Departmental Head (C, Planning) – B T Tefri
The company employs 89 people in the head office, 656 people outside the head office

Tasks

- Preparing quotes and outline contracts (buildings, roads, emergency repair to river banks and sea defences, rail).
- Dealing with subcontractors.
- Drafting contracts.
- Project supervision.
- Deadline enforcement.

National characteristics

- Poor regularity of power supply.
- Poor road and rail transport.
- Difficult topography and seasonal heavy rains which cause further transport difficulties.
- Poor internal telephone service. Supplemented by radio communication.
- Scarce access to international currencies.

Your brief is to look for likely departments within the company requiring effective MIS tools and which have a high probability of being able to maintain and sustain a new system. You have been able to glean other useful information on a series of transect walks and informal interviews:

- Company turnover has been static for the last three years. There has been a linked reduction in customer demand.

- The accounting section has been seriously undermanned for three years and has suffered from considerable manpower loss (particularly younger staff).
- The Senior Accountant does not sit on several senior committees.
- There is a small computer unit using very old machines and turning out very poor payroll and costing information.
- Morale among senior staff can be seen as being fairly poor.
- One family has members in several senior positions. This family link tends to be the information/operational spine of the company.
- Junior staff are generally well trained and frustrated by poor promotion chances.
- The outlook is surprisingly good. Contracts being negotiated and European Union grants would indicate that growth will increase at 7 per cent per annum for several years.
- The three major departments within the company – Planning, Policy and Works show a certain amount of internal friction. Loyalty to family appears to be a bone of contention.
- The Planning section deals with contractual details and some works design.
- The Policy section exists to lead discussion with major customers (government departments, private companies) and contractors and set outline policy statements.
- The Works section is the business end. It employs 75 per cent of staff, carries out and/or supervises construction and maintenance. Works is directed by one of the Ario family.
- The Works section employees man all regional offices.
- Your project donor/financier is an international bank. They are looking for an area to invest $300,000 initially in MIS activity.

Given this background, produce the rich picture for the organization. Prepare the rich picture as a brief for yourself and possibly as the basis of a seminar to brief the donor.

Some hints
You have three key areas: the world, the regional offices and the department. Obviously there is conflict in the department and the prominence of the Ario family cannot be overlooked. As this is a document for the donor you can be quite frank in your views of the scenario.

Don't attempt to appear to be all knowing. There will be a lot of details which you will not have. For example, how does the organization's administration fit into all this, what role does the existing computer unit have and how well trained are its staff?

Be sure to make a list of items that you will require more information about.

Part 2: On root definitions and systems models
Working from the rich picture go on to prepare root definitions for:

- The analyst (you).
- Hypothetical – for the donor.
- Hypothetical – for the managing director.

Include all your own doubts and problems with the job in your own CATWOE. Remember, how do the terms of reference fit with what you have found out in the rich picture? Do the regions need help? Are they getting it? Should other individuals and agencies be questioned?

Presumably if (for example) the analyst finds that the regions could do with information systems support in the line functions of the organization, whereas the customer and bank feel that the core concern is central office MIS detail, this will show up in your consensus CATWOE.

Part 3: Developing a systems model

Outline the top level system model of the initial MIS you would set about designing. Pay particular attention to your view concerning:

- The limits of the initial MIS.
- The products of the initial MIS.
- The dangers for the initial MIS.

Your existing work will probably have indicated that the organization contains numerous subsystems (eg management, strategy, policy, planning and works). Your MIS will need to focus on these type of subsystems. How will you deal with the 'issue' of the regions?

One attempt at a model answer is given to the exercise in Appendix 3.

CHAPTER 6

INFORMATION MODELLING: MAKING A WORKABLE SYSTEM

KEYWORDS/EXPRESSIONS: entity model, functional decomposition, events, entity/function matrix, data flow diagrams, attributes, performance indicators

SUMMARY: The systems model leads on to a more quantitative approach: information modelling. During this phase the subject of the problem is broken down in terms of entities, functions, attributes and events (and indicators if needed). The ground is prepared for the proposed information system. Entities correspond to things that we wish to keep information about. Attributes are the qualities (or fields) which compose the entity. Functions are the processes which work upon the entities and attributes to produce information products such as indicators. Events are the triggers which cause functions to operate.

Introduction to information modelling

The second, more quantitative stage of the methodology involves adapting and developing the systems model for the proposed information system developed in Chapter 5 in such a way as to produce the plan of the main content and processes for a workable information system in line with the requirements of major stakeholders. This stage is important if the information system is going to be a management information system (MIS) type application and if you need some say in setting out the key features of the information system for yourself. As we set out earlier in Chapter 4, it is not so important if you are eventually going to purchase your software ready made.

Assuming that you need to work out exactly what your information system is going to be like in terms of files and functions, once the analyst and the stakeholders have reached agreement (even if this is quite tentative) on the overall picture of the situation and on the root definition of the system to be designed then information modelling can begin. This stage can be very drawn out. The devil is very much in the detail. To achieve a high measure of accuracy in terms of information modelling the task can take a considerable amount of time to work itself out in great detail. A criticism of this tendency is the observation that by the time the information model is completed the needs of the system have dramatically changed or the system is no longer needed.

Other books deal very effectively with the extended development of information models making use of a variety of different methodologies (Bowers 1988; Dennis and Haley 2000; Maciaszek 2001; Weaver et al 1998).

In terms of the present task *we do not want to spend our time on lengthy academic review, we need to think about what our information system is actually going to do and attempt to produce an outline system which is practical and workable.*

We now need to identify (in liaison with the stakeholders of the system):

- What key information products are required? and therefore:
- What do we wish to keep records of data about (entities)?
- Of what are these entities composed (attributes)?
- What functions are carried out on the entities?
- What are the triggers or events which fire the functions?

At any one stage in the analysis and design process it is difficult not to think of the manner in which the current stage will affect those which follow. This is a very useful feature but one which analysts and designers in the past have undervalued. It can be argued that at each stage of the analysis it is best to attempt to banish all past and future analysis from your mind. This ensures that analysts do not attempt to take elements of the analysis out of context, eg to specify the hardware and software for a system before having carried out the information modelling stage. The problem with not thinking about other stages is that the links between stages are ignored and we end up with a six stage methodology, with six stages, none of which interrelate with the others. Therefore our task at this stage and at every other stage is to keep a clear notion of the ideas which led to

AUTHORS' NOTE: In this chapter we discuss the intellectual tools which non-specialists can use to model their information system. The tools described have a lengthy and well tried track record but other approaches do exist, most notably object orientated programming (OOP). It is useful to look briefly at OOP but not all reviews are positive. David Avison has described object orientated information systems development as 'the latest silver bullet' (Avison 1997). Wainright-Martin et al (1994) describes OOP as follows:

'Objects are self-contained software modules that perform a given set of tasks on command. By connecting a number of these objects, a software engineer can create a complete, working application almost as easily as assembling a stereo system by plugging together a receiver, tape deck, and CD player.

The difficulty arises in creating an object that works properly and is robust enough to be used in a variety of applications... [T]he object orientated approach (is) ideal for the large-scale, team development cycle typical in the corporate setting' (page 190).

We will not build on OOP ideas in this chapter partly because we are more focused on developing non-specialist's intellectual tools for thinking about and describing information flows and partly because, as Wainright-Martin puts it, the OOP is a 'quintessential black-box' and our task here is to increase the understanding of information flows not obscure them in functional black boxes. For further material on OOP see sections of Moreton and Chester (1997), or Tozer (1996) or Cats-Baril and Thompson (1997) and there are numerous websites to visit including www.w3.org/OOP/

the current analysis, keep in mind the main needs of the stage to come and concentrate chiefly on the work in hand.

To be aware of how our current work fits into our overall analysis is useful but to make any decisions concerning hardware, software and training would be to reduce the value of the entire analysis exercise and would make a nonsense of the process. We will eventually want to make decisions in terms of implementation but this is not the time. There is great value in having a nominal idea as to what combinations might produce the system we are designing but these ideas should be held lightly until the final stages of the analysis (whichever route through the methodology we select). The reason for this is quite simple. Any joint discussion of hardware and software with stakeholders can raise false expectations, unnecessarily bring pressure to bear on yourself to deliver, and most importantly, rule out the possibility of making changes to your planned system. If stakeholders perceive that the system which they have so far agreed to is to be changed they may consider this to be regressive. This in turn can cause problems in the relationship between the analyst and the stakeholders. This stage of the analysis also has meaning in terms of our learning. Table 6.1 shows the elements of the learning organization in relation to information modelling.

With these thoughts in mind we will now look at the major features of the second stage of the analysis.

Table 6.1 *Learning organization and information modelling*

Discipline	Value in information modelling thinking	Outcome?
Systems thinking	We can get away from this if we are not careful. This stage can become very focused on the parts of the system and not the whole.	A system designed as a whole if the approach is truly systemic.
Personal mastery	This stage takes us through the team mastery of the problem context into a model which can be made actual. In information modelling we gain mastery over the data and information detail of our organization.	Ownership and control over the information system.
Mental models	Each of the four main elements of information modelling includes mental models.	Improving the accuracy of the eventual system.
Shared vision	The information model should be a shared vision of the eventual information system.	Improving the clarity of the vision of the transformation.
Team learning	The team continues to develop the participatory approach at this time.	Consensus on the way forward.

Entities, attributes, functions and events

We are going to try to reduce our proposed information system to four features. In order for our analysis to be accurate we need to spend a little time defining them. It is important to realize, however, that these four elements are meaningless without the information products which are their *raison d'être*. A problem for many information systems has been the tendency to develop information systems which are functional and efficient but which are not used because they do not generate the information which stakeholders need.

Entities: An entity is something about which records are kept. The definition is intentionally vague in its meaning. The need for a degree of flexibility is essential because the entities in a system can range from the major individuals who are working within the organization (eg senior managers, chief accountant, etc) to operational and strategic information sources (eg staff records, sales records, payroll, land use data, profitability, research and development, etc).

Attributes: that is, the attributes of the entities. For example, if the entity is a land use planning system, the attributes might be rainfall, climate, percentage of the land use which is arable, percentage of the land use which is pasture, percentage of the land use which is urban, etc. On the other hand, if the entity is an MIS dealing with company performance, some of the attributes might be gross sales for years x to y, gross profit, net profit, number of staff employed, staff salaries, etc.

Functions: Functions are actions which take place within the information systems and concerning entities. Therefore some of the functions related to a small computer maintenance business might include update the customer ledger, update the supplier ledger, keep inventory of the companies stock, register sales, register bad debts, register sales staff mileage. Functions set out in this form are fairly chaotic. To understand the web of functions which make up even a basic operation we make use of a hierarchy tree. For example the major function:

Update customer file

might contain such sub-functions as:
Receive sales data
Receive bad debt data

The first of these items might then contain sub-sub-functions like:
Add new customer data
Edit old customer data
Delete archive customer data

This is a very simple example, and quite often you may need to go into quite a lot more detail. However, it is also true that in breaking down the core functions which are essential for the information system in its first phase the analyst often discovers that things are much more simple than was first envisaged. The breakdown of the functions or functional decomposition, will work its way out to a tree structure as shown in Figure 6.1.

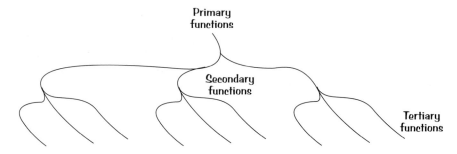

Figure 6.1 *A tree structure*

Events: Events are triggers which make functions occur. For example in a training organization a potential participant for a short course wanting to enrol is an event which triggers the function 'process application'. This may in turn trigger off other functions – 'check vacancies' or 'assess sponsor'.

If we try to put the entire scheme together in one particular case it might appear as follows:

An ENTITY   a database concerning borrowing for small scale landowners

has
ATTRIBUTES   Reference number
Contact date
Land use type
Credit to date

carries out
FUNCTIONS   Add new record
Sort records on family name and region
Assess creditworthiness

at specific
EVENTS   Seasonal events
Financial events

In order to provide information products:
PERFORMANCE
INDICATORS   % bad debtors
                % in flood plain
                region
                Rates of repayment
                in certain income
                bands

This simple example shows the way the entire system fits together. We will now go on to look at each element in greater detail.

THINK POINT: Can you, for your own organization, think of three major entities, three major functions and then break down one of the entities into attributes and consider an event which will trigger one of the functions?

But what is the information that the information process generates?

Entity models/tables

Entity models or tables are usually the primary components looked at by analysis and design teams. If we do not know what we want to keep records about then we have not got a system view to work from.

It is possible to start off the analysis with a review of information products, functions or entities. For the purposes of this book we feel it makes sense to begin with the entity (the nouns or objects of the system so to speak) rather than the function (the verbs or actions of the system) although we must not lose sight of the information products which this all exists to support. Also, for the purposes of the continuity of this multiperspective methodology, we feel that the clearest correlation between the HAS and information modelling is from system model to entity model/table.

What are the major items about which we wish to store information? It should be remembered that all entities will contain attributes and also have associated functions and we will eventually want to link all these items together. The process of arriving at a definitive mapping of entities can be argued to be a slightly academic exercise as there is room for judgement in the selection. Two things are vitally important and have been pointed to many times by other authors: getting a complete picture and at the same time not *flooding* the analysis with information. We will discuss this in greater depth shortly. The process of producing a table of entities can be seen in Figure 6.2.

This is far from being a straightforward process. You may need to simplify your analysis down to one or two basic entities.

Earlier on we mentioned being complete in terms of our entities whilst at the same time avoiding *flooding*. By completeness we mean that no major thing about which you wish to keep information is missing. Flooding refers to the potential complexity of the final model if we were to map out every single entity which comes to mind. At this stage we want to map out major entities only. In fact the process of reducing complexity down to the key components of study is an important lesson to learn. It will always be possible to increase complexity and even have levels of entity model later on. In Table 6.2 we list all the major entities for our department

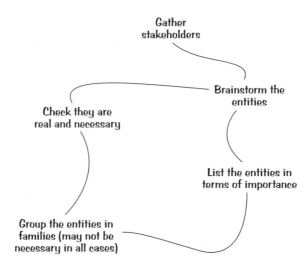

Gather
stakeholders

Brainstorm the
entities

Check they are
real and necessary

List the entities in
terms of importance

Group the entities in
families (may not be
necessary in all cases)

Figure 6.2 *A procedure for organizing entities*

AUTHORS' NOTE: We realize that information modelling is a topic which is dealt with in great depth elsewhere and for mastery of the topic further study is necessary. In this book we wish to empower the non-specialist to produce a model of the system which is to be produced. The model may not be complete and may not be entirely accurate but it should be the basis for later development. Our aims are for modest and understandable information systems.

of roads MIS as set out by a team of non-specialists. In the table they have tried to keep in mind the main systems in the systems diagram set out in the previous chapter.

Table 6.2 does not demonstrate a complete picture of the data in the department but does indicate that there are a number of things about which we wish to get information and that these things (entities) are related to other entities. From this point we can link together certain groups of entities and then produce a final map showing all entities and their relationships with each other. In Figure 6.3 the team (including analyst and main stakeholders) have linked all the entities by means of lines defining the relationship in a preliminary diagram.

Sometimes the analyst may find it helpful to make a table of notes relating to the diagram concerning the nature and direction of the entity relationship, eg Departmental Finance is *monitored* by Accounting

The reverse (Accounting monitored by Departmental Finance) does not seem to be too silly so confusion might arise without this type of clarification. For those who are interested in such things, the name for this type of explanatory note is 'anchor point notation'.

The major insight that we can give concerning your entity model construction is that it may take many attempts to get the model clearly defined. Lines should cross as little as possible, and for most purposes we would recommend that you

Table 6.2 *Main entities for the MIS*

Entity	Relevant system from the systems diagram	Links to other entities
Management	Management and administration	Employee database, heavy equipment inventory, roads register, accounting and planning
Accounting	Management and administration	Management, departmental finances, preliminary budget, final programme
Soils test laboratory data	Design	Roads information
Roads information	Construction and maintenance	Soils test laboratory data, regional and project data and roads register
Roads register	Construction and maintenance	Roads information and management
Departmental finance	Management and administration	Accounting
Planning	Design	Final programme, preliminary budget, management
Final programme	Management and administration	Accounting and planning
Employees	Management and administration	Employee database
Employee database	Management and administration	Employees, management and regional and project data
Regional and project data	Projects and regional and data collection	Employee database, preliminary budget, heavy equipment inventory, roads information
Heavy equipment inventory	Mechanical	Management and regional and project data

should reduce the situation to about 20 entities. If there are more than this you are probably dealing with a very complex problem and unless you have existing analysis and design skills we recommend that you try to begin by reducing the scope of your analysis to a subset of your original terms of reference. In our example here we have reduced our analysis to four key areas as derived from our system model:

- Programme planning and finance.
- Personnel records.
- Roads register.
- Equipment inventory.

It is possible to reduce the entities still further. Table 6.3 provides one view.

> THINK POINT: Before going on, take a close look at Figure 6.3. Can you see how we might construct a simpler entity model? Could we prune this one back to essentials? Have a good think about this before going on.

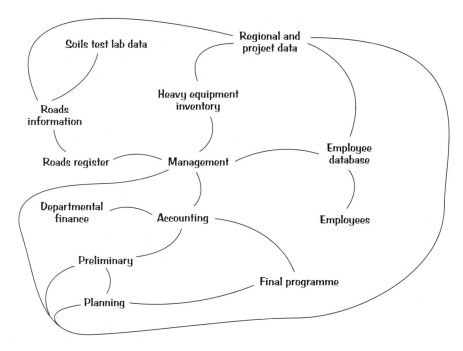

Figure 6.3 *A preliminary entity model*

When you are satisfied that you have:

• identified and listed your major entities, and
• modelled them in a diagram or table which makes sense to you and to the major stakeholders

you are ready to go on to the next stage. It is quite important to realize that data within entities can change into data in other entities, eg in a training institution an applicant could become a student who in turn will become an ex-student. In the example we have above the accounting entity transforms data in the preliminary budget entity into information for the final programme entity.

Table 6.3 *A simplified entity list*

Entity label	Function
Management	This is the sink for all information, everything ends up here
Regional and project data	This is the source for all information
Preliminary budget	Secondary entity, drives information from regional and project
Personnel records	Secondary entity, drives information from regional and project
Roads register	Secondary entity, drives information from regional and project
Equipment inventory	Secondary entity, drives information from regional and project

Table 6.4 *Storing information on entities*

Name of entity	Number of attributes in entity	Potential number of records in entity	Volatility of records	Suggested person-hours/ year to maintain the entity
Personnel records	35–40	Approximately 1500	10% per annum	40 hours
Etc...				

It is not the purpose of this book to go into considerable detail on these issues. Entity modelling (and all the following stages of this phase) can be developed in great depth. If you feel that you require greater detail we refer you to books on data analysis (see Suggested Reading). Our main theme is not to provide an academically polished model but to make use of existing analysis and design tools and produce practical and reproducible analysis and design products. In some fields such approaches are called 'reasonably quick and dirty'.

At this stage it is important that you keep a note of the potential size of entities – that is, will they contain hundreds, thousands or more information or data elements – and about how often the data changes in the system. For example, you might end up with a notion of a system with 60 data elements, 40 per cent of which you might expect to change each year. This information will be very important for the next stage of the analysis. One way of recording this type of information is shown in Table 6.4.

In this example the analyst is trying to ensure that at this stage the size and level of change of the entity is at least considered. As an extra a guess at the labour required to maintain the entity is suggested. This gives an idea of the financial cost of this element of the system. At this time it is not essential or possible to be exact in the vision of the entity. But it does help to think these issues through early on. There is no point in planning an entity which will lead to a database which cannot be sustained.

Amount of time devoted to analysis so far:
Total for this stage (entity modelling) = 2 days
Cumulative total update = 9 days

Working on the estimates of time we set out in the first stage of our approach we suggest that two or three days should complete this phase of stage 2.

For now we are assuming that you are ready to go on to mapping the major attributes as related to the entities.

Attributes

For the development of the system it is useful if we begin to identify key attributes of entities. Thinking back to our introduction to the chapter the reason for this is

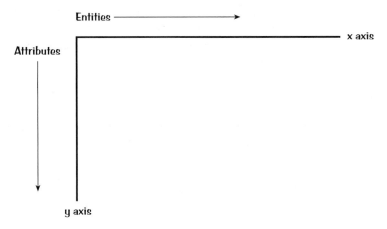

Figure 6.4 *Entity–attribute matrix*

because the attributes we set out here should form the basis for the fields of our eventual database for the MIS (in the primary case we are using in this example).

One way of carrying out this exercise would be to create an entity/attribute matrix as shown in Figure 6.4.

This can be a little tedious but it is worth the effort. For each entity on the x axis the attributes are listed on the y axis. This should result in a comprehensive listing of all major attributes. One reason for *not* doing this would be in the event of having a lot of attributes related to any one particular entity and not much else. In this event the matrix would become rather ungainly. Ten or eleven entities would produce possibly hundreds of attributes. It is probably easier to just set out each set of attributes against each specific entity. A simple example of attribute listing is shown below.

Attributes for the Roads Register Entity

Name of road
Date of construction
Personnel involved – engineers, overseers
Duration
Cost
Benefit as projected in original report
Source of finance – external, internal
Total quantities and costs of:

- cutting
- filling
- gravelling
- culverts
- bridges

etc.

If necessary the analysis could go into much greater detail if time, resources and need demanded. The amount of detail you need is again your decision. It is not intended that at this stage you should be thinking of the actual database structures which might be required to accommodate the data sets which you begin to generate in outline.

This example of attribute mapping focuses on setting out the analysis as an aid to computerization. Each entity can be clearly seen as a pro forma for a record and store of data. A group of records is a file. Each attribute is a field in an entity. Sometimes this type of approach is appropriate. For example, if the analyst knows that he is required to design an IT-based system and is familiar with database design there is little point in not setting out the attributes in this manner. However, if the information system under design is not primarily a data store – for example if you are more concerned with setting up a website for promoting and marketing a specific product or service and the information system is largely descriptive and advertising orientated then this type of analysis stage is not necessary.

Amount of time devoted to analysis so far:
Total for this stage (attribute listing) = 1 day
Cumulative total update = 10 days

One day should see this phase completed

Functional decomposition

This may sound rather a mouthful but, as with so many analysis and design terms, the reality is quite straightforward. Decomposition as used here refers to a hierarchy of tasks broken down into their component and even sub-component parts. This is used to show the major functions and the way in which these consist of other simpler functions. A simple example would be to demonstrate digging a hole in a road (see Figure 6.5).

You might think that this is a trivial example but demonstrates the way in which decomposition works .

The breakdown of the whole into its parts is known as top-down decomposition. In Figures 6.6 and 6.7 we demonstrate the decomposition of functions at two levels for the department of roads.

> THINK POINT: try it for yourself. Take one of your standard tasks and see if you can break it down into a series of decomposed tasks. A major point is to try to get tasks of the same intensity or degree at each level. A great deal of modern project management relates to functional decomposition (that is, assigning tasks and different levels of tasks to different individuals).

It is important to notice how there are three major functions – planning and accounting, administration, and the roads information collection. This does not mean that these are the only functions. It means that these relate most closely to

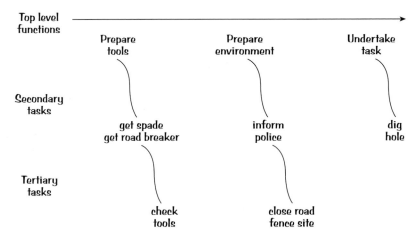

Figure 6.5 *Decomposition of digging a hole in the road*

the job we have been set in our terms of reference, the greatest areas of need as shown in the rich picture, the consensus view arrived at in the root definition and the new systems outline as given in the systems model. As a learning exercise, the information model has provided us the with opportunity to focus on three core areas, considered by the team and the stakeholders to be of primary importance. We need to restate that this is a subjective process and different analysis and design teams and different stakeholders would, in the same context, almost certainly select different information priorities. However, in this case it is not surprising to see that the major areas proposed functionally for an MIS in a government department are administration and major inventories. Also the planning and accounts areas are fairly clear contenders for new information systems design as invariably our priorities will initially be focused on repetitious and well structured tasks.

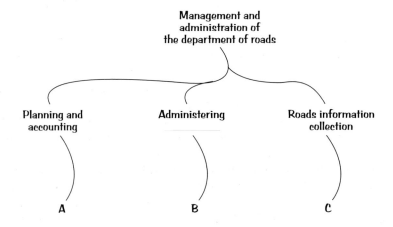

Figure 6.6 *Top level decomposition: The department of roads*

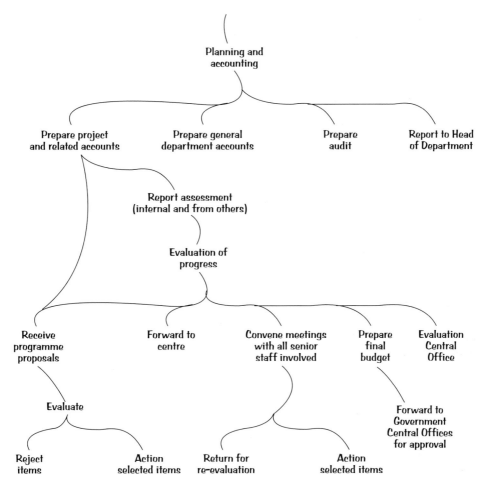

Figure 6.7 *Level 2 function chart: Planning and accounts*

The level 2 chart develops the decomposition of the planning and accounting function. A point to note on this chart is that there are two paths to 'receive programme proposals'. Ideally this should always occur following the 'report assessment' and 'evaluation' stages. However, there are times when this is not possible and an informal short cut is taken.

In another example taken from a training college and shown in Figure 6.8, functions were mapped out much more closely with the final computer system in mind. This does require a little explanation. The training college example is very specifically related to generating information products (performance indicators or PIs) for a training college. Much of the detail is abbreviated (FTL = Full Time Lecturer), but it is not important to understand the detail of the example. The decomposition is dealing specifically with generating information PIs. In fact there are numerous PIs altogether but we show only four here. The purpose of this example is to show that functional decomposition can be very specific to an IT

AUTHORS' NOTE: This takes us into the area of the discretion of the analyst and professionalism again. In some cases it is the responsibility of the analyst to remove unwieldy pieces of activity and in others to conform the new design to some tried and tested (if 'informal') activities. The way in which the individual analyst deals with this type of 'informal' information processing reality entirely depends upon the specific situation in which he or she is working. Sometimes the problem owner may not wish to have this pointed out but will still require you to work round it. It is another example of the analyst having to sometimes make use of a subjective evaluation of an 'economy of truth' in terms of his or her actual reporting. In our view the discovery of informality of this type is important for the organization's self learning and should normally be discussed and reviewed by the stakeholders – it is a learning benefit from analysis and design.

THINK POINT: Are all these entities and functions legitimate? Do they all have corresponding entities and functions ranged against them? What would be the outcome of a functionless entity?

related system, just as was the entity map for the college which we showed earlier on. This functional decomposition is intended to provide the basis of computer programs which will run the functions.

Double checking on entities and functions

Even the simplest of information problems will by now have generated quite a complex picture of the work to be done. When your experience of the information system indicates that it is getting complex it is useful to supplement the analysis with a little double checking to make sure that the picture of entities and functions being developed is sensible. One way to carry out such a check is to make use of an entity/function matrix. We have already mentioned entity/attribute matrices. An entity/function matrix operates on the same principle.

As with our previous example, the easiest way to demonstrate this is to give an example (see Figure 6.9). The rule is, if there are any functions without entities or entities without functions, or – more difficult to check – missing entities or functions, this matrix should be able to pick up any problems.

This stage of the analysis is timed out as follows:

Amount of time devoted to analysis so far:
Total for this stage (functional decomposition) = 2 days
Cumulative total update = 12 days

It is estimated that in many contexts this stage should take no more than two days.
    Summary so far:

• A clear, if preliminary entity model – enough for us to work from. We know what we want to collect data about.
• A listing of the key attributes or the exact types of data within the entities.
• An idea of the size and volatility (the rate of change) of the data in the entities.

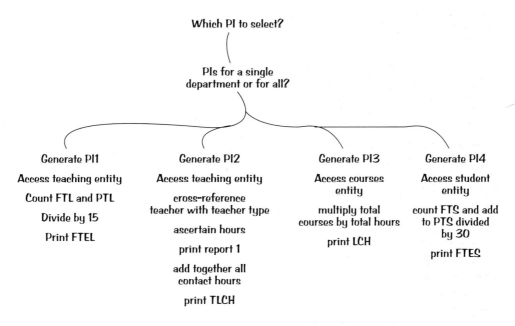

Figure 6.8 *Functional decomposition for performance indicators*

Entities

	Manage-ment	Accounts	Planning	Roads register	Regional and projects	
Administering	X	X			X	
Planning and accounting	X	X	X	X	X	
Roads information collection				X	X	
Report assessment	X		X			
Evaluation of progress	X		X			
Receive programme proposal	X					
Functions						

Figure 6.9 *A semi-completed entity–function matrix*

- A correlation of the relationships of function to entities and also some understanding of how these functions decompose in the organization.

The next stage of the information modelling involves building in the events which will trigger the functions which will move and mould information within the entities which have the attributes ('which lived in the house that Jack built!').

Events

To undertake event modelling the analysis makes use of flow diagram type drawings. In our experience flow diagrams are a useful tool for modelling the input of events which will trigger functions in the system.

The flow diagram examines and demonstrates how information flows in functional hierarchies. Within the diagram the information flows from left to right through the functions. The functions are shown in boxes. Events come in from the top driving the functions. See Figure 6.10. A key item to be aware of is the avoidance of ambiguity in terms of terminology, eg what 'entities' behind the functions are referring to at any one time? In this case we are looking at a shortened outline of the events which trigger the functions in the planning and accounts major function as related to the management, administration and planning entities. Ideally the flow diagram will provide the analyst with another element of learning about the organization:

- Where have events which trigger functions arisen?
- Do these events as modelled check with the realities of the present situation?
- Has the team missed out any major functions in the analysis to date?
- What is the degree of risk of an unlooked for or unwelcome event arising?

Generally, it is necessary to produce flow diagrams of major or complex areas. It is not usually essential to model the events for all functions.

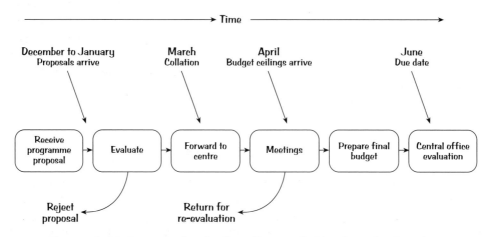

Figure 6.10 *An example of a flow diagram linking into the functions*

In this case you see that it is useful (and possible!) to put concrete dates to the events.

In terms of the second, information modelling, phase of the rapid appraisal approach the analysis will be complete when the events for the major functions which will form the core of our new information system are mapped out. Stage two of the analysis can be set out in total as shown in Figure 4.3.

At this stage much of the concrete detail of the eventual information systems has been produced. It may be that much of what the team has discovered is partial and limited. Nevertheless, a view of the information model has been achieved and this will (at the very least) help the team in their dealing with systems suppliers and developers later on. The process of stage two has continued the vital process of the team gaining ownership and confidence over the information and data flows within the organization.

Amount of time devoted to analysis so far:
Total for this stage (Event mapping) = 2 days
Cumulative total update = 14 days

A further two days should be sufficient to prepare the data flow diagrams as and when necessary (it is not envisaged that all aspects of the analysis will need this stage).

Tying it all together

The finalization of the information model should not take place without the overall schema being presented to all major stakeholders for agreement. For this procedure the analyst will need to produce the information model in such a form as is readily understandable to non-specialists.

It may be that the outcome of such a consultation process will be the need to rethink the information system; ownership of the information model extends beyond the analysis team. The information model should provide a good basis for understanding the likely extent of the system. This in turn will have repercussions for the cost of the system. It may be necessary to think in terms of several phases to eventually produce the system which the model shows. This is also useful thinking to surface at this stage of the analysis. When the stakeholders of the system are content with (or at least are willing to sign off) this stage of the model the third stage of the analysis can take place.

Conclusions

The information model provides quantifiable details for the insights of the systems model. During this stage the team may have to rethink the systems model. It may be that implications of the model are unworkable, too expensive or too widescale in terms of their implications. *This kind of discovery is all right.* One of the purposes of this approach is that the information system can be adjusted in reaction to further study, that the approach is a learning approach encouraging a learning organization. Between the human activity stage and information modelling there should be a feedback loop allowing for further refinement of the proposed system.

When the information model is complete it can be put to one side although never forgotten – it is the basis of the system to come (on paths 1 and 2). We need to keep reference of the amount of data and the number of entities which will need to be planned for. This information can be carried forward to the next stage of the analysis.

Exercise

At this stage we are assuming that you have compared the results of the exercises at the end of Chapter 5 with the model answer set out in Appendix 3. Having arrived at a systems outline of the new system the crunch has come. We now need to turn our systems model into the outline information system. The way we shall do this is to set out major entities, attributes of key entities, functions and triggers or events.

Your exercise is to:

- Make an entity table of the company as described in your top level conceptual model. Only focus on key entities. Try to keep it simple.
- Related to your entity modelling work, set out the major functions related to a primary entity. Think about how many of the functions might be coped with by an automated system and how many of them could not.
- Set out what are the triggers/events which will be most important for the system.

Some hints
Entity table construction. If there has been any discussion about the situation for regional offices this must be put behind us now. The terms of reference are explicit and therefore we need now to break down the conceptual model systems into entities about which we wish to store information. Primary entities might include planning and administration. These two will in turn be served by others. The top end of the entity spectrum is the issue of strategy for the company. Once you have drawn the entity table take a look at the suggested answer in Section 6 of Appendix 3.

In listing attributes for the entities only concern yourself with the primary items.

When working on the functional decomposition focus on the key issue of strategy. Work out the preparation of strategy function with particular emphasis to the hierarchy of sub-functions which help to provide the strategy formulation necessary for effective management. A key issue here will be understanding what the competition is up to. Feel free to go down two or even three levels in the decomposition. When you have completed take a look at the example worked out in Section 6 of Appendix 3.

When you come to look at flow diagrams, again focus on an element of the strategy formulation (for example, the events noted which would contribute to the effective monitoring of major competitors).

You might like to make use of the cruciform diagram shown in Figure 4.3. In this diagram format you can produce a cross working from information products back to the entities, etc. For some information systems this works well – especially if there are not many events and the information system is expected to produce a limited number of distinct information products.

CHAPTER 7

TECHNICAL NEEDS, SOCIAL NEEDS: GETTING THE RIGHT BALANCE

KEYWORDS/EXPRESSIONS: socio-technical systems, future analysis, social objectives, technical objectives, social alternatives, technical alternatives, best-fit solution

SUMMARY: This section covers the development of the implementation of the information system. We have learned a lot about the organization both in qualitative and quantitative terms. If we have pursued paths 1 or 2 we have gained insights into the information flows and stores as well. At this stage, common to all three paths, we are interested in considerations of hardware, software and people used to operate the outline system. The integration of a variety of alternatives in terms of their costs, resource implications and constraints leads to the expression of the actual tasks which will be accomplished by the various human and computer aspects of the system.

Introduction to socio-technical systems

It is not essential that the third aspect of the methodology should directly build off the information modelling stage. The main reason for this relates to the various ways in which our approach can be used. If you are using path three you will not have undertaken information modelling at all. On the other hand, if you have undertaken information modelling this will have provided you and your team with an outline of the structure which the eventual information system can make use of. We could even go so far as to say that the process will have identified for us a database structure:

- Entities = files and records.
- Attributes = fields.
- Functions = processes and necessary actions to take.
- Events = the triggers which prompt the functions.

The items which might be of most importance for this stage of the analysis are:

- Details of entities.
- Details of number of attributes.
- Details of potential number of records.

If you do not have this information don't worry. Following the third path you have an idea of the transformation which you wish to achieve and of the systems which will contribute to this transformation. In this stage you will generate a plan of the mixture of skills, attitudes, technology and training which will provide the transformation. The third aspect of the total methodology can stand alone. It is a holistic systems analysis and systems design process in itself.

Stage three, the design of socio-technical systems, provides the capacity for us to specify the nuts and bolts of the actual system itself in terms of human and IT tasks, human and IT requirements. After all, a system which is beautifully designed but is completely inappropriate for the people who are available to use it or the environment which will support it is not much use at all. Therefore it is essential to consider the way in which people carry out their work, the vested interests and politics of the local situation and the way in which the new system can best be fitted into it. What we set out in this chapter is based upon the work of Enid Mumford and the ETHICS approach (see Suggested Reading).

The process of the socio-technical design stage includes the outlining of:

- Job design.
- Specification of the human and IT (if appropriate) tasks.
- Specification of decisions about staffing and training requirements.
- A detailed technical IT specification (if appropriate).

The analysis depends for its background context on the rich picture (especially for issues such as local power supply, availability of spares/servicing, etc).

The job which the analysis team is called upon to perform is to outline the various alternatives available to the stakeholders to provide decision-makers with relevant and sensible plans for action.

The overall structure for the stage is shown in Figure 7.1

The outline set out in Figure 7.1 demonstrates a seven-stage process:

1 Scenario plan the future for the information systems context – this is the attempt of the analysis to build into any new information system some redundancy in terms of the system being able to deal not only with the issues of the context of the present moment but the situation as it continues to develop. Most information systems are built to deal with yesterday's issues.
2 Outline the social objectives and technical objectives – this stage sets out the general social needs of the system (improving job satisfaction, increased professionalism, etc) and technical objectives (improving the timeliness of operations, holding and analysing data efficiently, etc).
3 Then outline the social and technical alternatives – the measures in the social and technical fields which can be taken to meet the social and technical objectives.
4 Having done this, generate a number of 'mixes' by putting together the social and technical alternatives into different options. Here we show three. There should be at least two but there could be many more. There are always many ways of developing an information system.

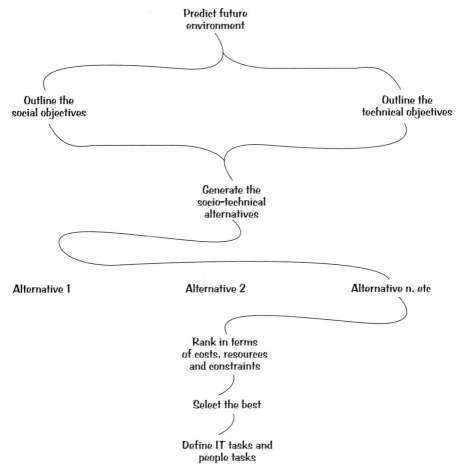

Figure 7.1 *Principles of socio-technical design*

5 Rank the alternatives in term of their costs, resources, constraints and benefits.
6 Select the best alternative mix – the 'best fit' solution. This is an important point. Our mix and match of social and technical alternatives to meet our needs will rarely appear to be ideal. We will select the *best* and not necessarily the *perfect* alternatives.
7 Finally we work out the human and IT tasks to meet the best fit solution.

In terms of the learning organization, this process helps us in a number of ways (see Table 7.1).

Taking the outlines of Figure 7.1 and Table 7.1 as our starting point the analysis begins to develop as follows.

Table 7.1 *Learning organization and socio-technical systems*

Discipline	Value in socio-technical thinking	Outcome?
Systems thinking	The stage encourages holistic thinking within the boundary of the transformation we wish to make. All our linking of people and technology relates directly to this wholeness.	A system designed as a whole if the approach is truly systemic.
Personal mastery	Socio-technical modelling provides the opportunity for teams and stakeholders to define both their technological requirements and their work practice.	Growing ownership and control over the detailed social and technical aspects of the information system.
Mental models	A difficulty identified with much information systems work is the focus on a 'solution' to deal with a problem. This concentration on a solution can lead the problem solving team to believe that there is only one answer to any specific problem. In this stage of the approach the team gains a map or mental model of a range of alternatives which can be applied to the context. The identification of choice is a powerful outcome.	Developing the coherence of the socio-technical plan.
Shared vision	Stakeholders are drawn in here again. They need to be in agreement about what is expected of them, what resources they will have to do it and what problems they might realistically expect.	Improving the clarity of the vision of the transformation.
Team learning	The team continues to develop the participatory approach at this time. Again there is a switch of focus and different qualities will be needed.	Consensus on the way forward.

Predict future environment analysis

To review social and technical resources and constraints for the development of efficient information systems without thinking about the future of such systems would be a short-term attitude and would almost ensure the redundancy of the new information system at an early date. We cannot know what the future will bring but we can make some speculations and develop some scenarios on the nature of changes. The consideration of future conditions may well help information systems planners to avoid some of the problems identified in Chapter 1. The study of future environments and conditions was originally expressed in the 'future analysis' theory but scenario planning now has a rich literature (see Suggested Reading) and there are journals dedicated to futurology (eg *Futures Journal* and *Futures Research Quarterly*). Essentially the analysis used here has four major foci: uncertainty; future changes; risk; and threats.

- Working from what is known about the context of the information system it is possible to make a prediction of the kinds of change which are possible (be they technological, legal, or economic, etc). This requires a careful consideration of the context and situation of the organization in which the information system is to be sited and, possibly with the help of structure plans (if they exist), predict the mid-term development of the institution (three to five year plan). This analysis stage should provide some idea of the type of expansion, contraction or change which will occur and which the incoming system will have to deal with.
- The likely outcome of the system in the future – what will be the effects of an improved information system? There are all kinds of disruptive and/or constructive events which may be related to the development of a new system (laying off staff, employment of computer professionals, development of new grades to cover computer staff, etc).
- What features of the proposed system are more susceptible to change? Where would you expect the new system to change first? Can this be planned for? For example will data collection procedures change, will the existing departmental structures be maintained?
- What is the extent and horizon of the system? This requires a long-term view (five to ten years). This will comprise enlightened guesswork but it gives one a sense of humility in the initial design and requires speculation as to how what is planned today may be either the building block for further developments – or redundant in the long-term future.

The end of the stage is to set out the new system within the context of continuing development in the organization and the wider world. The study provides the analysis with a means to see the proposed information system in the context of a process of change in time.

This type of study can be quite detailed. Generally, however, it is quite a short procedure. In the case study of the governmental roads department our findings (in brief) were:

- Prediction of the kinds of change which are possible: Major issue: There appears to be the potential for fast growth for the department for the next five years; major investments in infrastructure (running to over 10 per cent of the department's annual budget). It is expected that the investment will lead to increases in employment within the department in terms of technically competent personnel. At a more political level, it is expected that the department will have a widening national responsibility in terms of maintaining existing roads.
- The likely outcome of the system in the future: Given the mood in government as a whole and the spirit of the age, the greatest efficiencies would seem likely to occur in terms of finance and staff administration. More specifically there may be a reduction in unskilled staff employment and a tendency towards widening use of technologies of all kinds. The project is linked to related investment in improving national communications.
- What features of the proposed system are more susceptible to change? The assumption is that the senior management team will feel the changes first. This

may take the form of fairly widespread disruption and unsettling changes in practice for several years to come. This may well require training and motivational support.

• What is the extent and horizon of the system? Eventually the system will probably extend beyond the narrow centralized system to all the regional and district offices (again, this links to the communications investment).

The future scenario analysis can be far more detailed if time and circumstance (and need!) demand. One means to undertake this analysis is to encourage stakeholder teams to draw rich pictures of a variety of possible scenarios and then develop action plans of how the various scenarios could be achieved. Similarly a SWOT analysis, such as that discussed in Chapter 4, could provide the insights to deal with the four questions. However you and your team go about answering the questions concerning the future and no matter how hesitant and preliminary the findings, all following analysis and design will need to keep in mind these considerations. They should be built into the information system planning, and influence choices in terms of the needs of the organization to cope with a new information system and the capacities of technology to cope with developments.

The next job is to agree and set the outline social and technical objectives of the system being created.

Outline social and technical objectives

Social objectives refers to the expectations of employees and major stakeholders. The technical objectives refer to capacity of the organization as a whole to react to key issues. For our case we can set out the twin objectives as follows:

Social objectives of the proposed information system

• To be relatively self-sufficient.
• To provide a quick service.
• To provide job satisfaction.
• To provide professional satisfaction.
• To improve professional status of the department.

All these objectives are arrived at following consultation with all major stakeholders. This is a vital point. The social objectives of an information system, broadly to be seen as the expectations of the information system in terms of the human beings who are going to be working with it, will vary from site to site. No two information systems being planned for organizations will have the same objectives. Often the social objectives of a system are undervalued. Management do not tend to feel that the social needs of a system are as critical for system development as technical issues. Thinking back to the systemic/reductionist arguments of the earlier chapters we cannot overemphasize the need for social issues to be adequately planned for. Having outlined the social objectives, the next task is to return to our system model and information model to set out the technical objectives for the incoming system. In the case of our example these are as follows:

Technical objectives of the proposed information system

- To inform management.
- To improve timeliness.
- To improve communication.
- To increase information processing capacity.
- To provide a long-term facility.

THINK POINT: Consider your own organization. Could you outline the range of social objectives which your colleagues might expect from a new information system? Would you expect the objectives of different colleagues to change with different sections of the organization (the lateral dimension of the organization) or seniority (the vertical dimension of the organization)? What types of variation would you expect to find and why?

These are the primary tasks which the stakeholders are expecting the system to undertake. In our example the objectives are quite brief and broad. They could be very specific – for example this is a single technical objective of a management system for a large trading company:

To provide daily commodity movement statistics – in the form of 34 agreed performance indicators on 15 key commodities for all managers above grade 10.

As we have said before, your own position will indicate the depth of detail you will need to go into. There may be need for the analyst to grade objectives, particularly if interviews generate quite a lot of them.

Generate social and technical alternatives

The social alternatives refer to the description of different ways of organizing individuals to undertake the work required for the system whilst at the same time achieving the social objectives. Technical alternatives should offer a range of means of meeting the information processing requirements. The issue of technical alternatives does require the analyst to understand the basics of what each type of alternative might mean. For example, one view of the range of technical means to work an information system might be as follows:

- An entirely manual information system.
- A manual information system with aspects capable of being automated (for example those produced by the Kalamazoo company).
- A mixed manual information system with some IT aspects. PCs installed on a stand-alone basis.
- Information system based entirely on stand-alone PCs.
- PCs networked together.
- PCs networked onto a more substantial mini or mainframe computer.

If you are not familiar with hardware and software options don't worry – you are in good company. With the incredible continuing development of computer power it is almost impossible even for professionals in the industry to keep up with developments. As a very general briefing Table 7.2 provides an overview.

Each option offers benefits and costs. In any analysis there is a need to consider in some depth what the information system team is ready and able to provide analysis for and what it would be confident to recommend (as well as what the organization can cope with). The organizational, team and self learning you will have achieved by this point in the analysis will be vital. The warrior type of analyst (first described in Chapter 3) is often overstretched at this point and has a tendency to select systems which are either organizationally inappropriate or too demanding on the limited skills of the non-specialist analysts (or both). In our example the alternatives worked out as follows:

Social alternatives
- S1 In-house training of existing staff and organizational change to provide the complete computer service.
- S2 In-house staff trained to supervise newly employed, pre-trained staff.
- S3 Trained new staff employed.
- S4 Make use of short-term agency and contract consultants – outsourcing?

As you can see the social alternatives are ranked from S1 to S4. Essentially we are looking at ways of manning a PC-based system. The range of options ranges from the use of existing staff, trained in the skills required, to the use of short-term consultants (or even outsourcing). The technical alternatives are as follows:

Technical alternatives
- T1 Minicomputer-based system.
- T2 PC network.
- T3 PC stand-alone.

Note that we have not included in our logical alternatives the possibility of using a manual system. This is because the alternative was not relevant following discussions with the funding agency (and thinking back to our root definitions in Chapter 5). This is a real-time limitation on any analysis and again reiterates the importance of the terms of reference on analysis and design routines.

Rank the alternatives

The next stage of the analysis is to mix and match the various alternatives together and then to list all the alternatives and reject any that are immediately not feasible. For example:

S1 T1	reject outright on grounds of cost
S1 T2	proceed with analysis
S1 T3	proceed with analysis

Table 7.2 *Some generalized observations about different information processing systems*

Information system	Selected features
Non-computer, manual	Subject to basic analysis errors (the human factor). Well understood; often these systems have been around since the organization began and they are well understood by their 'guardians'.
Manual but computerizable	Often these are new systems, breaking with the traditional pre-computer systems. Basic error avoidance through methodical practice. Partially understood by some members of the organization, well understood by a small minority on the 'inside'.
Mixed manual/PC	Old practice and new – often the worst of both worlds. Basic software employed on stand-alone systems. 1000s of records processable by the basic software and the PC. Reduction in analysis errors over manual systems but often confusion between the two systems running in parallel. This reduction in analysis error will be true for all the computer-based systems. Increase in input errors because, although the software is usually error free (if it is well tried and tested software) the input of data to the computer can be laborious and raise numerous new errors – this will also be true for all the systems set out below. Maintenance required for the PCs and for all the following computer systems.
Stand-alone, PC-based	Basic software employed of the 'office' variety (word processor, spreadsheet, database, communications). 1000s of records processable. Potential adoption problems if the technology is seen to take people's jobs. Training needs to be developed at this stage. Mixed manual/PC systems have a parallel system to fall back on if the PCs fail. In this case there is dependence on the PC and this in turn means skill levels must be raised and spread among a wider number of staff.
Networked PCs	Basic software supplemented by some quite complex networking packages. Potential adoption problems resulting from the social implications of the network set out above. Training needs can become very high here most specifically for those entrusted with the maintenance and management of the network and the related shared files.

Information system	Selected features
PCs linked to minicomputers and higher systems	Substantial changes in practice can result again. PCs, once trained for and introduced, tend to be used by the majority of members of an organization and they are inclusive, encouraging participation and thinking about how the system can be improved by all. Once the computers become more powerful they also become more remote and there can be a return to the days of the computer guardians or high priests, keeping the uninitiated away.
	Specialized software is often used by such systems.
	100s of 1000s of records processable.
	Large potential adoption problems as the organization gears up to a computer priesthood and the interface problems this can cause.
	Training needs can be very high especially for the programmers and managers of the system.
	Sometimes these systems require specialized, protected environments.
	Considerable maintenance requirements.

S2 T1	reject outright on grounds of cost
S2 T2	proceed with analysis
S2 T3	proceed with analysis
S3 T1	be wary of costs
S3 T2	proceed with analysis
S3 T3	proceed with analysis
S4 T1	proceed with analysis
S4 T2	proceed with analysis
S4 T3	proceed with analysis

Working from our example we now need to find the optimum combination of alternatives. We need to consider each pairing in terms of their implications for *costs*, *resources*, *constraints* and if needed (although not usual) *benefits* (if thought necessary). These factors can be assessed using one of many methods. Three are outlined below.

Cost–benefit analysis

They can be arrived at by a process of cost–benefit analysis – whereby each alternative combination is costed and its benefits assessed. Internal rates of return and net present value are key to this approach. However, this can be a lengthy process and

AUTHORS' NOTE: Of course one can be much more sophisticated than is shown in the example we have discussed here. For example you may have set out the initial alternatives so that multiple social and technical combinations could be selected. In this scenario S factors could relate to: training, management change, reduction in organization hierarchy, introduction of lifelong learning package for staff. On the other hand, the technical alternatives might relate to T issues like: digitize data, produce organization intranet, develop website, use fast modems for communication between different sites. In this type of scenario there would be complex mixes of S and T alternatives (eg S1,S2,S5,T1,T4 as one set).

provides a purely economic framework for the consideration of the system. This is not an approach which fits in with the holistic approach adopted by the authors of this book.

Tabulate and grade

They can be set out on a table and graded against each other on a ranking of 1 to 9. This is a qualitative and subjective approach but a team can try to arrive at a consensus view. For example we set the number values as follows:

1 = very good
2 = good
3 = quite good
4 = better than average
5 = average
6 = worse than average
7 = quite poor
8 = poor
9 = very poor

Our alternatives could then be set against each other as follows in Table 7.3:

The idea behind this ranking systems is that the alternatives with the lowest totals would indicate the more appropriate choices. This procedure can also be quite time consuming especially if undertaken by a team.

Table 7.3 *Ranking the alternatives*

Alternatives	Costs		Resources		Constraints		Totals
	Social	Technical	Social	Technical	Social	Technical	
S1T1	4	4	3	3	1	1	16
S3T1	8	8	7	8	6	9	46
etc.							

List major factors

An even simpler rule of thumb would be to just set out the major factors against each aspect, For example:

S1T2 In-house staff and PC network
social costs – training in use of software and network
technical costs – software, hardware purchase
social resources – some trained staff
technical resources – some existing PC hardware
social constraints – none of real importance
technical constraints – power supply, climate

S3T1 Trained new staff employed and minicomputer-based system
S4T1 Make use of short-term agency and contract consultants – outsourcing?
and minicomputer-based system
social costs – high cost new staff, training in use of software and network
technical costs – very expensive software, hardware
social resources – none available at present
technical resources – none available at present
social constraints – introducing new staff to practices
technical constraints – power supply, climate

By using this method expensive alternatives can be rapidly peeled off. There might
still be trouble however, if there are very close alternatives to compare. In this case
it might be thought justifiable to fall back on the second method off assessment.
The result of this phase will be a ranking of the alternatives in order. Our ranking
from our exercise were as follows:

1 the best alternative S1T2 In-house staff and PC network
2 S1T3
3 Joint third: S2T2, S2T3
4 Joint fourth: S3T2, S3T3, S4T2, S4T3
5 Joint fifth: S3T1, S4T1

For the purposes of this exercise it was decided to work with the best combination
and, in applying the limitations which it will inevitably provide, attempt to relate it
to our information model arrived at in the last section.

An important point to recognize is that the decision concerning the information
system is vital but so is the transparency of the process which led to it.

Human and computer tasks

The final stage of the socio-technical specification is to outline for the new
information system in terms of tasks for people and IT.

People tasks

The people tasks which your team sets out must deal with the wide range of issues
and potential problems which you have thought of in your future analysis as well
as the range of data tasks which were implied by the information modelling carried
out in phase two of our approach (if you undertook that stage). These tasks can be
broken down along a number of lines but for our purposes we provided a four way
division into management tasks, input-output tasks, training tasks and
maintenance and support tasks.

In general terms these tasks can be structured as follows:

- Management tasks:
  - Overall management of the system.
  - Management of an effective reporting procedure.

- Input–output tasks:
  - Data input to the system.
  - Selective output from the system.
  - Specialized report generation.
  - Interpreting the output.
- Training tasks:
  - Training senior management in familiarization.
  - Training assistant managers and administrators in use.
  - Training data entry staff in operations.
  - Training technicians in IT maintenance.
- Maintenance and support tasks:
  - Repairing faulty items.
  - Regular servicing.

Several points can be made concerning this type of checklist. As a rule, in our practice we have observed that training should always begin with the top management. If undertaken effectively this ensures that the system will be supported and retain its annual budget, etc. One problem which is constantly recurring is the potential alienation of managers through assuming their commitment without training. IT and related information systems are generally seen as being pretty threatening to those who are on the margins. If a system is planned and the senior staff are not given strong support in its uses and values it can often happen that the system is under-used by other staff and lacks the political support to really gain thorough acceptance. Second, the outline which we prepare now will not be worked out in detail at this point. It will be the task of the final stage of our approach actually to set out the major aspects of the configuration in its final form. Here we are attempting to provide ourselves with the overall guidelines for the coming system. Third, we need to gain the assent of all major stakeholders at this stage to the tasks which we outline. All such tasks will have immediate and recurrent costs on the organization and the donor. There may be need for the analyst to reduce his or her expectations in the light of what is financially feasible. This point also is true for the next stage, IT tasks.

IT tasks

These will tend to be rather easier to structure at this level. Generally two levels need to be considered, the data and the equipment.

The data. This refers to the actual items which will need to be accommodated. The type of data which our government department needs to be stored and retrieved is as follows:

- Roads register data.
- Heavy equipment inventory.
- Employee records.
- Project data.
- Accounts data.

- Other items (misc.), eg:
  - word-processed documents,
  - spreadsheet matrices,
  - database files,
  - graphics files,
  - road design files.

The equipment. At this stage the equipment prescribed can be set out by general function rather than actual hardware and software. Thus, with our department we could specify:

- Networking of data to key personnel (approx. 16 units) – multiple access to files.
- Quality output as required.
- Draft output as required.
- Equipment to deal with power fluctuations and power down (potentially hours).
- Capacity and facility to archive (approximately 40 megabytes in year 1).

Amount of time devoted to analysis so far:

Total for this stage (socio-technical) = 6 days
Cumulative total update for paths 1 and 2 = 20 days
Cumulative total for path 3 = 13 days

This stage could be completed in six days.

Conclusions

There are various points which the chapter demonstrates and which we would like to express in general conclusions.

- At this stage the analysis and design team do not need a detailed knowledge of the technology. This can be sorted out later on either by the team making use of the numerous trade magazines or with the assistance of computer sales companies (more on how to deal with these characters later on in Chapter 10).
- The alternatives can be arranged in any type of order. Analysis will be subjective and no doubt different stakeholders and members of the team will have different preferences at this stage. The ranking of the alternatives provides the opportunity to set out in a more democratic fashion which are more or less appropriate.
- Always bring the stakeholders into this stage of the analysis. You will need to explain and justify the socio-technical combination which you finally recommend.

The end of the stage should be a clear and agreed overview of the technology and social requirements for the system in question. This provides the third 'view' of the information system under development. In the HAS stage we perceived the needs for the system and set out its main components. In the information modelling stage we worked on the data and the information which such a system will work with. In this third stage we have set out the technology we will use and the social requirements. Following this stage, depending upon the path you are using, you are either ready to go onto the human–computer interface or technical subsystems.

Exercise

We have outlined the development of the social and technical systems which will make up our final system. Your task is to do the same.

First, working from the example you have to date, set out the range of social and technical alternatives which will meet the information system you have modelled. Remember your terms of reference and your budget.

Then, work your way through the analysis. Give reasons for arriving at the conclusions you have.

Some hints

One way of simplifying the social and technical objectives outline is to set out some of the larger social objectives (as first set out in the CATWOE stage of the HAS) and set against each the related technical objectives, eg:

Social objective	Related technical objectives
Improve planning	Technical skills
	Automated features
	Networking decision-making

The alternatives arising from the objectives might be fairly standard (eg ranging from retraining staff to adding new staff on the social side and manual to networked PCs on the technical).

Resulting ranking is probably best carried out by using the table method – comparing costs, constraints and resources. It would be best to set out all the details of the table here. When you have finished compare your answer to those set out in Section 7 of Appendix 3.

CHAPTER 8

THE HUMAN–COMPUTER INTERFACE

KEYWORDS/EXPRESSIONS: technical interface, social interface, security interface, design procedure, priority access

SUMMARY: It is essential that the user be able to work and communicate effectively with the computer. This chapter works out some of the details of the tasks which were discussed in the previous chapter. Various potential problem areas are reviewed including work styles, sources of discontent in terms of new work practice, dialogue systems (the way in which computers communicate with users) and the security of different user groups. Security can be seen as a way of protecting the system from the user as well as a means of safeguarding valuable and sensitive information.

Introduction to the human–computer interface

If you are using this book to assist you in analysis and design as set out in Chapter 4 you will have arrived at the human–computer interface following the three previous stages of human activity system (HAS), information modelling and socio-technical system design. By this stage you may feel that there is still more you don't rather than do know concerning the information system which you are planning. One thing you must be clear about by now, however, is whether the system which you are planning will contain IT. If the system does not require an IT system, this stage still has value in terms of thinking about the interface which your manual system will have but the focus and detail of your work will be different. If you have decided that IT will be required then this stage provides you with insights into effective design. We assume that you have a fairly clear understanding of the tasks which the computer and the various users in the system are going to undertake. We do assume that you know that the computer systems are going to communicate to users and that users will need to be assisted in what can appear to be an unequal struggle. Our next job is to:

- explain what an interface is;
- look at the principles of good interface design; and
- review examples of design.

The human–computer interface refers to the environment in which the user and the hardware come together to perform the information system operations. The range of functions which can be carried out include:

- The input of data.
- Checking data for errors.
- Making enquiries concerning information items.
- Producing reports at certain events (remember our information modelling?)
- Management, security and monitoring.

However, the manner in which these tasks take place and the social implications involved in different work practices need to be understood if the system is to work well. Key issues pertaining to work practice should have already been described in the HAS stage in Chapter 5. If they were significant they will have also been structured in terms of alternatives in the socio-technical stage in Chapter 7. Quality of work life is an important aspect of the total design. The interface set up here needs to provide end users not only with a technically sound system but also with a work situation which maximizes work interest at the same time as minimizing the negative aspects of technology (eg the potential for de-skilling and reducing job satisfaction).

Therefore, when dealing with the human–computer interface we are dealing with a wide range of issues, such as those set out in Figure 8.1.

Always keep in mind one golden rule: you are thinking about information systems for users not for computer experts. If your system is to be used it has to be not so much 'friendly' as recognizable and useful to those who are going to use it. This may seem a simple idea but it is one which appears to be profoundly elusive to 80 per cent of those involved in information systems planning.

The contribution which this stage can make to a learning organization is set out in Table 8.1.

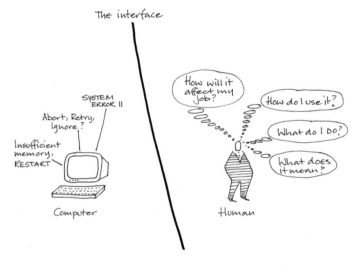

Figure 8.1 *The interface and the two parts of the struggle*

Table 8.1 *Learning organization and the human–computer interface*

Discipline	Value in human–computer interface thinking	Outcome?
Systems thinking	The challenge of this stage is to keep the vision of the whole despite needing to focus on very specific issues. The manner in which we address a number of different views of the interface should encourage a holistic overview.	Interfaces which are designed with the organization as a whole in mind whilst providing for the needs of groups and individuals.
Personal mastery	This mastery will now extend to the way in which technology and humanity interface with each other.	Systems which people can feel in charge of. Sharing the ownership of the system.
Mental models	Each interface must be modelled and tested in the organization context.	Clear boundaries assigned to each level of the interface.
Shared vision	As with the previous stage, stakeholders are encouraged into this stage – the interfaces have to be 'theirs', they have to drive the creative element of this stage.	An agreed and participatory vision of the system.
Team learning	The team learning of this stage is often within the context of worries and concerns of workers and users with technology. The learning is often related to understanding that apparently benign systems can be very worrying to those who do not share in their vision and creation.	Insight into the organization and its use of technology.

The nature of the interface

At root the computer has to be able to deal with any of the range of tasks which have been identified in Chapter 7 and give a response which is understandable and useful. For this to occur smoothly the designer must plan around the three major interface aspects of computer systems:

1 Keyboards, the computer pointing device (be it a track ball, mouse or graphic tablet), scanners and digital cameras are used for handling all aspects of data input and – in some cases – for manipulating data.
2 Monitors in many forms (different resolutions, different sizes, flat and conventional) are for the display of information and data. The first device for output from the computer.
3 Printers and plotters for hard copy of reports, etc. The second output device from the computer.

Depending upon your situation (eg the capacity of your organization to fund IT related work, the skills of colleagues, the extent of the system which you are planning, etc) you will require support in the development of the interface. Usually programmers would set up the nuts and bolts of the interface mechanisms. These mechanisms are designed in outline by the analyst in an interactive process with the range of ultimate end users of the proposed system. As we have already indicated the object of the analysis is to bring together two apparently contradictory and divergent themes:

1 to provide the computer with clear, concise and unambiguous data and commands;
   and yet
2 to provide the wide range of different users with appropriate interfaces which, while being clear and unambiguous, are also 'friendly' (or at least not hostile) and provide facilities for dealing with mistakes and accidental entries as well as the correct ones.

The latter theme involves the second, social, aspect of our system. In outline this means the way in which we deal with the potential problems arising from what is often seen as a confrontation between the users and the PC. One starting point is to look at existing communication forms (standard data collection forms, reports, etc) within the organization and attempt to copy those which are most appropriate. The purpose of the exercise is to allow the user and the computer to 'understand each other'. To make this possible from the user's point of view we will need to try to facilitate understanding of what is going on inside the 'box'. Much initial user training is often required in this area.

Some interfaces

The technical interface

Information systems can only be flexible up to a point. Despite the fact that in recent years the technical interface has been 'humanized' with the advent of graphic interfaces (first on the Apple Macintosh and then more recently with Windows on the PC) and computers with speech recognition facilities, it is not possible to have a system which can be adaptive to any type of user that happens to come along. However, this level of flexibility is not usually required. The team designing the information system will normally be involved in looking at certain types of user, their basic requirements and then trying to match (by a process of interaction and participation) the right interface for the right user.

It is not difficult to think of examples. Data entry staff, will probably have very specific, fixed needs from an incoming system. They will generally be familiar with existing manual input to registers, ledgers, etc. The basics of these operations should be well known and so our interfaces can be matched to what is already understood.

Researchers, managers or planners on the other hand are likely to want to talk about targets, aggregates, trends, etc. They will probably want to be able to manipulate large volumes of data quickly and may well be uncomfortable using limited interfaces. The sorts of interfaces you plan for these different categories of staff

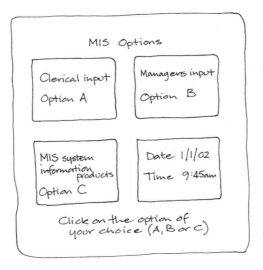

Figure 8.2 *Analyst's sketch of an MIS introductory screen*

ought to reflect those differences. An example will illustrate some of the problems which we regularly encounter with monitor display.

Figure 8.2 shows an analyst's sketch plan of an initial monitor input screen to a management information system. As you can see there are three key options: clerical, managerial or MIS products. Put yourself in the position of the users of this system. Three broad bands have been planned for:

> THINK POINT: Before going on, if you were setting out the specification for an interface for managers, clerical staff and information users what sort of things do you think would be important to include in the introductory screen? Similarly, what do you think you would need to avoid at all costs?

1 Clerical workers inputting data.
2 Managers for controlling the system.
3 Information consumers needing to know things.

Clear and easy to understand? Maybe but complaints about this type of interface include:

- General: too vague. Users would like to know more about what option they want. 'Tell us what to do and where we ought to go next!'
- Clerical comments: Generally OK but 'not what we are used to'.
- IT Managers comments: 'I resent the feel that I am sharing a system. I would rather be physically unconnected to the clerical and information product aspects. This presentation does not feel secure enough. I need less guidance and menus and more sense of control.'
- Information users: 'I felt that the system throughout gave information that was pre-planned. There should be less patronizing menus and more capacity for users like me to formulate questions.'

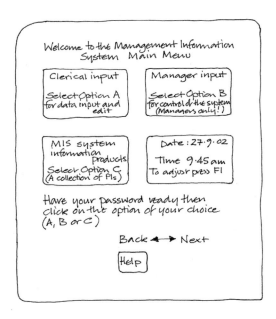

Figure 8.3 *Analyst's sketch of an improved introductory screen to an MIS*

Some of these comments go outside the scope of this single menu display but it does go to show that even a simple introductory menu can have problems. One attempt to improve the system is shown in Figure 8.3.

The main criticism of Figure 8.3 is that the designer had gone too far! This screen is too busy, too full. It tries to say too much and still does not segregate out manager from clerical functions or really tell users what to expect from decisions they make. Possibly a better approach would be to start off by asking each user if they want one of the three options as shown in Figure 8.4, and then proceeding with the relevant options for each group.

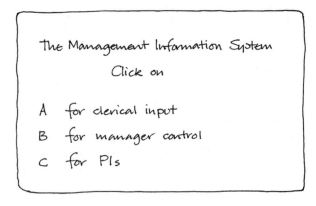

Figure 8.4 *Yet another example of an improved introductory screen to an MIS*

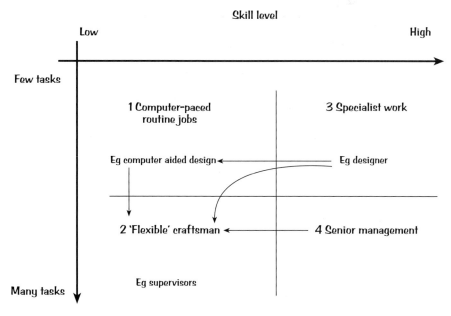

Source: Willcocks and Mason (1987)

Figure 8.5 *IT and work*

However, variations in what users require from the interface should be seen as only part of the dynamic operating between the two aspects (human and technical) of the proposed working system.

Social issues

Automation will tend to radically change the nature of work itself, often concentrating decision-making in the hands of a few managers while simplifying work procedures for other groups. Willcocks and Mason (1987) have attempted to structure the impact of technology on job by use of a matrix. We develop a version of this matrix in Figure 8.5.

AUTHORS' NOTE: Anecdotally, and as also shown by Willcocks and Mason, from our own experience we might argue that the reverse 'flow' is also possible in certain cases (see Figure 8.6).

The matrix demonstrates the manner in which a variety of jobs can lose skill content because of higher levels of automation (the assumption being in this case that cleverer computers and systems are taking the place of an existing installation).

Therefore, individuals can make use of incoming technology to improve their situation within the organization. Whether information systems can lead to job expansion or contraction the overall need is for the social impact of computer systems to be understood prior to installation. Willcocks and Mason (1987) argue that a series of implications follow automation when this is related to a 'scientific management-based approach':

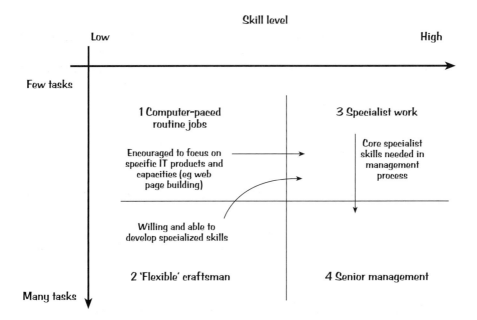

Figure 8.6 *Alternative impacts of IT on work*

- The division of mental and manual tasks.
- Maximization of specialization in skills.
- Minimizing skill requirement.
- Minimizing training and learning time.
- Achieving full work load.
- Minimizing variety of work.
- Creating short-cycle, repetitive jobs.

To determine whether all or part of this list of implications occurs requires the analyst to consider the human–computer interface in terms of job interest and job content.

There are a number of strategies which can be adopted so that de-skilled work and relatively dull computer work can be improved. These include such approaches as:

- Goal orientated working procedure – whereby the staff are given a sequence of short, mid and long-term goals to enhance job interest.
- Working teams – to share a series of low interest tasks.
- Vertical work groups – to distribute a range of working procedures around a group, rotating the higher value tasks to encourage interest.

The design of the social interface will usually require the analysis and design team to think about what the information system will mean to the end users and what strategies might be best considered to deal with potential problems. We shall return to this in the section on 'Considering the social interface'.

Security

The final interface issue we deal with here is that of security and the issue of user exclusion from certain aspects of the automated system. The issue of exclusion arises because *an inexperienced, unauthorized or malicious user allowed free access to a computer-based information system can cause intentional, wilful or unintentional harm to that system.* Two apparently contradictory positions need to be reconciled:

1 to allow users to make the most use of the system; and
2 to protect the system from the user and others. (Gold 1997)

This is dealt with in more depth in the section on 'Considering the security interface'.

Working on all three interfaces provides the analysis and design team with rich learning opportunities and further potential for understanding the way the people in the organization work with and react to technology.

Considering the technical interface

At this stage we are setting out the design of the overall system and should not be too concerned with implementation and the problems which may well arise at that stage. It is quite important that we feel free to design the 'right' system rather than the one which is most practical. The two things may be identical or it may be that we will need to gradually work towards the system which our team believes to be best.

The provision of information to users requires us to look at the manner of the dialogue which will take place. Willcocks and Mason suggested a range of methods for implementing dialogue. These methods are shown in Table 8.2. The table shows eight ways in which the technical interface between user and machine can be handled. In our example early in the previous section the second option – 'menu list' – was selected and various problems arose with this. It is quite possible to have several different interfaces for different types of user. For example, in the previous section we identified three different system users – clerks, managers and information consumers. A single menu-based system was planned. Possibly a better system might have been to provide:

• Clerks with the highly controlled menu system.
• Managers with natural language so that very precise commands can be given.
• Information consumers with a graphic interface.

Each of these options requires separate programming and therefore designing and implementing this type of technical interface design will be quite costly.

The first point in any interface design exercise is to be sure that the analysis team have identified the range of users working in the system. In the case of the example shown in the previous section, method 2 was universally adopted despite

Table 8.2 *Ways to implement dialogue between user and computer*

Item	Dialogue type	Meaning
1	Form filling	Form displayed, blanks to be filled by user
2	Menu list	A set of options displayed, user keys in choice
3	Question and answer	Computer displays a range of questions
4	Function keys	Multiple function keys, some programmable by users
5	Natural language	Dialogue in the user's natural language
6	Command language	Limited number of commands available
7	Query language	User requests in specified language
8	Graphic	Icons, buttons and symbols used to convey meaning

Source: Willcocks and Mason (1987)

the problems identified by the users. The reasoning behind this approach was that menu driven systems are one of the *safest* methods, boxing users into limited options within the system. To get round potential problems with three user groups being supported by one system the menu system was supplemented with method 6 because there were a variety of user groups, each needing a distinct information product from the information.

Another point to keep in mind when selecting the right interface for the right user is that any specific operation will involve the system in a number of exchanges. For example to provide an administrator with staff information involves several different dialogue exchanges, For example:

- A review of the staff/division listings.
- Determining whether a required individual is still employed.
- Confirmation of department.
- Confirmation of priority to look at sensitive material.

And this structure does not take into account the problems of accident, incomplete information listing, forgetting the staff member's registration number or incorrect spelling of his or her last name. Without becoming unnecessarily concerned the analyst must realize that the potential for errors to arise in any system are almost countless. Systems should be provided with facilities to deal with such issues as:

- Incorrect initial data entry leading to problems with search and retrieval.
- Incorrect retrieval information.
- Insufficient data available for specific request.

At this stage it is worth noting where potential errors can enter the system (eg basic data entry by clerical workers), the types of expected error (eg misspelling, double entry), and the type of error checking that will be required (eg random checking of spelling – one record per one hundred, computer check of record to see if it already exists, etc) and the action to be taken (eg providing a prompt to edit).

The case study: Specific issues

In the case of our government department there were a number of special items that had to be covered in our analysis. An initial concern was that almost all computer software is written in the English language. In our case although much of the internal information in the department is in English, much of the input and the output is produced in the local languages. Moreover, many of the junior staff have only a very limited grasp of English. However, following a further stage of analysis the team were satisfied that the system would mainly be used by senior staff who tended to work most closely with the English language and that the manual system would run side by side with the incoming system so the facility to support information integrity (in case of loss or damage) would be available from that manual system. The junior staff acting as operators on the incoming system would be selected in terms (partly) of their good grasp of English. So the team could design our dialogue working on the valid assumptions that:

- English is the language medium.
- There will be various levels of interaction.
- Interfaces will need to be designed for each level.

The levels of user we identified were as follows:

- Senior managers.
- Computer unit staff.
- Clerical staff.

The next problem was to set out the principles of the user interface most appropriate to each user level. Computers tend not to be too friendly in this area. For example one very standard microcomputer system on sale throughout the world would give you the following message:

Abort, Retry, Ignore?

If there was a problem with the computer system. This is not a very informative message. Today things are improving but basic systems still come up with messages like:

Error 11, RESTART?

What is error 11? What will happen when the restart happens? The user does not know what the result of any particular action in the context of the problem will be. For the three groups in this case the team now need to think about the types of dialogue which will be most appropriate.

Senior managers

This group should not require a detailed knowledge of the system as such. They will require information 'summaries' upon which they can either formulate further enquiries or make a decision. With this brief in mind the team can specify a design for the interface to be used:

- Menu driven.
- Access via code number.
- Summary screens of data.
- Urgent request facility.

AUTHORS' NOTE: We will go through the details of this design stage by stage but it is useful to explain the basis of a menu driven system. For most of the specialized work which will be carried out on the databases it will be possible to pre-write menus of commands from which the user can select a function. For example, on logging in, a senior manager might see something like Figure 8.7. In this case the manager is not required to know any more than which function he or she requires. This menu will lead to another and so on.

Note: the code or pin number refers to the security of the system and the issuing of code numbers which are to be confidentially held by all users. We will be looking at this area in a little more depth in the section on 'Considering the security interface'.

IT unit staff

This includes all individuals who are working directly with the computer system in terms of its day-to-day running and operation. The group might include:

- The IT manager(s);
- IT advisers;
- IT trainers;
- IT operators; and
- IT technicians.

The group is diverse in terms of responsibilities and activities; however, for the purpose of our exercise we assume that they should not require sophisticated intermediary dialogue devices between them and the IT. There must be some form of priority system whereby junior or untrained staff cannot gain access to sensitive material (eg access to details concerning salary, etc).

Clerical staff

This group is not included under the general heading of IT staff because they will usually be involved with the inputting of data from specific sections of the department and therefore are not under the direct control of the IT unit. It is the responsibility of this group to enter data into certain systems such as the employee database, the heavy equipment inventory, the accounts system, soils laboratory data, word-processing, databases, spreadsheets.

The reason why the analysis team chose in our example to delegate the work to discrete sections of the department is threefold. First, it conforms to the overall methodology of user driven systems which we outlined in Chapters 1–4. Second, the sections mentioned already run manual versions of these systems. Third, the data in these bases may be sensitive and should not be widely known outside the confines of the section itself, senior management and computer management sections.

Figure 8.7 *Sketch of a possible manager's MIS menu*

In your examples you may decide that there is good reason to keep all data input and edit operations initially under the control of a central data processing unit. This may be appropriate in the early stages of implementation specifically if the system is quite new and does not build upon existing manual practices.

Clerical operators will require facilities from the computer such as:

- menu driven;
- access via code number;
- summary screens of certain limited types of data;
- help facility; and
- urgent request facility.

This may look similar to that which we prescribed for senior management. However, the detail will not take the same form. The level of help will be of the same type but the clerk is only supposed to be inputting data initially and possibly editing selected data later. No other access to the files is provided. The urgent request facility will operate to allow the clerk to forward notification of potential errors to the computer manager.

AUTHORS' NOTE: if you do want to do this you might be overridden by offended section managers who see their prestige as threatened by the removal of certain even quite mundane activities to the new computer unit.

Considering the social interface

We have already identified the probability that an incoming computer system will have a variety and range of impacts on staff morale, job mobility and staff seniority. The system you are planning may lead to massive social upheaval in your organization.

Not all change can be known in advance but a range of measures should be set out in advance to ease the implementation of the new system.

There are many issues which the analysis and design team may need to confront but here we will focus on de-skilling and under-skilling (see Figure 8.8).

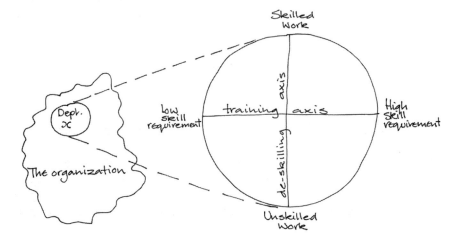

Figure 8.8 *Social issues: De-skilling and under-skilling*

- De-skilling: the capacity of IT facilities to reduce the expertise and/or sense of worth of an individual.
- Under-skilling: The capacity of an organization to fail to recognize the importance of training existing staff in the use of IT.

As shown in Figure 8.8, the two forces can be seen as operating on linked axes. For each section of an organization which is adopting a new information system the planned system can be evaluated in terms of:

- the likely impacts on existing skilled staff in terms of de-skilling; and
- the need of the new system for existing staff to be trained in new areas.

Ideally any de-skilling tendency should be countered by those staff being retrained in the new technology. This is not always possible.

The case study: Specific issues

In our case the impact of the new system was generally seen as being positive. In the short term a certain amount of staff displacement would be encountered but this would run to no more than approximately 4 per cent of the total workforce. The perceived wisdom from meetings with stakeholders in the new system was that this level of disturbance was well within the tolerance level of the organization. Measures undertaken were as follows:

• Maximizing pre-installation briefings to provide workers with as much detail concerning the new system as possible prior to implementation (thus spreading understanding and ownership of the system at an early date).
• Detailed and long-term training inputs for all levels of staff. A core staff was identified which would be the focus of the new system. This core to be provided with relevant training and longer-term outlines of potential future training.
• A degree of sensitivity to be agreed with senior managers concerning the displacement of existing staff. Sensitivity measures might include:
  – offers where possible to work with the new system;
  – re-allocation to other, similar departments;
  – 'generous' redundancy.

Considering the security interface

We will look again at security measures for the system as a whole in the next chapter but, for now, we will focus on the essential work security of discrete user groups.

The focus for the interface is to balance usability with security. As Figure 8.9 shows in the form of a glass tube filled with fluid, it is very difficult to increase

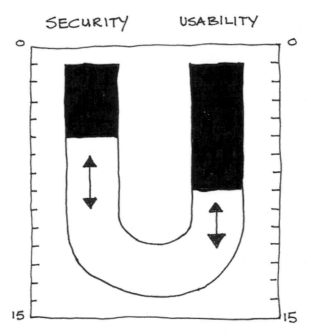

Figure 8.9 *Trade-off between usability and security*

security without decreasing usability and vice versa. Sometimes as systems become better protected they can become harder for users to gain access to.

Therefore, the security which any one system requires will be a function of the level of hazard in the operational environment as assessed by you. If systems are locked in offices with physical access restricted to key staff then security within the interface can probably be quite slight. If, on the other hand, systems are in open office space where anyone can gain access then quite stringent interface procedures might be needed to protect the systems from casual access and/or abuse. 'Stringent interface procedures' generally imply password and pin number systems.

The case study: Specific issues

In our case study we required a certain amount of security, although it was not thought necessary to physically lock computer systems away. When a manager first enters the system, the computer might inquire as shown in the designer's sketch shown in Figure 8.10. *This screen might protect, but it might also deter. Security is thus a compromise between safety and use.* Users will get no further unless name and user code match up with those that the PC is expecting. If this is not so, the potential user might, after several attempts, see something like the sketch in Figure 8.11 – even if there is no monitoring procedure available at all! Often a severe message will put off most of the unwary. For example, most PC systems can easily be adapted to use basic menu systems. Also, many basic database packages come with menu systems available.

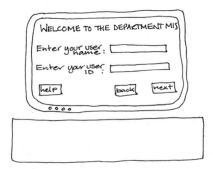

Figure 8.10 *Sketch of an entry screen*

The code will also indicate the type of user (eg manager, technician or clerk). The summary screens of information will appear at the end of the process of working through the layers of menus. For example the senior manager may wish to see if a certain road project is running to schedule. He or she could select the roads register in the first menu, within the roads register another menu would give details of the services available one of which might be:

Figure 8.11 *Sketch of an illegal access screen*

Inspect present progress?

Having selected this the computer would request details of the particular road by region, district and project and could then give the manager the most recent project report.

As a final note, the *urgent request facility* mentioned for managers refers to a method for diffusing potential frustration as well as providing the manager with a direct means of communicating, via the computer-based information system, with the people who run the information system. With this facility the manager can be provided with means whereby he or she can enquire about certain details which may be causing confusion and require further explanation. This could easily be expanded on most available PC networks to allow the user to send messages to other users of the system as well as to the IT staff.

Implementing the interface design

It is not usually the responsibility of the analyst to create databases and become involved in processes of database debugging although the analysis team may well find itself in this position. All we can suggest here is that if the team find themselves dealing with database set-up/installation as well as analysis and design then read on to the database aspect in the next chapter; see the specific texts dealing with databases in 'Suggested Reading'; and follow all database manuals closely in terms of set-up procedures.

The analyst's brief normally runs to suggesting likely software packages which can carry out the types of operation as outlined in Chapters 3 and 4. In situations where computers are being brought into an environment for the first time there is often a degree of flexibility in the adoption of the results of the analysis, and often systems are designed at the point of contact in direct response to the users' wish – this type of approach is known as prototyping.

Amount of time devoted to analysis so far:
Total for this stage (HCI) = 5 days
Cumulative total update for path 1 = 25 days
Cumulative total update for path 2 = 20 days
Cumulative total update for path 3 = 13 days

The interface can take quite some time to get right for all users but we feel that the major principles for interface design in the problem context can be outlined in five days.

Conclusions

The interface as set out here has three major aspects:

1 The technical interface: what is seen and how information is put in.
2 The social interface: how the organization copes with new systems.
3 The security interface: how systems are kept secure and at the same time used!

As with the previous chapters all recommendations in these areas are by way of rules of thumb for incoming systems. However, if these three areas are planned for the final system has a much higher chance of success than might otherwise be the case.

Exercise

- Set out the range of impacts that your information system will have on the existing working relations within the company. Who will be de-skilled, where may there be staff conflict?
- Set out a series of measures that you feel will satisfactorily deal with these conflicts.
- Set out the security procedures that you feel will be appropriate for the new system.
- Set out examples of ideal screen interfaces for your system.
- What measures would you plan to ensure reducing staff resistance to the new system?

When appropriate, take a look at the model answer given in Appendix 3.

CHAPTER 9

TECHNICAL ASPECTS: WHAT IS NEEDED?

KEYWORDS: technical aspects, applications, database, retrieval, maintenance, management, monitoring and evaluation (M&E)

SUMMARY: At this stage of the analysis we begin to design the various component parts which will make up the final information system – we gain a vision of the whole. The components which we deal with here concern the way information activities are coped with by the system, the database structure which contains information items, the production of reports and other output, the management and maintenance of the system and finally monitoring and evaluation.

Introduction

So far you will have undertaken one of three paths to arrive at the technical design stage. As an *aide-mémoire* take another look at Figure 4.6. No matter which of the paths you have adopted you will arrive now at the stage of technical design (there is no escape!).

Technical design refers to the stage which is concerned with outlining and then combining key components of the information systems which can usefully be planned independently. The six areas which we will focus on here are:

1 Application.
2 Database.
3 Retrieval.
4 Management.
5 Maintenance.
6 Monitoring and evaluation.

The components link together to produce what we might refer to as a 'technically workable system' as seen in Figure 9.1. This shows that this stage is ideally based upon the results of previous stages, for example, the application area is based upon events

AUTHORS' NOTE: This raises a problem for teams who have taken paths 2 and 3 through the methodology. Will this stage be irrelevant for you? The human activity system reviewed in stage one and the socio-technical systems design are informative for all stages and provide some basis for all the six aspects. Even if you have taken the third, minimal path through the analysis and design procedure you will be able to make effective use of the rules of thumb which we apply in this stage of the design process.

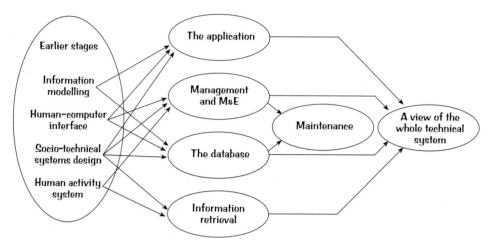

Source: Avison and Wood-Harper 1990

Figure 9.1 *The technical aspects: The 'whole' technical system*

identified in Chapter 6, information modelling, the socio-technical system identified in Chapter 7 and the human–computer interface worked through in Chapter 8.

Before we look at each of the items in detail we can begin by discussing what each of the six areas actually involves (our interpretation here will be different to previous interpretations by other authors).

Application. The application is the core aspect of the system which is being implemented – eg management information system, web-based holiday sales system, intranet decision support system, geographic information system, payroll system, accounting system, etc. The application is the 'to do' part of the system, it is all the functions which we wanted carried out on entities (if you undertook stage two, information modelling) or, at a higher level, it relates specifically to the transformation we set out in the human activity system. Generally this means that application refers to activity within the system to provide the information desired.

Database. The database is also central to the new information system. All information systems are centred on a database somewhere or other even if they are not called such. If you have taken paths 1 or 2 through this book you will have structured the basics of one or several databases already and you will be familiar with the ideas of 'entity' and 'attribute'. If you have taken path 3 then this may be a new idea. The database for your system will be the thing (or things) which store information which your application will work on to produce the key information products (eg reports, etc) as and when required. Going back to the human activity system stage, databases are implicit in the systems set out in the systems models.

Retrieval. The retrieval aspect is the component of the system which produces the information products, be they maps, reports, performance indicators or whatever. These will have been indicated in several stages in the methodology so far.

Management. Management controls the overall system. It deals with security, backing up and all stages of activity within the system. Importantly, management also has the responsibility for maintaining user ownership and interest in the system and for being responsive to user initiatives for change. Management must learn as well as manage. Management is usually in overall control of both of the following areas.

Maintenance. This keeps the system going. Under the general title of maintenance we include the planning of preventative and corrective maintenance procedures.

Monitoring and evaluation. Central and often ignored or under-represented in information systems implementation, monitoring and evaluation will increase the odds that a working system stays working. Monitoring and evaluation, or M&E, provides both management and maintenance subsystems with vital information with regard to the overall health of the system. It is also the main tool which management has for learning and inducing participation in the ongoing system.

Having introduced the area we will now go into the details of planning each of the six aspects and linking them in one overall schema ready for implementation. In terms of the learning organization, this stage of the analysis and design process can enhance the development of learning in the ways shown in Table 9.1.

The application area: What we want to do

This element is concerned with the development of what the information system has to do, these are the 'transactions within the system'. One example of this part of the process comes from Chapter 6. In the information modelling stage we suggested that activity could be set out, even at that early stage as a computer program. If you are not familiar with this take a quick look at Figure 6.8, it will either serve to remind you or introduce the concept.

The figure shows the manner in which four performance indicators (PIs) are produced by a software package. The package does not interest us at this stage nor is it important to understand what is going on in detail. The important feature to recognize is that the PIs are the key information products which we want, the diagram shows what is required to generate each of these PIs and what information databases (or 'tables') need

THINK POINT: Take another look at the six aspects of this stage of the methodology. Now think about the information processing within your organization. Under the six headings can you set out some examples from your own context? Who is the manager? What is the application? How many databases? What is the form of retrieval? Who does the maintenance? Is there effective M&E?

In answering these questions you should quickly see that the six aspects can be applied rapidly as means to think about the information systems you already have. To take the next step and apply them as mental levers to think about the information systems you are planning should not be such a major step.

Table 9.1 *Learning organization and technical aspects*

Discipline	Value in technical aspects thinking	Outcome?
Systems thinking	The technical aspects are a technical system when combined. Here the team can develop a strong vision of boundary and (therefore) an understanding of what is in the systems and what is outside.	The clear demarcation of the new systems boundary. If the team is going to submit this plan to a professional information systems company at this stage, they should be sure of what they want the system to contain and do.
Personal mastery	Not only should the process of considering the 'humanization' of the information system be an empowering process for user and analysis team alike but also the result should be that the user will have a greater sense of control over the work environment.	A real sense of individual and shared ownership over a complex technology.
Mental models	Both analysis team and user community can gain valuable insights into what can often appear to be an information systems 'black box' if the stage is completed with discussion and participation.	Consensus thinking about the roles of each technical aspect.
Shared vision	The development of the M&E aspect should encourage the team to think about sharing learning, ownership, authority and responsibility among information systems users.	The beginning of procedures for 'bedding in' the information system with and by users (not imposing it on them).
Team learning	As above, the M&E stage helps the team to develop the view of extending ownership and learning throughout the system.	The organization becomes part of the team even as the analysis and design team is part of the organization.

to be open to allow the applications to work effectively. PI1 produces information on Full Time Lecturers (FTL), PI2 on Total Allocatable Lecturer Contact Hours, PI3 on Lecturer Contact Hours and PI4 on Full Time Equivalent Students.

If you have undertaken the work effectively a programmer could take your application outline and prototype (or using the rapid application development – RAD – form of prototyping) a software structure which could do the job. Alternatively, a pre-written package, off the shelf, could be purchased and rapidly adapted to do the job required. For example the Sun accounts package is used by numerous organizations as the key application in the accounts department while ARC INFO is a geographic information system applied in numerous locations. Small contextual differences between organizations are not important when purchasing applications which have a general value.

The main skill to develop for this phase is to think through the applications sequentially and hierarchically, eg *how many applications do I have and what shall I call them?*

Within the overall application of MIS I have:

- Application A: Product listing.
- Application B: Relative product value in terms of return.
- Application C: Best performers in the last x months.

etc.

What does each application involve?
Application A.

- Open product database.
- Index the database on product name.
- Produce listing of products including present gross return for financial year.
- Print out listing.

This process can be developed to a high degree of detail if required. In this book we assume that the team will want to gain the overview.

AUTHORS' NOTE: The previous paragraph demonstrates that this stage of the methodology can be used in at least two different ways:

- As a means to plan out the aspects of a new system which is to be written as a one-off by a programmer or, more usually,
- As a requirements list to be built into a specification for a software package already written.

In the latter case the work during stage four on the HCI will also be important. The interface specification is already produced and should be developed as software is selected – more about this in Chapter 10 – software purchase.

The case study

For the department of roads the application of key concern was the roads register. For this register particular applications outlined were:

- Present cost status. This referred to the running cost of a particular section of road. The figures would need to be comparable between different regions.
- Amount of use. The physical amount of traffic which a specific road has to cope with.
- Environmental impact. What effect has road x had on the surrounding countryside? Details would need to be given in terms of specific indicators such as: physical factors (land slips, etc); economic factors (economic inequality between different regions connected by the road(s), etc); social factors (migrant labour in and out of region, etc).
- Present maintenance status. The maintenance record of a road or section of road. Current tasks required to be undertaken.

THINK POINT: For your own organization think again about the main applications. What is the main 'to do' element of any existing information system? If it is an MIS it is probably the bit of the system which produces the PIs or major information products. How might the application be improved in your view?

Tasks for each of these applications were set out and agreed with stakeholders.

The database area: The data store

If the application is the centre of the system to the user, the database is the core to the IT people. Without it there can be no applications or reports. Although the database is central it can be quite simple to outline so long as you have a complete listing of all the information items which should comprise the final system. If you have undertaken information modelling you will have a list of entities and attributes which can be carried forward, if you did not complete that phase you will need to consider:

- What are the things which you want to keep information about? (registers, listings, people, contracts, etc). These are entities.
- What are the main features of these entities? (for example a student register might contain surname, first name, term address, home address, past marks, disciplinary records, etc). These are attributes.

THINK POINT: Can you set out 10 or so attributes (or fields) of one of the major databases in your organization's information system?

Constructing and testing databases should not be trivialized and in this book we are careful to explain that we are seeking to gain understanding of new information systems in a sustainable if rapid way for non-specialists – the view and the detail can always be developed and improved upon. However, non-specialists gain in understanding of IT-based systems if they have an understanding of what data is important to make this system work well.

Of the 10 or so attributes which do you think are the most vital data items for the system to work well?

Rather like the applications area there is no great mystery concerning the development of this stage, it requires you to think through what the major entities are and then give as complete a listing as possible of the attributes required, keeping in mind that this stage is intimately linked to the applications. The application aspect cannot undertake work if key attributes of key entities in the database subsystem are missing.

The case study

Continuing the theme from the applications subsystem, the major entity was agreed as being the roads register. Some of the working out of attributes was as follows:

List of major attributes for the roads register
- Name of road.
- Date of construction.
- Personnel involved – engineers, overseers.
- Duration.
- Cost.
- Benefit as projected in original report.
- Source of finance – external, internal.
- Total quantities and costs of:
    - cutting
    - filling
    - gravelling

etc.

The retrieval area:
What we want from the system

The retrieval area provides the team with the opportunity to:

- Structure the content of reports and other output.
- Agree the timing of reports and other output.
- Prepare the presentation of reports and other output.

There will be key events when certain information products are required:

- End of the financial year.
- Enrolment of new staff.
- Completion of a project.
- Marketing of a new product.

At these events information of certain types will be required. The form and presentation of the information is also important. One of the most powerful functions of modern IT-based information systems is that retrieval can be automatic and fairly effortless (from the point of view of the user anyway) if planned for. On the other hand, if a system has not been properly planned the production of reports can be almost as time consuming as undertaking the process manually. The retrieval area should link in closely with the application and database areas but can be planned as a separate function. The planning process requires the following action:

- Assess which reports are required. Make allowances for reports required at a given time (eg end of the financial year) and those which are required at any time (eg the current activity of staff in a design agency). List these reports and indicate when they are required.
- For each report set out key information or indicators which should be included. This can comprise a listing. When producing the list keep in mind the applications area. Applications should produce all the workings for these reports. There should never be a report or other retrieval operation without a link from an application. Similarly there should never be an application which does not produce, or combine to produce some form of report.
- When you are sure that your listing of all retrieval products is complete and that the content of each of these is similarly set out think about design. There are two golden rules in the design process:
  1 Clarity and simplicity.
  2 Recognizability – resemblance to existing reports.

Reports can contain far too much information. Reports can be highly unstructured. For the clarity of a report it is advisable to work with an agreed template. A template is a structure which all reports in a given context will obey. For example a promotions record report taken from a personnel register might be as follows in template form:

Surname:

First name:

Home address:

Work address:

Grade:

Payroll number:

Last three promotions:

THINK POINT: Think about the kinds of reports which you get in your organization. Are any of them IT generated? Could any of them which are not so generated be so? What do you get from reports which you do not need? What do you not get which you could usefully apply? In the university sector we get lots of information but it is often not digestible. A pile of printout is no substitute for one well produced pie graph.

But, do you need to know sex and age? Does 'work address' mean 'name of department'? What does 'grade' mean? Does a promotions report need to contain details of the payroll number? Certainly this form is short but will it tell a manager what he or she needs to know? What obvious information is missing?

The retrieval system should be planned to provide information at a time and in a form which is useful. The caveat to this is the need to produce all designs in cooperation with the major stakeholders who are going to make use of the reports.

The case study

Following discussions with the major users of the applications it was decided that existing report forms would be copied and reproduced by the system. There was a certain degree of inflexibility concerning reporting. The IT-based information system was seen largely as a way of speeding up the existing process, the range of new options in terms of reporting was largely ignored and/or not seen as being important. This is a situation which occurs quite regularly. A popular response to this is to design reports around the existing documents but to leave provision in the system for change and further development. Most software packages allow the user to continually add reports.

The management area: How to control the system

Management covers a wide variety of issues (see Figure 9.2). For our purposes we will focus on:

- Controlling the information system with an operating system.
- Job priority control – what to do and when (issues of continuous workload and seasonal workload).
- Security – access, debugging and back-up.
- User support – including mutual learning.

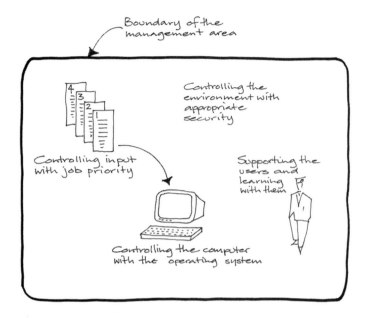

Figure 9.2 *Management issues*

Controlling your system with the operating system

This section will not teach the use of the operating system. The object is to point at needs for good management and suggest ways to achieve these needs.

Inevitably understanding the operating system (eg Windows NT, Mac OS, Linux, etc) is the bottom line for good management of the hardware and software. Yet training in the use and control of operating systems is a component left off many training schedules. This is a point worth noting and carrying forward to your plan of training needs at the time of implementation. The operating system allows the user to:

- Control the IT itself effectively, eg:
  - understand error messages;
  - check disks for errors;
  - control output.
- Handle software properly:
  - install software;
  - back-up files;
  - back-up disks.

Although the operating system can be laborious and difficult (in fact it can often be the source of many problems for new and old user alike) it is essential for it to be managed well if your information system is to work effectively. What problems can arise without effective management of this aspect?

- Computer error:
  - overloaded hard disks;
  - fragmented files.
- Software error:
  - incorrectly installed;
  - incorrect screen/printer driver;
  - software/hardware mismatch.
- User error:
  - files lost – no back-up;
  - disks lost – no back-up.
- Cost:
  - unnecessary use of potentially expensive outside agencies;
  - lost time;
  - lost work.

Effective training or literature are the major means of avoiding problems. For most purposes a good book is good enough if you already have some experience. For the new manager – look to a good training programme to start off.

Job priority control

That is, what to do and when (issues of continuous workload and seasonal workload). Priority is often a balance between four factors

1 The job being done.
2 Staff seniority (more senior staff tend to expect quick access).
3 Limited computer time available.
4 Computer frailty.

AUTHORS' NOTE: Seasonal work (eg annual accounts) cannot be moved around. There is need to schedule IT availability for key times of the year. Continuous workload, such as order entering, inventory updating, etc, can be slotted in on a more casual basis. Freak loads cannot be planned for. This is the percentage of time that you build in to deal with unexpected eventualities. One way of dealing with this is to make public that the IT is available for 12 hours/day and to hold the extra 4 hours as a buffer against need.

These four factors can be balanced by the following rule of thumb method:

- If IT power is scarce it is useful if you can arrive at an agreed working day for the machines. A standard applied in many locations is 16 hours/day. If all users have a networked computer on their desk (for example) this issue is less relevant.
- Review all existing work. Assess for seniority of demand in terms of: seasonal cycles of work, continuous workload and freak loads.

When you have assessed the workload produce a weekly, monthly and annual schedule indicating on and off IT times. Most importantly, circulate the schedule with a note indicating the need for discussion and agreement on your plan. It is best if the schedule is known by all users (even if they do not all agree with it). Once agreed, an annual review is useful but otherwise never deviate! It is always a good idea to hold back some IT time in the event of emergencies. This should be time which you do not mind seeing the IT being used but is generally not available for the user.

Security

A most important aspect which includes access, debugging and back-up.

As we indicated in the last chapter when dealing with software security at the level of the user interface, as you improve access, so you can lose control! Loss of control of the system is to be avoided at all costs. As you increase control so the user has less and less access! This is also highly undesirable. Most security involves organizations in coping with a paradox.

The individual manager sets his or her own balance. Three major aspects of security are hardware safety, software safety and user safety.

Hardware safety

IT units need to be protected from a variety of enemies. These will vary with location and sophistication of the unit but include:

Excesses in climate. Climate is of particular importance. Hot, dry, dusty spells in rooms with no air-conditioning can be fatal to PCs. Humidity can be a danger. Basic precautions include the following:

- Rooms with many PCs in them should have doors which make a good seal. An ante-room is a good idea.
- Air-conditioning in computer rooms removes problems of over-heating. Keeping blinds and windows closed is an even cheaper option.
- For very sensitive equipment ensure that air-conditioning provides a positive air pressure so that air will rush out of the room if a door is opened.
- Carpets on the floor remove dust from the atmosphere. But care needs to be taken when vacuum cleaning the carpet.
- During very humid periods, moisture extractors can be fitted in the room.

Power supply. This refers to irregularities in power supply and its criticalness will depend upon firstly your location and secondly the sensitivity of your equipment. Some software is very prone to problems with power supply cuts – for example, some database software will corrupt files if they are open when the power goes down. Obviously you must assess your own risk but there are three levels of protection you can apply:

1 Total: an independent generator designed to cut in when the mains supply goes down.
2 UPS or Uninterruptible Power Supply: these are battery based and will guarantee you 30 minutes or more work time after power goes down.
3 Voltage stabilizer: this will regulate any peaks and troughs in your supply. If you are in doubt, get an electrician in to check on your supply.

Theft. Local conditions will again prevail, but unfortunately hardware and software are attractive to thieves. Levels of protection include:

- Situation of the computer room on the second floor of the building.
- Electronic burglary devices.
- Bars on windows.
- Security staff.
- Searching of staff on entering and leaving the work rooms.
- Access to key holder only.
- Securing all computers and peripherals to desk surfaces.
- Providing user identity cards.

Accidents. By their nature these are difficult to plan for. The computer manager should get to know the level of risk in the environment. Some of the favourite items to guard against include:

- Tea and coffee being used to irrigate computer systems!
- Disks being erased.
- Keyboards being dropped on the floor.
- Keyboard being hammered by over enthusiastic typists!
- Computers being left on overnight.

Most of these items are dealt with if the manager obeys some basic IT systems maintenance disciplines:

- Ensure that all operational staff know what they are supposed to be doing and are kept up to date with systems development. This means that staff training and workshops for users to discuss problems and learning areas should be continual.
- Ensure that all software is copied and protected prior to release. Copies of software should be periodically examined for corruption.
- Ensure that all hardware is kept in a good state of repair. Measures to provide for this include monthly checking for keyboard failure, screen burn, drive alignment and general trouble-free operation
- Servicing (annual). Be careful in your selection of agency! Many servicing agencies are not all that they seem to be. It is worth getting a number of quotations for work and then taking a look at the servicing department of the shortlisted companies.

Software safety
We have already mentioned keeping the software in a state of physical safety in terms of regular backing up. Another issue is that of selecting software which offers a clear upgrade path. Often it is difficult to see if software products will still be around in a few years time. The best indicator is to go for products which are well supported and have a strong existing customer base. This will be an item which will attract growing attention as software continues to grow as a percentage of the total cost of an information system. Two other items arise:

1 Staff taking liberties. Bringing in their own software and working with it on office machines.
2 Sabotage.

Both these items are hard to deal with. Physical protection includes vigilance of staff and threatening notices.

Software protection includes the use of lockable keyboards and passwords. Some software does now come with software password control. Also packages can be purchased. These come with their own password protection which can be used to keep away the non-expert. But beware: on PCs there is no complete software protection as yet.

Another software threat comes from computer viruses. These are small software packages, written by people who either have nothing better to do with their time or who wish to disrupt information systems processes. Viruses can attack any computer system and are transported onto systems (generally) in the form of copied software or via email. Viruses are preventable if you do not copy software and have some form of vetting incoming email. If you get a virus there are quite a number of potential symptoms:

- The temporary interruption of key jobs. This appears to be a common problem. No sooner does an agency or department become dependent upon an IT assisted system than the system becomes corrupted and ceases to function. The implications are particularly worrying where decisions are delayed in such critical areas as: health care, agricultural planning and product profitability. Close to the root of this problem is the inability of manual practices to cope when the IT fails.
- The closing of IT departments. Again this seems to be becoming increasingly regular. In one case, an IT department in a university was closed to students because it had just been cleared of viruses for the third time and staff did not want to have to go through it again!
- Unnecessary and expensive hardware replacement. Sometimes hardware is replaced mistakenly when the real fault lies with the software. On several occasions in the authors' experience fixed disks have been replaced, and even thrown out when the real fault lay with a virus.
- Slow and/or faulty data presentation. Too often IT output is seen, by IT people it must be said, as being adequate in itself. Results of calculation are not checked effectively and the garbage which eventually comes out can be used, unknowingly, in management decision-making. With the proliferation of management information systems based on computers and the related spread of viruses decision-making is threatened. One of the primary indications of the presence of many boot sector viruses is the slowing down of computer processes.
- Project failure. This is the bottom line. Computer facilities can produce tremendous value, they can also be the weak link which cause projects to fail partially or completely, in the short- or long-term. Without efficient local data collection, verification, validation, storage and processing the risk of some form of failure is increased. This is so with manual systems; the risk is even greater when systems are computerized. An extensive literature exists on the various faces of such failure (see Suggested Reading).

What can we do? First and most importantly, effective management of information system facilities needs to be focused on. There is evidence that at present absolutely minimal attention is being focused on the management of resources. Second, culturally and politically sensitive analysis and design should precede all installation. Overly technical approaches to analysis and design produce admirable technical systems. These, however, often break down when put into the social context. Analysis and design needs to understand the context for information systems and recognize that information systems are social systems. Third, planning should be central to pre-computerization and manual systems can often be strengthened and run parallel with incoming IT-based systems. This is a matter of common sense. Any information system requires a degree of contingency planning to ensure that systems can be provided in the event of major breakdown.

User safety
We will deal with user support shortly. User safety is improved by:

- Priority access being in place. Users need to know when and how much access they have.
- Passwording in place. A hierarchical structure of passwords can be set up in most systems.
- Training is sufficient and maintained. Training schedules for all staff should be outlined. Users often have a better idea about what they need to know than computer 'experts'. We shall return to the need for mutual listening and learning processes to be in place between users and IT staff.
- Unauthorized use is guarded against.

User support
User support as we deal with it here has four major themes: access, control, back-up and feedback. We have already dealt with access.

Control
It is important to note that almost all access to and use of IT involves concepts of control. It is also important to note that control is rarely uncontested and needs to arise from processes of negotiation. Control without negotiation can be experienced as tyranny. Matters relating to control include:

- Control over unauthorized physical access.
- Control over unauthorized access to sensitive software.
- Control over access to other users' workspace.
- Control over user files. If the application which the user is working with is producing data for a third party and that data is critical for decision-making (eg MIS information) then the user may well need to be guided in appropriate security measures such as: always working with copies of files and regular backing up of files.

User back-up

The manager needs to provide:

* Supervision to hands-on users.
* Training in the use of new packages. This will probably mean at some time the computer unit will need to provide the users with a curriculum of training activities including basic introductory programmes, advanced programmes and programmes in specific applications. Further, training usually needs to be differentiated between basic operator skills, advanced operator skills and expert user skills.
* Regular updates on latest developments. This is a great way of keeping the curious happy, eg with a regular newsletter or a weekly/monthly bulletin.

User feedback

There is little point in providing users with support if there is no capacity for the user to provide the computer manager with feedback as to the success or otherwise of his/her endeavour. Throughout this book we have been focusing on the additional value which the analysis and design process and the subsequent information system implementation can provide an organization in terms of learning (about core business and organizational well-being). The emplacement of learning mechanisms is vital if a new information system is not to fall foul of the types of problems which we identified in Chapter 1. To this end, useful facilities include:

* Regular team meetings: the team being defined as all 'users and suppliers of the system'. Focus group forums are a good mechanism for drawing out learning and problems.
* A regular, formal user committee attended by the manager.
* A well advertised complaints procedure.

The maintenance area: Keeping the system going

The lifetime of IT equipment is not a subject which encourages universal agreement. A computer committee might advocate seven years for minicomputer hardware, a microcomputer manufacturer might expect 18 months for the desk life of a fixed disk. Much will depend upon the wear and tear that the equipment receives and upon the level of maintenance provided. Generally speaking computer maintenance has two major components: *preventative* and *corrective*. Precise details of maintenance procedures can only be given when firm information is available concerning the location of the system and the type of hardware and software to be used. However, in practice we can set out the major requirements of preventative and corrective maintenance as shown in Figure 9.3.

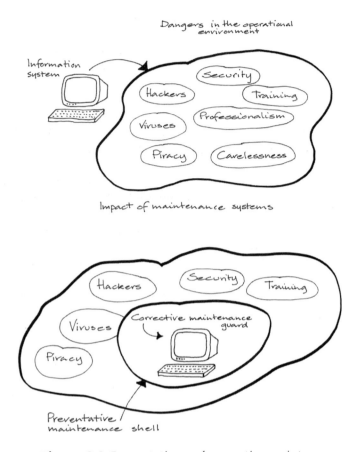

Figure 9.3 *Preventative and corrective maintenance*

Preventative maintenance

Taking as our theme the idea that all information systems are set up in situations of hazard, a preventative 'shell' is essential to provide the system with the bare chance of survival. Features of the shell might include:

- Daily supervision of the users – this includes the development of appropriate security measures set out in the management subsystem.
- Regular, quarterly servicing of all hardware.
- Annual servicing down to computer component level.

Corrective maintenance

Within the preventative shell some unexpected problems will arise. To deal with these problems rapidly and with minimum disruption to users a corrective 'guard' is useful. The guard might include the following aspects:

- In-house understanding of basic fault finding. Operators and supervisors can be trained in fault identification.

- In-house maintenance technician or a 24-hour call-out procedure agreed with a local maintenance company.
- Security procedures linked to monitoring and evaluation of key indicators (eg wear and tear on machines, incidence of disk theft, incidence of new software appearing on machines).

The monitoring and evaluation area: Learning about the system

The working system is never static: changes constantly occur. The way to plan for the events is to implement effective monitoring and evaluation (M&E). M&E in a project cycle can be seen in Figure 9.4. Monitoring and evaluation is our primary means for making sure that the system is producing the information users require when required and also that this is occurring at a cost which is proportional to the benefit. Although M&E is a detailed subject in its own right (see Suggested Reading), there are at least three levels of rapid M&E which we can plan for in our rapid planning approach, namely rule of thumb, key indicator and logical framework.

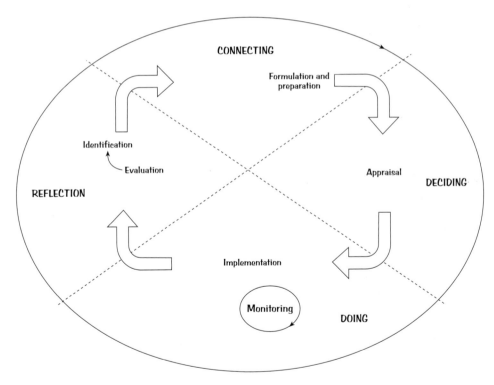

This diagram builds off earlier work by Coleman and Kolb (Coleman 1987b; Kolb 1984)

Figure 9.4 *Monitoring and evaluation in a learning project context*

Rule of thumb

Monitoring

This comes before and complements the maintenance of the system. Monitoring should be constant and refers to the wear and tear on the computer facility as well as the operational smoothness of its day-to-day running. Monitoring can take various forms:

- Informal periodic review of users within the context of focus groups.
- Formal analysis of user habits (eg a questionnaire dealing with assessment of time spent hands on, assessment of good and bad habits, such as: typing skills, login/logout procedure, disk care, complaints concerning supervision).
- All answers need to be carefully interpreted in the light of the obvious user biases.

Evaluation

This can be annual and can cover such aspects as:

- The general physical condition of equipment compared to previous year.
- Evidence of theft and/or wilful damage.
- User complaints and/or suggestions.
- Staff complaints and suggestions.

Key indicator

M&E should deal with all aspects of the information system – technical, personal and social, soft and hard, formal and informal. This can be seen in broad terms as relating to:

- The human activity system (HAS).
- The information model.
- The socio-technical system (STS).
- The human–computer interface (HCI).
- Technical areas.

For example, if all these areas are regularly monitored for problems and issues and the resulting problems evaluated annually and appropriate action taken your system should be fairly successful. For the purposes of the exercise here we will not go into great detail concerning the way in which key indicators are identified and monitored. At this stage it is useful if we have some idea as to the components which are most prone to change. In our own example these were as shown in Table 9.2.

The task of the planner is to assess which if not all of the indicators are to be monitored during the run time of the project and what results would constitute the development of a problem. Second, the planner will want to identify several of the indicators which can be evaluated at the end of the project cycle.

Table 9.2 *Selection of areas needing M&E (as related to the Multiview methodology)*

	M&E focus	Critical indicators to monitor and evaluate
1	Human activity system	New conflicts of interest. New departmental linkages. Widescale changes in senior personnel. Changes in the economic climate. Changes in the political arena.
2	Information modelling	New functions imposed. Substantial reworking of old functions. Changes in decomposition. New entities. New attributes. New events.
3	Socio-technical	Changes in the organization's 'vision' of the future. Changes in personnel responsibilities. Changes in the economic performance of new IT. Costs of IT.
4	Human–computer interface	Changes in operating systems. New software. Changes in the approach to dialogue (eg voice operated systems).
5	Technical areas	Changes in the system's performance with use. Increasing error levels. Retrieval difficulty.

The logical framework

We will have more to say about this approach in Appendix 2. For now, the logical framework has been developed in a number of contexts (see Suggested Reading). It is a four by four matrix for developing thinking about a project but it can also be used to model and monitor project progress and project impact. See Appendix 2 for more detail.

An issue of risk?

In the development of any information system there is risk involved. Quite how the issue is managed is up to the assessment of the analysis and design team and the rigours of the specific context. However, we have found

> THINK POINT: In your own organization think about what you would want to monitor to see if:
>
> - the information systems were functioning properly and
> - the users were making the most of them.
>
> Let your thinking take in both social and technical features which are both formal and informal.
>
> How much effort would you be willing to put into M&E? How could you 'sell' the cost of this effort to the organization? What would be the benefits arising from good M&E?

it useful to have an easy-to-apply method to make assessments of information systems at this stage, prior to purchase.

Assessing risk value

One risk analysis which is of general value is that set out by Hughes and Cotterell (1999). What follows is adapted from this book with some additional elements.

Some risks will be relatively unimportant whereas others will be of major concern. Some are likely to occur and some are unlikely.

The probability of a risk occurring is the *risk likelihood*. If it happens it is known as the *risk impact*. The importance of the risk is known as the *risk value* or *risk exposure*.

Hughes and Cotterell calculate risk as follows:

risk value = risk likelihood x risk impact

The estimation of the cost and probability of risk is a problematic issue and I will not deal with these here – generally they are time consuming to generate and unreliable measures. However, there is still great value in developing some form of quantitative measure of the risks evident in any information systems development process.

Likelihood is usually developed as a subjective valuation between 1 and 10 where 1 is considered to be completely unlikely and 10 is just about certain.

Impact measures are assessed in a similar manner and take into account the total risk to the project including such potential costs as:

- The cost of delays in gaining information.
- Cost overrun on reports development.
- Compromises on quality set against schedule.

What follows in Table 9.3 is an example of a risk value assessment.

Table 9.3 *Risk assessment example*

Risk number	Risks drawn out from M&E	Likelihood	Impact	Risk value
1	Changes to requirements specification of data gathering	8	8	64
2	Data entry takes longer than expected	4	7	28
3	Staff sickness affecting analysis activities	5	7	35
4	Staff sickness affecting non-critical activities	10	2	20
5	Coding and analysis take longer than expected	4	6	24
6	Pls demonstrate errors or deficiencies in design	1	10	10

Prioritizing the risks

When a risk analysis has taken place a number of options are available to the stakeholder:

- Reducing the risk exposure by reducing likelihood or impact.
- Drawing up contingency plans to deal with risk should it occur.

It is important that the major risks are given more attention to ensure that costs for contingency (for example) do not multiply on low risk items.

Putting it all together: The technical package

The final package can be seen as a specification which will maintain an information system within what is always assumed to be a hazardous operational environment. The linking together of aspects or areas into one whole should be occurring throughout the design process. Figure 9.5 is one view of the wholeness we are seeking.

Amount of time devoted to analysis so far:

Total for this stage (Technical aspects) = 5 days
Cumulative total update for path 1 = 30 days
Cumulative total update for path 2 = 25 days
Cumulative total update for path 3 = 18 days

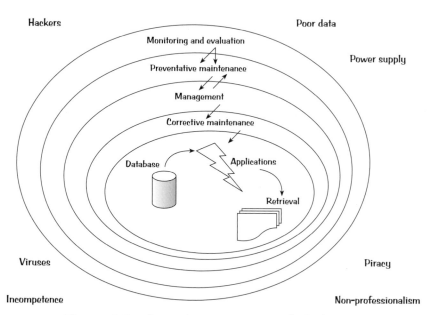

Figure 9.5 *Information systems as technical areas*

Conclusions

This stage of the analysis has provided the outline of the completed system. The only requirements which remain are for the outline hardware, software, and training to be followed by an implementation strategy. Make sure that this is the case! Go through your technical areas and make sure that the system which you outline only requires practical details. If your system is deficient at this stage (for example if the system does not provide enough detail for a software package to be described) rectify the point now.

Exercise

Using the model from the book set out, in outline, the overall details of the new system in the form of a briefing document for senior company staff. The document has to be accessible to a range of different readers and therefore should be quite general. In the document you will need to allude to the total system. This will include items on all the areas outlined above but focusing in particular on:

- The database and the applications aspects.
- The management aspect.
- The M&E aspect. This should include some references to type of M&E procedures, expected problem areas, contingency plans.

Take a look at the model answer in Appendix 3.

CHAPTER 10

THE TOTAL DESIGN, TRAINING, HARDWARE, SOFTWARE AND IMPLEMENTATION

KEYWORDS/EXPRESSIONS: training choice, software selection, hardware selection, implementation strategy

SUMMARY: The chapter works on the assumption that you have worked through one of the three paths and that you are now ready to embark on the range of training, hardware and software specification and information systems implementation issues. Some brief outlines are given of the types of problem which can arise during this phase.

Introduction to implementation issues

In the previous chapters we have concluded our review of the stages of the rapid multiperspective approach to planning sustainable information systems which we specify as requiring as little as 30 days (6 weeks).

It has been our intention to develop in a concise, stage-by-stage manner the means whereby the methodology can be applied to make sense of the information requirements of the organization on the one hand and the best fit solution to meet those requirements on the other.

The total design has been seen to require considerable labour but we suggest that elements of the methodology can be dropped if time is lacking or certain aspects can be adopted in an abbreviated form. Figure 10.1 demonstrates the unpacking of the total analysis, design and implementation model.

Although planning or analysis and design usually ends with the technical specification of the system, implementation issues will quite often be of concern to us – the learning team who have gone through the analysis and design stages are in a wonderful position to now progress the project through to implementation and beyond. In the next few pages we will look briefly at four areas of interest for implementation of the design:

1 Training.
2 Software selection.
3 Hardware selection.
4 Implementation.

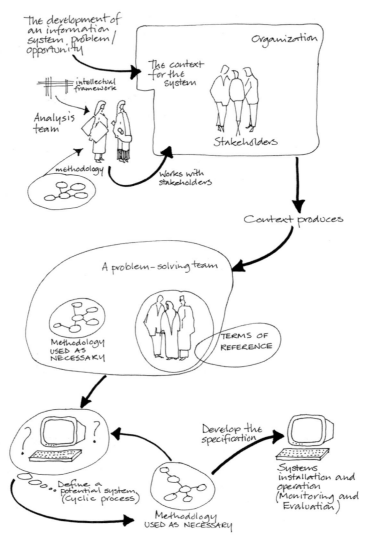

Figure 10.1 *Rich picture of the overall approach*

Training

Before developing the regime, what is good training about?

The communication of skills

Information system and particularly computerized information system use is not intuitive as a rule (despite the development of what are sometime claimed to be intuitive graphic interfaces). The process of training is usually involved with passing on hands-on skills and confidence in a new system. Other items which may need to be communicated include: theory principles, specialist data preparation and fault finding.

Communication requires that the two sides of the informing process are working on the same wavelength. The training programme which you specify might attempt to enhance communication by use of the design factors set out in the following list:

- User needs are clearly determined in cooperation and partnership.
- User capacities are evaluated/self-evaluated.
- A training pack is planned with a balance of training items and procedures included. The emphasis is on continuous learning not 'one-stop' training.
- A sequence is set out and agreed for training.
- A schedule is designed and agreed.
- Milestones of achievement are mutually identified by potential trainer and trainee.
- Final positions are jointly evaluated.

The short cut to effective communication and therefore training is identifying, first, what the user needs to know and, second, what he or she already knows. The human activity system (HAS) and the socio-technical design should have indicated some possible answers to these questions, continuous dialogue between the team and the user groups will aid it.

One means to effective communication lies in the development of the teaching/training package, the precision of its sequence and the organization of its schedule. We need to set out the *content*, *sequence*, and *schedule* of events. We will deal with this more fully later in the section (see 'Specific training issues to be aware of').

Repetition of skills out of the training room context: Self confidence and self reliance

Training is only effective in so far as the skills developed in the classroom can be replicated at the work place. *This of course is obvious!* However, it is essential that training be developed with this object in view. The following list sets out some means to achieve self confidence and self reliance:

- Including in the training programme plenty of points where the participant has to work on his or her own, eg self-assessment exercises and reflective self-examinations of skills.
- Exercises containing trial runs requiring the use of new skills, eg demonstrations and simulations.
- Project work, where the participant can develop their own themes with the existing training material.

The results of not achieving self-sufficiency and self reliance can be many and varied. The catastrophic outcome would be the folding of the project. Lesser outcomes might be the extreme annoyance to the organization running the new information systems as numerous requests for help come in from worried users, the lowering of morale among newly trained staff and criticism of the training unit that they are not doing their job properly!

One vital aspect of training is the evaluation of performance. It's all very well performing the training and assessing that the users are up to the job in hand. However, one should always expect the unexpected. Training is only one aspect of computer installation, for example:

- Hardware and software faults can lead to total system collapse or at least the undermining of staff morale.
- Humidity or dust can lead to system faults.
- Poor data collection, validation or verification all have their problems.
- Trained staff may have a high premium on the local labour market and well trained staff may leave projects and departments shortly after completing training.

Not to mention the training related problems such as:

- New software being used which bypasses the existing training.
- The development of new tasks which have not been trained for.
- Large increases in data collection and therefore data processing which alters existing and expected working practices.

All these points indicate the need for monitoring and evaluation some time after the completion of training and the return of individuals to their departments. Many analysis and design teams will already have these type of contingencies planned for from the information provided in Chapter 9. Such an evaluation might make use of the original rich picture concept set out in Chapter 5 and is best carried out by an individual not directly related with the original training but briefed on the training terms of reference and achievements.

Specific training issues to be aware of

There are a number of easy-to-identify issues which can impede your progress with a training schedule. We will, very briefly, run through three of these here.

Senior manager intransigence

Generally speaking, the more senior a member of staff, the greater may be his or her reluctance to adopt the training schedule. This is further complicated if the manager is powerful enough to either daunt the trainer or just tell him/her to go away! As we have already discussed in Chapter 2, computers threaten many individuals' views of themselves and of their organizational role. Computerized information systems can offend managers' concepts of what constitutes an effective organization. Also, computers can threaten the employment of individuals.

If a training programme is likely to come up against this type of problem certain factors can be usefully applied:

- The key to winning over reluctant participants is empathy. Understanding the origin of reluctance and sympathizing, while at the same time attempting to dispel needless worry, is half the battle.

- Remember, participants will respond better to training programmes if they are convinced that the training is 'on their side', empowering them and improving their personal mastery.

Wide range of abilities relating to IT in any organization

It is often the case that computer training sessions tend to have a wider range of abilities among participants than many other forms of training. Being 'quick' with a computer is not an indication of intelligence. Rapid response to a computer can demonstrate that the participant is good at reading instructions but is not in fact making any mental effort to *understand* the content.

It is not possible or desirable to have all students working at the same pace. However, order can be imposed on the potential chaos of a class all moving at different paces by:

- The use of exercises to encourage the faster individuals to reflect on their learning and make them really take in the content. This provides an additional level of quality to training.
- Self-assessment tests to indicate that milestones have been reached.
- The use of a graduated series of instruction which all can work through at their own pace.

> AUTHORS' NOTE: A graduated series of instruction is useful but does severely limit the capacity of lectures and presentations, if this type of teaching is used, to come at the 'right' time for everyone.

- Projects which encourage fast and slow participants to work together.

Jargon

Jargon puts off the newcomer and confuses everyone. It also indicates that the training is not on the same 'side' as the participant. It sets the training apart and reduces comprehension. On the positive side, the occasional use of jargon can be effective in intimidating the aggressive or obstructive individuals ('Have you tied your hexadecimal bootstraps yet?')! But seriously, it is to be avoided at all costs: jargon is generally a negative component. The training programme devised by the team will need to create a common language which provide the trainer and the participant – the learning team – with a format in which both can communicate effectively.

Software selection

We have already indicated that most applications used in information systems design and development (be they websites, MIS, payroll systems, land assessment systems or otherwise) make use of a database. We have also mentioned that in terms of the case study used in these notes a range of standard packages will need to be employed including word-processors, databases and spreadsheets. What we have not yet covered is the area of selection procedure (see Figure 10.2).

There are quite a number of methods for the selection of software. The task is to match the perceived requirements of the users to the capacities of the packages available. The type of information which is needed for the specification to be exact includes the following:

- *Size.* How much data is there going to be? How many records per annum (or quarter, or whatever discrete time unit you are going to use) do you expect to add to the database? How large will the database be?
- *Volatility.* This refers to the regularity with which you will be deleting old data items and adding the new ones which will keep the base up to date. For example, if 50 per cent of the data is to be removed and new entered each year and there are 120,000 data items – this equates to a considerable degree of volatility for a small organization. If you have taken path 1 through the methodology then information modelling will have indicated to you answers to both these questions.
- *Response time.* At what speed is the data required by the user? Generally speaking the larger the data set, the slower will be the response time even if a very powerful computer system is used. There is need to select the database system which will meet your requirements in terms of speed not just at the present but, using our future analysis in phase three of the methodology, try to put a figure on the rate of expansion of the system up to the mid term (five years).

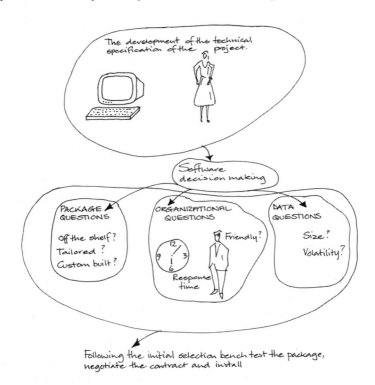

Figure 10.2 *Some features of software selection*

With this basic data set identification information covered, issues of the range of software options available to you needs to be looked into next. In general terms there are three areas of software which might be explored:

- *Software packages.* These are pre-written and cover an enormous range of applications at the time of writing. What we tend to assume is: 'if I have a software requirement, someone, somewhere in the world has already had that requirement and has produced a package to meet it'. Of course this may not always be the case especially in the developmental/research areas but it is not a bad working assumption. A review of software catalogues and magazines can identify quite a range which can then be reviewed more closely.
- *Tailored packages.* This can be quite expensive and is often required as well as the first option. The tailored package is a development of the standard product. It may involve you (or a hired expert) in adapting elements to your specific requirements. Items to be wary of include: poor tailoring leaving considerable bugs for you to discover, getting involved in this without thoroughly checking the ready-made market and using spurious experts!
- *Custom-built packages.* This is undoubtedly the most expensive and most problem-prone area to deal with. All the items to be wary of, which we mentioned above, still need to be considered. It is a good practice to get any expert group producing such software to give written guarantees and dates for delivery (as well as cost!). Much modern software is produced with quick build tools which provide developers with the ability to significantly reduce development time.

Case study

For our own example we estimated that any one of a range of software packages would carry out the major database functions which we would be engaged in. The main, specifically *technical*, requirements were:

- For the database system to be multi-user.
- Similarly, spreadsheet and word-processing packages should have multi-user facilities.

Specific developmental factors included: packages used must be readily available in local markets (remember, our example is set in a developing country), and all selections should be well established products which had the widest chance of being locally serviceable in terms of training.

Realistically we work on the assumption that most software provided for and by developing countries will be pre-written. This will partly be due to the enormous range of software already available and the prohibitive cost of custom-built software. General points to keep in mind are the following:

- On reviewing a series of software options, which of the packages actually do the job which you have specified in the logical model of technical specification? Does the package provide you with the levels of control which are essential for successful running?

- Does the software fit the outline hardware configuration which we are forming? Will the software shake hands smoothly with the operating system?
- How well do the performance times of the software rate? Can a trial data set be run on each system for comparison with standard workloads?
- Can the system be made as user friendly as was set out in the human–computer interface of the methodology?
- How adaptable to change is the software?
- Is the vendor for the package(s) in question honest, legal and decent and if not is this acceptable?

Hardware selection

Having made a choice of software which meets the needs which your analysis has arrived at you are now ready to specify hardware for the system. Again there are a number of key factors that have to be considered (see Figure 10.3).

The process involved with hardware selection can be outlined as follows:

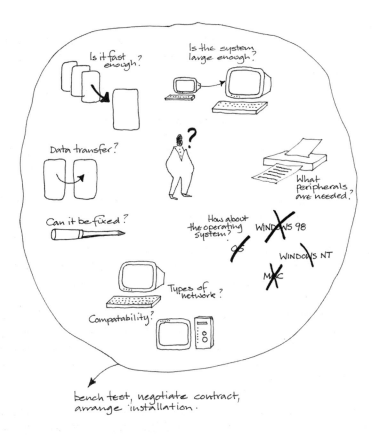

Figure 10.3 *Some features of hardware specification*

- System evaluation which includes: information gathering on potentially appropriate systems (eg trade magazines and visits). Following this the team needs to identify vendors, request details of total cost (which includes all hardware components, hardware training, hardware support/maintenance). Other important questions include: is hardware flexible enough to adapt to the user environment? The end of this stage is to produce a shortlist of potential systems.
- Installation evaluation. Here we think of such issues as what precise local factors will affect installation? For example, humidity, temperature, dust, seasonal fluctuation in atmospheric conditions, the recurrent budget for spares, the availability of spares locally and the availability of finance. More specifically, how easy is the system to use?
- A useful approach to adopt is to request details of existing users. In discussing the system with existing users particular attention can be paid to runtime problems in similar environments but beware defensive attitudes following 'bad' decisions (individuals are rarely likely to tell you if the system they have bought has been no good).
- Finally, test drive (benchmark test) the proposed new system.

Case study

For our example we decided upon a PC network. Our final hardware selection was for a locally available and serviceable PC-based network supplied with uninterruptible power supplies.

Implementation

Following the nuts and bolts of hardware and software purchase, implementation is the next stage. Several factors need to be kept in mind:

- In new environments rigorous management techniques will need to be applied (see Chapter 9, the management subsystem).
- Staffing will need sufficient initial and recurrent training in the use of the technology (see the sections on training structure in this chapter).
- The monitoring and evaluation procedure will have to be continued on an annual basis. Initial (within three year) success should not create undue complacency.

Actual systems installation can take a number of forms (see Figure 10.4). The precise form will depend upon the circumstances in which you are working and the perceived benefits of each approach as perceived by yourself and the major stakeholders. Kozar (1989) lists four considerations to keep in mind when selecting the installation structure:

1 *Stress considerations*. The least stressful of the four approaches is probably the parallel system. In this case there is a fall-back and the various agencies within the host institution should not feel too 'exposed' with the new system.

2 *Cost considerations.* Although the parallel approach appears the most costly, purely in terms of keeping two systems running at the same time, it may reduce some runtime costs because of the reduced stress on operators and managers. This is yet another example of the local environment being the major force in the adoption of a system.

3 *Duration considerations.* This refers to the speed for systems uptake and the length of time which it is envisaged that the system will be partially implemented. Again the parallel approach would appear to be the most costly in terms of duration. Users of the old system are more likely to hang onto functions which they know and are happy with.

4 *Human resource management considerations.* Resistance is one major factor in terms of staff consideration. The rich picture at the beginning of the analysis should have provided us with some idea of likely centres of resistance. All implementation procedures should be based around a strategy for ensuring minimum disruption to key personnel. The parallel approach should provide the major problems in terms of staff selection for two systems. The cutover approach will produce the most stress in terms of sudden workload and untried procedures.

Conclusion

With implementation the information system moves from the planning and design phase through to operation. You are the proud owner of an information system 'solution' as the technology salesmen like to put it. However, it is dangerous to think of the development process as now being over. Your problems are probably just about to begin! The new information system *will* have teething problems; hopefully your monitoring procedure will pick these up before they become too acute and your maintenance shell and guard should keep the worst of the environmental hazards at bay. As we have hinted throughout, the greatest concern in the field of information science is undue complacency concerning the power and efficiency of information systems. A healthy attitude to cultivate is that your learning curve is just beginning, the first year or two after installation are often the most valuable in terms of gaining experience, this period can also be quite painful!

The Multiview methodology
The first five stages of the foregoing analysis should provide you with tools which will allow you to plan and develop information systems for most organizational requirements. Any information system you design will have to be as dynamic as the organization it is going into. If the system cannot adapt to the changing needs of the organization then you will have problems. Our intention has been to demonstrate not only good practice in information systems planning but to emphasize the need for caution and the capacity to adapt to changing situations. Ultimately the information system is part of the wider social system and this in turn is part of and dependent upon the global system. The sources of potential interference and disruption are almost endless but this realization should encourage rather than disincline us to plan as effectively as well as we can.

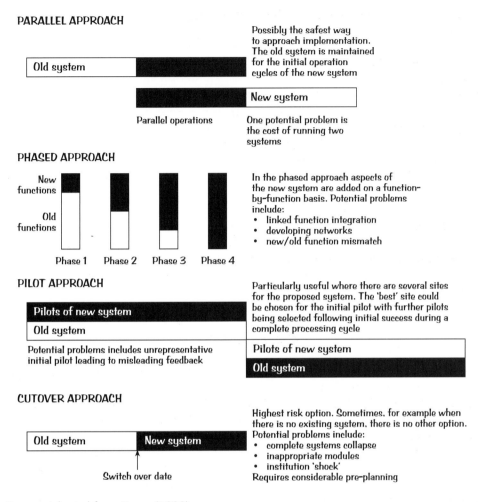

PARALLEL APPROACH

Possibly the safest way to approach implementation. The old system is maintained for the initial operation cycles of the new system

One potential problem is the cost of running two systems

PHASED APPROACH

In the phased approach aspects of the new system are added on a function-by-function basis. Potential problems include:
• linked function integration
• developing networks
• new/old function mismatch

PILOT APPROACH

Particularly useful where there are several sites for the proposed system. The 'best' site could be chosen for the initial pilot with further pilots being selected following initial success during a complete processing cycle

Potential problems includes unrepresentative initial pilot leading to misleading feedback

CUTOVER APPROACH

Highest risk option. Sometimes, for example when there is no existing system, there is no other option. Potential problems include:
• complete systems collapse
• inappropriate modules
• institution 'shock'
Requires considerable pre-planning

Source: Adapted from Kozar (1989)

Figure 10.4 *Installation approaches*

The learning organization methodology

We have attempted to demonstrate throughout this book that the process of information systems analysis and design throws up a range of powerful opportunities for organizations to learn about their internal processes. There is also a terrific opportunity for teams to develop and generate real knowledge about the organization. This team-based knowledge base can be seen as being a compatible and linked outcome from the analysis procedure. Analysis and design teaches the organization about its data and information processes, the learning organization provides unique insights into the knowledge within the organization.

As a total picture of the learning which can be gained from using our approach see Table 10.1.

Table 10.1 *Sustainable information systems and learning organization*

Discipline	Value in sustainable information systems development	Outcome?
Systems thinking	Information systems can be seen as being remote objects and problems to users or they can be seen as being part of the organization as a whole. Systems thinking encourages us to see information systems as part of the complex whole which is the organization.	Arising from our focus on wholeness and not dealing with information systems in a piecemeal fashion comes systems which are better geared to deal with real needs, provide more relevant information and grow and change with the organization.
Personal mastery	Each stage of our approach provides opportunities for the team involved to develop their confidence and understanding of their own organization as well as its information flows.	From the empowerment of being involved with, if not architect of, an information system come a range of potential personal mastery outcomes: • Over the informing function. • Over the function of the organization as a network. • Over group processes within the organization.
Mental models	Within our approach you are encouraged to model your context from many (multiple) views or perspectives. Each mental model, from the rich picture to flow diagrams provides a different and yet valuable insight into the organization's processes.	Many outcomes are possible: • The capacity to stand back from the context and consider it according to one variable. • The recognition that different perspectives are possible and all can have value. • The liberation of mind to show that no single way of thinking is absolute, 'true' or 'right'.
Shared vision	In our approach we have emphasized the value of shared thinking and working. The result is an information system which is more than a single view. Being the outcome of group processes it reflects that group and the various needs which it represents.	Outcomes include: • An information system which is for the organization not one individual. • Informing processes which support the organization's vision of what it should be. • Information systems which can evolve with the vision of the organization.
Team learning	Above all our approach is a team learning opportunity. The team should be selected carefully to represent the richness of the organization but once selected the team can learn cooperatively through the process of finding out how the organization actually functions.	Numerous potential outcomes, eg: • Team cohesion in the organization. • Technology supporting team working. • The establishment of networks within the organization. • More effective use of and valuing of the organization's knowledge.

APPENDIX 1

SYSTEMS ANALYSIS AND SYSTEMS DESIGN: METHODOLOGIES IN RELATION TO EACH OTHER

In our opening chapters we discussed the problems which organizations have with developing information systems. Problems seem to arise no matter what methodology is applied. In Chapter 2 we looked at the thinking behind methodologies to information systems analysis and design and in particular we looked at the reductionist and systemic tendencies in information systems thinking. Reductionist thinking is usually equated with traditional 'scientific' thinking. It treats the world as an object to be studied. Figure A1.1 is a representation of this type of approach.

The reductionist measures elements of wholes to understand them. By taking things apart and putting them back together again the reductionist gains understanding. The weakness of the approach can be that the whole is not given due importance being seen as being too complicated to understand in its entirety. By contrast we discussed systemic or holistic thinking which considers the whole and the processes which it includes. This is portrayed in Figure A1.2.

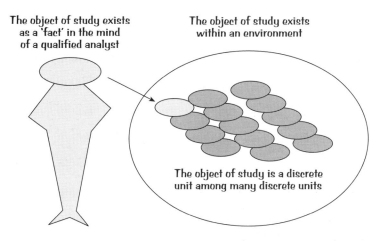

Figure A1.1 *Reductionist approaches*

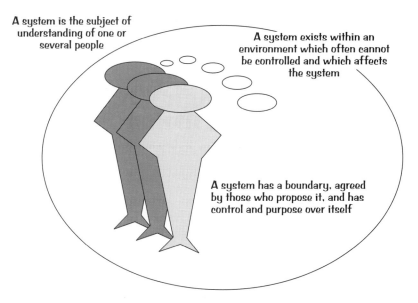

Figure A1.2 *Systemic approaches*

If we were to describe these two approaches we might draw out their main differences as shown in Table A1.1.

In this book we have proposed that the 'hard' approaches have tendencies towards the reductionist model and the 'softer' approaches tend to the systemic. This is not an infallible fact but an observation derived from experience (and assented to by many practitioners). For a thorough analysis and comparison of the range of approaches available the authors recommend that the reader see Avison and Fitzgerald's book (1995). For the purposes of this book we would like to indicate where we feel the various approaches 'fit' in terms of the tending to reductionist and tending to systemic, those which tend to people issues and which tend to the technology. We set out the methodologies in Figure A1.3.

Table A1.1 *A comparison of systemic and reductionist approaches*

Systems approach	Reductionist approach
The problem is shared by legitimate stakeholders in the problem context.	The problem is defined in the mind of the expert.
The system as a whole is reviewed.	A part of a complex whole is analysed.
The environment affects the system.	The environment is controlled.
The boundary of the system is flexible and dependent upon the perception of the stakeholder.	The boundary of the part is defined by the expert.

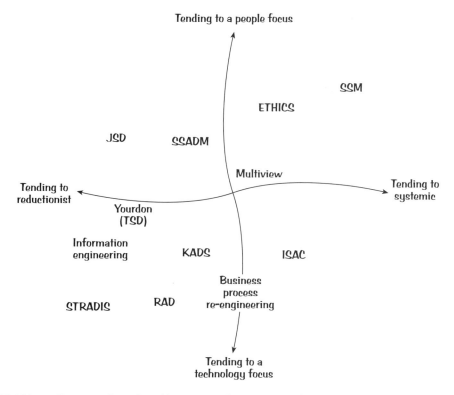

ETHICS = effective technical and human implementation of computer-based systems, ISAC = information systems and analysis of change, JSD = Jackson system development, KADS = an expert systems development methodology, RAD = rapid application development, SSADM = structured systems analysis and design methodology, SSM = soft systems methodology, STRADIS = structured analysis, design and implementation of information systems, YSM Yourdon systems method.

Figure A1.3 *Methodologies: Systemic and reductionist, people and technology*

None of these methodologies is 'right' or 'wrong', they are different and emphasize different types of tools and techniques. They are derived from different mindsets and do different things differently. In our estimation the Multiview approach is appropriate for the development which we have given it in this book because it is closest to the central point, offering the best chance to cover the widest range of issues across the breadth of the organization. Each of the five stages of Multiview looks at the organization and the information which it contains in a slightly different way. This provides the analysis team with a good chance of covering issues of concern and including in analysis the majority of problem items.

APPENDIX 2

THE PROJECT CYCLE: SEEING THE TASK IN PERSPECTIVE

The nature of the cycle

The object of this appendix is to set the systems analysis and systems design stage in the perspective of a total project. It is quite easy not to see the fuller picture when you are working on the detail of specific design.

Analysis and design can be said to fall into the stages of the project cycle known as *formulation* and *preparation*, and *appraisal*. This is not the place to go into great detail on these matters but it is useful to introduce the fuller picture, to set analysis and design in context and indicate key texts which can be pursued for a fuller appreciation. Figure A2.1 indicates the major components of most projects and shows five distinct phases in the project cycle with the monitoring function as being continuous:

1 *Identification.* This is usually very general and non-specific. The identification is usually of some general need or general issue such as: 'the need to improve the delivery of sales and purchase data from regional offices to head office in order to give the company competitive edge', or 'the need to increase the efficiency of core government operations by means of management information system functions'. The identification stage usually occurs without any reference to systems analysis and systems design.

2 *Formulation and preparation.* This stage is also known as feasibility. It is at this stage that the workability of and outline terms of reference for the project are decided. If those involved in the formulation and preparation stage think that the project will deliver the required end within the scheduled time then the real work of planning can begin. Sometimes analysis and design is involved at this time. Quite often an IT orientated project will make use of a systems analyst expert witness to provide details of the feasibility and cost of given project plans. The tools discussed in Chapter 5 relating to the human activity system (HAS) may be applied at this stage.

3 *Appraisal.* This is the major planning stage of the project. Appraisal requires systems analysis and systems design because it will be the appraisal document which will form the basis of the implementation plan. It will be during the appraisal period that we would expect the five stages of analysis and design (as we have described them here) to be undertaken. In conventional projects this stage would include some form of cost–benefit analysis.

4 *Implementation.* In our book we have set implementation outside the analysis and design stage but still within the analyst/planner's mandate of activity. This is often not the case for an entire project. There will often be many non-computer functions related to the project. For example in our case study used throughout this book there was a communications improvement function which was running with the analysis and design of the MIS and yet had no direct linkage to the analysis/planning team. Implementation will mean that all the threads of the project are now brought together.

5 *Evaluation.* Most projects should end with some form of evaluation, setting out the original themes for the project work and measuring the level of success in achieving these goals. If the cycle is to be a cycle then the evaluation should feed into future projects and thus pass on learning. This is often not the case.

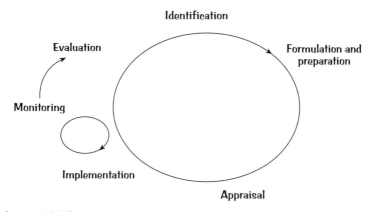

Source: Coleman 1987b

Figure A2.1 *Simplified project cycle*

In Chapter 4 we set out a project cycle drawn from Bell (1996) and building off the Kolb learning cycle of Reflecting, Connecting, Deciding and Acting (Kolb 1984). We feel that all cyclic project activity should be reflective and thus a learning experience.

In Chapter 9 we briefly described another tool for considering projects, the logical framework (or logframe). The framework is shown in Table A2.1. Whilst not providing a cyclic activity, it can be a profound way of considering the vertical and logical structures of an IT project. Popular project management tools such as PRINCE (see, for example, HMSO 1990) go into great depth in terms of the control and procedure in IT projects. As we have shown throughout this book, this type of control is often not possible for IT projects. Often staff, time and resource are not available or maybe, the project is just too small for the effort involved in PRINCE. The logframe on the other hand is now widely used across a range of projects (see Suggested Reading), has also been widely criticized but can be used at a number of levels:

Table A2.1 *The logical framework*

	Verifiable indicators	Means of verification	Assumptions or risks
Goal The higher objectives which the project will contribute towards (mention targets).	Measures (direct or indirect) to verify to what extent the goal is being realized – *strategic indicators.*	The sources of information necessary to realize the indicators at this level.	Important conditions and decisions outside the control of the project which must be true for the next level to be realized.
Purpose or root definition The sustainable effect to be achieved by the project.	Measures (direct or indirect) to verify to what extent the purpose is being sustained – *sustainability indicators.*	The sources of information necessary to realize the indicators at this level.	Important conditions and decisions outside the control of the project which must be true for the next level to be realized.
Output The results and outcomes that the project should be able to guarantee.	Measures (direct or indirect) to verify to what extent the output impact is being achieved – *impact indicators.*	The sources of information necessary to realize the indicators at this level.	Important conditions and decisions outside the control of the project which must be true for the next level to be realized.
Activities The activities that have to be undertaken by the project in order to produce the output.	Measures (direct or indirect) to verify to what extent the activities are being performed – *performance indicators.*	The sources of information necessary to realize the indicators at this level.	Important conditions and decisions outside the control of the project which must be true for the next level to be realized.

- As a 'thinkpad'. As a means to just consider the levels of the project.
- As a detailed analysis tool for thinking about the times and dates for various interventions.
- As a preliminary tool for developing a project which will require further tools (eg Gantt charts, work breakdown structures, etc).

Perhaps the greatest value of the logframe is that it can be done collaboratively or alone, in depth or superficially, in a quantifiable or quality orientated way, focusing on soft and/or hard issues and events, problems or opportunities. It is flexible. Figure A2.2 shows one way in which the logframe can be integrated into the project cycle.

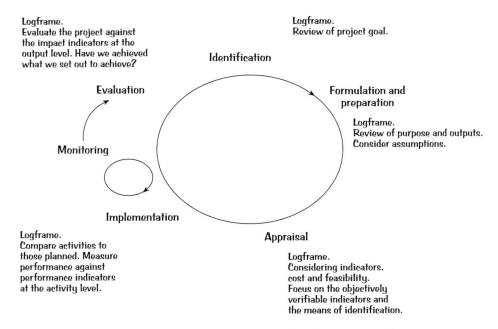

Logframe.
Evaluate the project against
the impact indicators at the
output level. Have we achieved
what we set out to achieve?

Identification

Evaluation

Formulation and
preparation

Logframe.
Review of project goal.

Logframe.
Review of purpose and outputs.
Consider assumptions.

Monitoring

Implementation

Logframe.
Compare activities to
those planned. Measure
performance against
performance indicators
at the activity level.

Appraisal

Logframe.
Considering indicators,
cost and feasibility.
Focus on the objectively
verifiable indicators and
the means of identification.

Figure A2.2 *The logframe within the project cycle*

In perspective

Systems analysis and systems design is usually a component part of any ongoing project. Throughout this book we have tried to indicate the importance of the analyst/planner being humble in terms of his or her relationship with those who will inherit the system which is being devised. Humility is also required with regard to these wider project considerations.

Any work undertaken will need to fit into a greater whole. To some extent all analyst/planners have to be multidisciplinary in their approach if they are to survive in the project environment.

APPENDIX 3

SOME THOUGHTS ON ANSWERS TO THE EXERCISES

Exercise in Chapter 1

In the first chapter we asked you to read the article 'GPs' network buckles under huge workload' and asked you to consider if any of the 'problems with information systems' identified in that chapter were relevant. Thoughts you might have come with include:

- Task–machine development mismatch. The system as first conceived could not deal with its own success. As the load increased so the system came apart.
- Maybe in the same line we have an example of over-ambition on the part of managers of the system.
- The system may have been conceived with a poor analysis perspective. It seems to have outperformed its capacity and maybe this might have been foreseen if managers and clients were included in the original planning

Other possibilities for comparison may occur to you. The point we would like you to carry forward is that the five examples of problems we have given you can be used as models to compare real situations with, in order to see if there are some fairly common basic problems with the information systems with which you are familiar.

Exercise in Chapter 2

There is not a right answer to this but the case seems quite clear on the evidence we have here. This case has quite large reductionist content. Reductionism should deal with technical and quantitative issues within a tight technical boundary. Such items abound, the 'bug', the number of courts, the size of the data and the need for reports to schedule. However, the problems and 'soft' features seem to predominate. Soft would cover the political and social problems for the information systems and draw a large boundary around the potential context. The original bid was 50 per cent lower than rival bids – how was this achieved? Would we not expect problems with such cost cutting? How will the delay rebound on the confidence of the agencies providing the funding? Might there be a case now for a re-negotiation of the contract or at least of the technical roll-out? Given the context, the need is to properly understand the nature of the problems and their real causality rather than applying a technical fix which might lead to the whole thing happening again.

Exercise in Chapter 3

This is a tricky scenario. The analyst will have to deal with a complex meshing of powerful interests (being paid by a publisher whilst working under a charismatic director and for an harassed senior administrator). On the other hand the need for technical ability is also evident. The information might be global, and be in a wide number of formats and for a diverse range of reporting and delivery needs. In our estimation the core need is for technical ability here. The NGO is in the UK and the budget for the project is given. In this sense the publisher is the major client and can push through the system. Although the ability to work in the context and to understand and draw out the needs of the NGO staff is vital, to get the basic system designed in a technically feasible manner might be thought to be the main consideration.

Exercise in Chapter 4

Strength. Software is pre-selected and the staff are well trained also, the project is a pilot and can therefore be allowed to learn from mistakes without expecting catastrophe.

Weakness. The hostility of the heads of schools so far.

Opportunity. The potential to 'sell' the idea to the schools in terms of showing from the pilot how they can gain control of their organization and access to additional funding by cooperation.

Threat. The potential for non-inclusion of the schools and therefore the further development of the hostility into open anger at what is seen as being useless additional bureaucracy.

In terms of the approach, path 2 might be best at the outset. There will probably not be a need to focus on the HCI if the software is pre-written and is known to work – the proviso being that the systems interface is sufficiently acceptable to British users. There may need to be participation on the structure of the application (and therefore information modelling) – it depends how much the US and British systems are alike.

Exercises in Chapter 5

The rich picture
There are some major points of note in the rich picture (see Figure A3.1). This is a picture for the analyst's use only. It indicates a decision-making spine based on the strong family interests running through senior management. The overriding message from the picture is ignorance. We simply do not know enough about the core management and administration functions of the organization. The worst

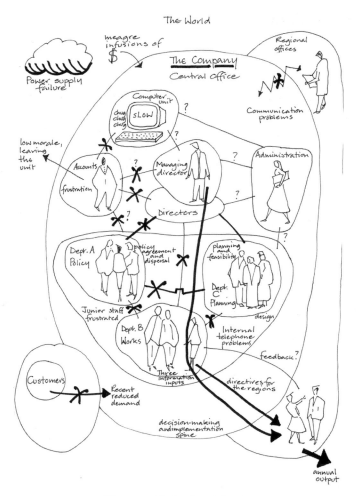

Figure A3.1 *The rich picture*

mistake we could make at this point is to disguise or ignore this ignorance. We need to know more about core functions. We have read between the lines and indicated a fair degree of frustration and anger in the management section. Initial indications would suggest that more details are required concerning:

- Present use of computing.
- Role and attitude of administration.
- The working relationship between the three departments.
- Attitude of the regional offices to head office practices. This is the result of a sideways look at the project. The project terms of reference are stressing MIS at headquarters level. The business of the company takes place in the regions. Are the terms of reference right?

These items could be further developed in a second rich picture.

The root definitions

The analyst

Client: Primarily the donor (the bank), secondly the company.

Actor: Self, senior and MIS company staff.

Transformation: MIS for key functions aimed at assisting key management with a unified purpose.

Worldview: Improved efficiency of operations and the reduction in internal wrangling. A sneaking feeling that the main problem is not so much the management function of the company but its line function, that is, the dirty work in the regions.

Owner: The company in the long term, the bank in the short term.

Environment: Company head office initially, then the regional offices. All work would need to take the regional offices into account.

The donor

Client: Primarily the donor.

Actor: Primarily the analyst working within the donor's terms of reference.

Transformation: Improving the efficiency and profitability of the company through improving the management function.

Worldview: Increased profitability.

Owner: The company.

Environment: The company head office.

Head of department

Client: Primarily the company.

Actor: Company employees working with the analyst. Responsibility for work undertaken is seen as being on the shoulders of the analyst.

Transformation: Efficiency, MIS functions, status of the company improved.

Worldview: Improved competitiveness and status.

Owner: Company and analyst.

Environment: The company.

Consensus

Client: Donor and company.

Actor: Company employees and analyst working to agreed terms of reference.

Transformation: Action to develop efficiency and profitability.

Worldview: Cost effectiveness.

Owner: The company and in the short term the analyst.

Environment: The company.

This consensus is not completely agreed. The view of the analyst is not quite that of the bank or the managing director. Putting the view in a cone format it would look like Figure A3.2. It is not possible for the analyst to alter the terms of reference for the entire project, but it is worth noting down at this stage that there is a divergence of views.

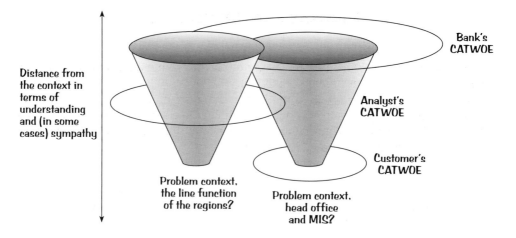

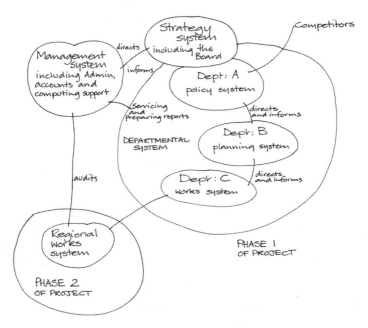

Figure A3.2 *Overlapping root definitions of the problem*

The top level systems model

The top level systems model (see Figure A3.3) takes some liberties with the rich picture. We assume here that there is a clear line of command between the three departments working its way out to the regional offices. We have taken a further liberty by salving our consciences concerning the need of the regional offices by setting out their needs as a second project. The other point of note is the strategy system lying outside and above the management system. The reason for this is the impact of the bank on strategy.

Figure A3.3 *The top level systems model*

Exercise in Chapter 6

The entity model

The entity model presented in Figure A3.4 shows that we have simplified the new MIS down to two primary areas – daily administration on the one hand and core planning on the other. Administration has to do mainly with equipment, staff and payroll details. Core planning is concerned with project progress. This model could be further simplified as in Figure A3.5 but we thought that this line of approach was too lacking in detail so we opted for Figure A3.4.

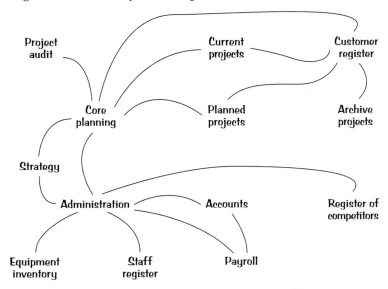

Figure A3.4 *The first entity model*

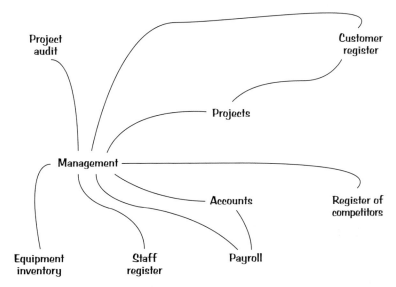

Figure A3.5 *Focusing the entity model*

Table A3.1 *The main attributes of the entities*

Name of entity	Names of attributes in entity	Potential number of records in entity	Volatility of records	Suggested person-hours/year to maintain the entity
Core planning	Project value Future projects Equipment			
Strategy	Accounts Audit			
Management	Projects Staff			
Accounts	Project details Payroll Equipment Materials			
Payroll	Staff name Address Grade Salary Allowances Tax rate/band Expenses			
Staff register	Staff name Address Record Grade Gender			
Equipment inventory	Name Age Location Value Depreciation			
etc				

Primary attributes

The details provided in Table A3.1 are only partial and would need to be further developed.

Major functions

The basis of all functions in the MIS is to support the strategy formulation function. Figure A3.6 presents our first logical level. Figure A3.7 develops the second level theme of strategy formulation. To carry the analysis one level further, we look at the details of the review of major competitors in Figure A3.8.

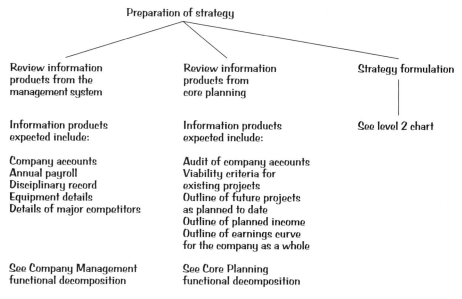

Figure A3.6 *Level 1 functional decomposition*

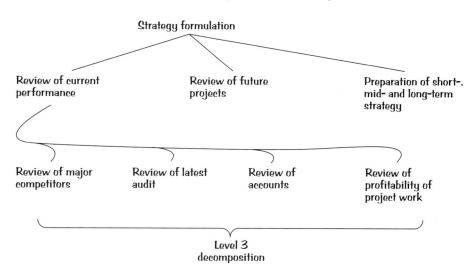

Figure A3.7 *Level 2 functional decomposition*

Key events

The flow diagram in Figure A3.9 shows the action of events upon the functions related to the review of major competitors.

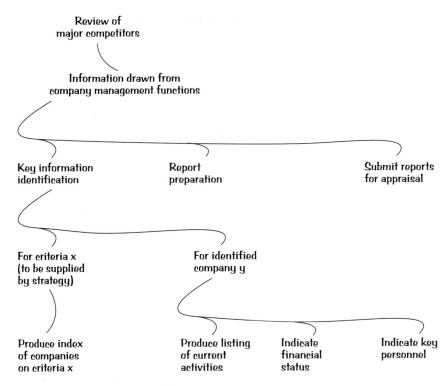

Figure A3.8 *Level 3 functional decomposition*

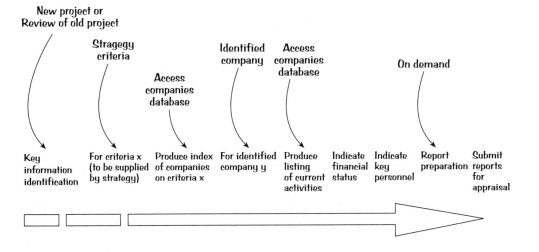

Figure A3.9 *Level 3 related events*

Exercise in Chapter 7

The approach taken to socio-technical modelling builds on that discussed at the end of Chapter 7. In Table A3.2 social objectives are seen to drive technical objectives, ie each social objective works its way out in one or more technical objectives.

Table A3.2 *Objectives*

Social objectives	Technical objectives
Appear credible	Improve communication
	Timely decision-making
Improve professionalism	Improve technical skills
Improve budget	Improve timeliness in budget planning
	Demonstrate effective budgeting
	Demonstrate efficient subcontracting
Improve planning	Technical skills
	Automated features
	Networking decision-making
Improve office management	Networking
	Standards
	Rapid processing
	Learning processes initiated

The alternatives arising from the objectives given are as listed in Table A3.3. The main point to note here is that we are linking social and technical alternatives in internal combinations. For example, T3 is a combination of T1 plus the PC network.

Table A3.3 *Alternatives*

Social alternatives	Technical alternatives
S1. Retrain key staff	T1. Computerizable manual system
S2. Retrain all staff	T2. PC stand alone + T1
S3. New Staff + S1	T3. PC network + T1
S4. New Staff + S2	T4. Network

The two best options shown in Table A3.4 indicate a desire to base any new system on new staff bringing in skills at present unobtainable in the organization. The difference between S3T2 and S4T2 is the level of retraining within the organization – all or just key staff. In terms of making a proposal based on this analysis it would be quite simple to indicate an expansion path for the incoming system, from a small, highly trained group dealing with the initial PC/manual system, gradually spreading out training to the wider community as appropriate. This would also link to the analyst's indicated preferred direction of the project as a whole – outward to the regions.

Table A3.4 *Comparing alternatives*

Alter-natives	Social costs	Technical costs	Social constraints	Technical constraints	Social resources	Technical resources	Total	Rank
S1T1	2	2	2	7	4	4	21	2
S1T2	2	4	3	6	4	5	24	
S1T3	3	6	4	6	5	5	29	
S1T4	4	7	5	6	6	6	34	
S2T1	3	2	3	7	4	4	23	
S2T2	3	4	3	6	4	5	25	
S2T3	3	6	4	6	5	5	29	
S2T4	4	7	5	6	6	6	34	
S3T1	4	2	3	7	3	3	22	3
S3T2	4	2	3	5	3	3	20	1
S3T3	4	3	4	3	4	4	22	3
S3T4	4	4	4	4	4	4	24	
S4T1	4	2	3	7	3	3	22	3
S4T2	4	2	3	5	3	3	20	1
S4T3	4	3	4	3	4	4	22	3
S4T4	4	4	4	4	4	4	24	

Exercise in Chapter 8

Impact of the new information system on the company

Because we have opted for a development path working off established manual practices and because there is an existing computer unit we might expect impacts of the system to be fairly minimal. This would certainly not be the case if a new and very powerful computer-based information system were being installed from scratch. The main problem will probably lie with the existing computer staff having to introduce and work equitably with the new, highly trained staff being brought in. Also, as a wide ranging change in practice will eventually follow the new system we might expect senior management to need a considerable degree of awareness training and general encouragement. There may be some displacement of clerical workers but hopefully most can be moved into the new areas of data entry and data edit.

Suggested measures

- General organization-wide awareness raising.
- Training on all new equipment for existing IT staff.
- General keyboard and computer package use training for clerical staff.
- Senior management awareness training.

Avoiding risks

We have avoided the worst risks for a new system by avoiding a networked computer option, although this may occur at some time in the future. A manual/stand-alone micro system can be made fairly secure by ensuring:

- That all machines are in safe zones (lockable offices with access only to authorized staff).
- A procedure for authorizing staff to access the system.
- Levels of access to any computer information. Access would work broadly on the lines of:
  - Level 1: basic data input;
  - Level 2: basic data edit;
  - Level 3: data edit;
  - Level 4: department-wide information retrieval;
  - Level 5: company-wide information retrieval;
  - Level 6: basic system fault finding;
  - Level 7: access to the total system.
- Usual software and data back-up procedures as set out in this book.

CONSTRUCTION PROJECT FORM 1A   SCREEN 1 OF 6

Name of project:

Location

Start date

Proposed completion date

Type of project (new or maint)

Initial budget

Officer in charge

Team size

Team details (numbers)

Senior managers

Senior engineers

Engineers

Labourers

DETAILS FOR MACHINERY ON SCREEN 2. HIT PgDn for 2.

Figure A3.10 *Form filling screen interface*

Screen interfaces

The priority with a mixed manual/micro system is for the two components to work well together. Standard paper forms will still be in evidence, particularly in the early stages of the operation. We would therefore expect that screen interfaces (in terms of data entry) would imitate these standard forms being based on a form filling practice as shown in Figure A3.10.

On the other hand, the managers who are going to be using the final information products will require a system which is menu based (see Figure A3.11). It is assumed, in line with the information given in Chapter 8, that computer staff will not require specialized screen interfaces.

Measures to reduce staff resistance

The key to reducing staff resistance is at least in part a function of the demonstration of:

- the value of the system to the individual user; and
- the fact that the system does not threaten.

Awareness training sessions can be an effective vehicle for this type of assurance. Awareness raising sessions involving computers too often tend to focus on the use of computers rather than the use of information systems. Ideally a simulation of the incoming system should be provided for the users and a range of normal tasks should be set out which will demonstrate to the user that:

- The system will make life easier.
- The system is open to change if there are problems – the user has ownership of the system.
- The system should result in a notable increase in the efficiency and work satisfaction of the user.

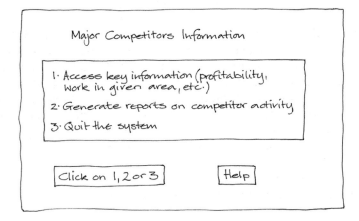

Figure A3.11 *Sketch of an information products screen interface*

Where there are problems (wide scale changes in work practise, changing job terms of reference) these can be introduced in the context of other positive elements (more pay, better conditions).

Exercise in Chapter 9

Technical briefing to all senior company staff

The outline of the new information system

The system arising from the review to date can be seen as having at least six distinct component parts:

1 An application.
2 A database.
3 Retrieval in the form of reports.
4 Maintenance of the system.
5 Management of the system.
6 Monitoring the working of the system and evaluating annual success.

Without going into too much detailed technical information now, we will set out the general details of the system. From our analysis and design the overall need for the application is uncontested. Strategy formulation has to be supported by information in the headquarters section of the company being made available in a packaged format. The information required for strategy is derived both from the general IT system and also from core planning. Therefore the overall application is designed as a management information system but more clearly – a strategy support system. The application is designed for interaction at three levels:

1 The production of strategic information products for senior managers
2 The input of basic data by clerical staff
3 The control of the system by computer staff

The main implications of such a system can be seen primarily in the information to be stored, that is, the databases. Initially the design team would expect that all project details would be required on a computerized database. This information would be cross-referenced with company information such as: payroll, staff details and equipment inventory. These information areas would be related to and further supported by information on current and past customers and a register of competitors. The activity of the system would be centred on the production of reports. These can be broken down into two key areas:

1 Reports for the support of strategy.
2 Reports for the increased efficiency of the company.

Reports in support of strategy

These would relate to the major areas of competitive advantage over other organizations, the review of current performance in specified areas such as cost control and project profitability, the results of company audit and analysis of future project trends – key areas to become involved in, old areas to drop.

Reports for increased efficiency
These would need to focus on the effectiveness and value of staff, staff costs as set against returns, the effective use of capital plant, internal accounting, staff records and staff turnover.

The applications, database and reporting areas would come under the overall control of management.

The management of the information system
In our case management would initially be undertaken by existing IT staff but would eventually probably become the responsibility of new staff to be employed. The central need for management is to ensure that the system is maintained secure irrespective of changes in the organization. Effective management requires that the following areas be effectively controlled:

The operating system of the incoming system. This includes ensuring that all user interfaces are in place and that levels of control are established through the use of the operating system.

Job priority control. Computers cannot provide all information to all users at all times. The central objective of the system is the support of strategy. Access to the system for this priority job would need to be ensured. Strategic decision-making is often quite unstructured and requires that the system have the capacity to respond flexibly to need. This may mean that one computer unit is constantly available for strategy enquiries. The information for the management and administration of the company can normally be scheduled in terms of the production of daily, weekly, monthly and annual reports. Clerical input has to function effectively if the information products are to be provided. Clerical use needs to be carefully controlled and information products need to be passworded off from casual or accidental access.

Security. Building on the items raised in 'Job priority control' above, security for hardware (power supply, theft and accidents) can be improved if effective control is exerted over the working environment. Because the system will initially be used by only a small number of staff the threats to hardware should be reduced through control over physical access to the machines.

User support. We have already mentioned a wide range of training support for the various user groups. Related to this should be effective day-by-day supervision of users (a function which can be provided by the computer unit staff) and a clearly defined line of communication, feedback and learning to and from the user body and those who control the technical system. This is important in allowing users to feel that they have some say in the future development of the information system and that their learning is important in the evolution of the system. A user support committee with attendance by computer unit staff should fulfil this need.

One aspect of effective management of the system is to ensure that regular maintenance is carried out. The initiation of a preventative maintenance shell linked to corrective maintenance guard is dependent upon the organization getting appropriate staff trained in these areas or of employing new staff who already have these skills. Given the hazardous nature of the environment in which the company operates (as depicted in the rich picture) the maintenance area will require development prior to system implementation.

Monitoring

Finally we come to the monitoring of the process of the system installation and the evaluation of preliminary information products. Table A3.5 indicates key items to monitor and the critical indicators to watch.

Table A3.5 *Selection of areas requiring M&E*

M&E focus	Critical indicators to monitor and evaluate
Human activity system	✔ New conflicts of interest between family members ✔ Changes in the local economic climate ✔ Changes in the relationships between headquarters and regions
Information modelling	✔ New functions arising from strategy ✔ Changes in decomposition ✔ New entities required ✔ New attributes for existing entities ✔ New events requiring new reports
Socio-technical	✔ Changes in personnel responsibilities ✔ Settling in of new staff ✔ Performance of technology ✔ Integration of manual and IT systems
Human computer interface	✔ New dialogue systems required relating to new information
Technical areas	✔ Effective user support? ✔ Regular monitoring at the level of the systems impact

The final evaluation of the system should occur following a three year run cycle to give the new system time to adjust to the environment. The evaluation should focus on the relative performance of the new system as set against the details of the systems analysis and systems design contained here. Of critical importance will be the reporting procedures – are the strategic reports being produced on demand and are these reports of relevance in developing better planning policies? Has the information system as originally designed been sustained?

GLOSSARY OF BUZZWORDS

action research The person undertaking research is part of the research context. The researcher tries to understand the context by linking theory with practice.

application The main activity of a computer-based information system (eg an MIS is an application).

attributes The basic features evident in an entity, for example the first name, second name, address, telephone number, etc in an entity called 'address book'.

bugs Faults in computer software. These usually arise because tailored or purpose-built software has not been adequately tested prior to installation.

case studies Examination of phenomena with no clear boundaries at the outset.

CASE tools Computer Assisted Software Engineering tools are software packages which assist analysts in the process of developing software packages. They were particularly designed to work with structured analysis and design approaches.

computer-based information system The computer is the processing basis and storage facility of the system which provides on demand a number of key information products requested by a specific user community or coalition of user communities.

conceptual model In this book this usually describes an activity model to achieve a transformation of some kind.

conceptual study A form of research also known as 'armchair' research.

consolidated computing The phrase used by Awad to define the second period of the computer age. Mainframe based and programmer orientated.

context The context of the system is vital to the workability of what is being proposed. For example a complex multi-user information system dependent upon a sophisticated support service would be contextually inappropriate in a remote location with few trained staff. This is an extreme case but the principle is that information systems requirements and feasibility vary with context.

data A wealth of meanings but generally thought to be unstructured, unverified, unvalidated material which is the basic foundation for information products. Some form of process must be undertaken to transform the data into information (eg sales data can be compiled as information on company turnover).

database The store for data.

debugging The procedure whereby a new item of software is analysed to make sure that it has no inadvertently built in faults or 'bugs'.

decision support system A computer-based system which provides users with the capacity to carry out 'what if' analysis (eg 'If I increase inflation by 4 per cent and decrease output by 7 per cent what does this do to my balance of trade?). Decision support systems or DSS are usually based on spreadsheets.

decomposition The process of working out functions to sub-functions and if necessary sub-sub-functions. Decomposing a task down to sub-tasks.

dialogue systems The screen formats and protocols which a computer uses to inform users and explain procedures.

drive alignment Relates to the ability of the disk drive to read the removable disks. If the drive is out of alignment then there will be problems with both reading and writing data.

eclectic In terms of information systems methodology this implies an approach to problem solving where a number of different approaches are brought together, linking the best or most appropriate parts of each, in order to arrive at a newly evolved approach. Multiview might be said to be an eclectic methodological framework.

eductive We tend to be familiar with deduction and induction but eduction is less common. It means to 'draw forth' and shares the same root with education. Ideally to educate is not to pump full of data but to draw forth the genius which each of us contains in potential.

entities The description of anything about which we wish to store data.

events The triggers which will spark off functions in an information model (eg the end of a financial year may be the trigger which sparks the function 'do the annual accounts').

expert imposition An attitude which is summed up in the anonymous quote 'I am the computer expert, please let me get on with sorting out your problem without interruptions!'.

field experiments Data is collected on the behaviour of the independent variable. The dependent variable is measured.

focus group Usually small groups of stakeholders in an enterprise who are brought together with a facilitator to gain quality information about specific problems and issues.

fragmented files Files which have been separated into many small pieces by software process.

functions In information modelling these are the activities which are associated with entities and which prompt information processing (eg the function 'sort into alphabetic order' may occur upon the entity 'store of data on library books'.

geographic information system (GIS) Numerous packages which handle spatial data (eg maps and satellite images) and produce composite maps, overlays, planning guides, route maps, etc.

hackers Any individual using a computer-based information system without authorization. In recent years this term has been most specifically related to users of the internet breaking into supposedly secure systems such as that belonging to the North Atlantic Treaty Organization (NATO).

hard Denotes a technocratic approach to problem solving.

hard disk A fixed disk drive which is usually located in the computer and is not designed to be removed. Hard disks are usually large, ranging from hundreds of megabytes to gigabytes of storage.

human activity system (HAS) A concept used and extended by Professor Peter Checkland in the soft systems approach to systems thinking and practice. The human activity concept includes initially understanding the problem context (often by use of a rich picture), discovering central themes with the root definition and setting out proposed activities.

human–computer interface The label given to work which attempts to make the connection between the human side of an information system and the technology as easy as is feasible.

information A product which has gone through a process which derived it from data. It is assumed that information provides the basis for knowledge which can in turn facilitate decision-making, eg company turnover information, derived from sales data, provides the basis for making knowledgeable decisions on production, marketing, etc.

information modelling A technically rigorous analysis and design technique. The technique is concerned with setting out what are the major entities of a system, what are their functions and attributes and what events will trigger the functions into activity.

information system The tendency is to confuse and conflate information systems and information technology. In this book we have tended to see an information system as any assemblage of technology and or people and or data which provides a user group with the necessary information to engage in intelligent decision-making.

internet The invisible global digital connectivity between computers of all types.

intranet Computer-based connectivity within an organization – usually based upon internet technologies.

isolated computing A phrase used by Awad to define the first period of the computer age. Firmly related to mainframe computers and mainframe systems.

knowledge A condition of being informed which, ideally, is the result of good information. Knowledge is the basis of good decision-making, eg knowledgeable decisions arising from accurately compiled information on company turnover data can be applied to make changes to the overall strategy of an organization.

laboratory experiments The researcher manipulates the independent variables. All 'noise' is controlled.

LAN – local area network A network of computers linked together on a particular site (such as in one organization).

learning organization An organization which is developing a 'blame-free' culture of understanding both in terms of its own internal processes and those which relate to its environment. The outcome of such a culture is heightened awareness, improved efficiency, professional satisfaction and enhanced capability to deal with change.

login/logout Terms for the process of getting into and out of a computer system.

lost clusters A cluster is a group of sectors allocated to a file. Lost clusters are just that.

mainframe A large computer, usually occupying an entire room – sometimes an entire building. This type of computer requires a very highly controlled environment, trained operators and a computer manager.

maintenance An aspect of the fifth stage of the methodology. Maintenance includes both corrective and preventative aspects.

management The technical aspect of the fifth stage of the methodology. Its focus is to control but also to learn and encourage participation from users.

management controls and constraints Awad's third period of the computer age, referring to the stage where computer functions began to be harnessed by the business managers within organizations.

management information systems (MIS) MIS are usually based on computers but do not have to be. Usually they are designed around the idea of supplying management at set times or on demand with key information products called performance indicators from an archive of historic data. MIS provide 'how am I?' information.

mathematical modelling In this form of exploration all variables are known. Therefore, analysis is reduced to a set of equations.

menu driven system A computer-based system which works according to users selecting a series of menu options in pre-designed sequence in order to arrive at the information products required.

methodology A term used in this book to refer to any approach for planning information systems although more properly it means the science of considering methods. Methodologies usually provide the user of them with guidelines and procedures for accomplishing tasks.

milestones Significant points for the evaluation of achievement. For example a milestone for the implementation of a new information system might be 'review progress on data incorporation into the computer system at the end of the financial year'.

mindset A mindset indicates all the aspects of an individual or group state of mind on a given issue at a given time. If a team is working on a rich picture in a participatory fashion, the picture could represent the mindsets of the analyst and the major stakeholders involved in producing the overall diagram. In this sense mindset implies our assumptions, beliefs, values and vision of the expected outcome.

minicomputer Not at the scale of a mainframe, nor yet that of the microcomputer or PC, the minicomputer is a large piece of furniture and requires support in the form of environmental control and skilled operators.

microcomputer or personal computer (PC) or desktop computer The range of machines which sit on the user's desk and act as stand-alone or networked facilities, generally used to operate a range of office software packages and internet utilities.

multi-user A computer system with a network that allows a number of users to use the same software at the same time.

Multiview An eclectic methodology initially designed by D E Avison and A T Wood-Harper and subsequently developed with other authors.

network Linking together computers so that they can share information, for example a client/server system linking internet and in-house intranet.

outsourcing The practice of letting third parties handle organizational functions. In terms of this book it relates to allowing a third party to control and develop the information processing function. Outsourcing avoids the organization covering the cost of information systems development. The risk is that a third party may not look after the organization's interests as well as internal staff.

partition The separating of a hard disk into several different logical disks. For example, the hard disk might be called drive C:. By partition we can make several logical drives (C:, D:, E:) on that single actual drive.

performance indicators An MIS will often be measuring a number of key factors to ascertain the relative success or failure of elements of an organization or of its functioning. The factors selected for this monitoring are often called performance indicators. Indicators can be of many types. An MIS can produce a range of different types of indicator, eg impact indicators (measuring a project's impact), sustainability indicators (measuring the sustainability of a region, country, etc) and strategic indicators (indicating the achievement of a company's strategic vision). Some professionals go so far as to say that an MIS without PIs is no MIS (ie MIS = PI).

phenomenological research Research which focuses on understanding the essence of experience.

pirated/piracy The illegal copying of software products.

presenting problem The superficial problem. Often this is not the real problem at all but a deeper problem lies beneath it as its cause. For example, on a project in Pakistan the presenting problem was the growing of opium poppies by small farmers. A simple problem of illegal behaviour? The underlying problem related to the lack of rural micro-credit facilities for these farmers to borrow money to develop new ventures in horticulture and saffron. When the micro-credit was available the illegal behaviour reduced.

problem context The situation in which an analyst and designer is working. The assumption is that an information system is required because something is not working as well as it might. Therefore, the system and the planner of the system inhabit a problem context.

prototyping This usually requires a programmer with access to sophisticated software tools to develop iteratively the MIS application in consensus with users and user teams.

rapid application development (RAD) RAD is a form of prototyping which makes use of CASE tools to iteratively produce systems quickly.

recipient community That group of stakeholders and users who will be the eventual information system managers, operators and clients.

reductionist What some consider to be the traditional and scientific approach to problem solving which claims to be objective. In a reductionist approach the whole is broken down to the parts which are then studied in isolation. Reductionism is often contrasted to systemisism.

retrieval The production of information from a database via an application.

rich picture The formal and informal structure, processes and content of the problem context visually set out as in a cartoon type format.

role of the user The fourth of Awad's periods of the computer age. At last the term 'user' is adopted and is seen as being important. Information technology begins to be orientated towards user requirements.

root definition A technique to set out the main transformation resulting from systems analysis. The definition as used in this text usually includes identification of the customers, transformation, actors, problem owners, environmental constraints and major assumptions of stakeholders.

screen burn If a computer is left on and not used for a considerable time the screen will eventually have a burnt-on image left. Thus, you will be able to see what has been on the screen even when the computer is off. This is easily avoided by use of screen savers.

social and technical systems analysis The linking together of human and technological resources to make the 'best' combination for the specific problem context.

soft A social sciences, empathetic approach to problem solving.

software–hardware mismatch The wrong software on the wrong hardware.

stakeholders Any individual with an interest in the existing or proposed information system.

stand-alone A computer which works independently from other computers. That is, a computer which is not networked.

structured analysis A specific form of analysis which makes use of some of the tools set out in this book. The main concepts are data flow diagrams, data dictionary, store structuring and process logic representations.

survey Also known as 'opinion research'. Sampling is dependent upon judgement and convenience.

sustainable A very important word. An information systems which is sustainable is one which can be maintained and will be the basis for evolution into the future. It is the obverse of a 'one-hit-wonder' system which does splendidly for a month or so but them collapses, or an information system which operates well but cannot be developed for future needs. One definition of sustainable which we particularly like is: not cheating on the future.

system The definition we favour is provided by Peter Senge (Senge et al 1994, p90):

*'A system is a **perceived** whole whose elements "hang together" because they continually affect each other over time and operate toward a common purpose. The word descends from the Greek verb sunistánai, which originally meant "to cause to stand together". As this origin suggests, **the structure of a system includes the quality of perception with which you, the observer, cause it to stand together.'**
(Emphasis added.)

systemic An approach to problem solving which is based upon a holistic approach. Pragmatic and sometimes subjective, systemisism is interested in understanding the complexity of processes and relationships in wholes. Systemisism is often contrasted with reductionism and confused with systematic (a procedural or cook book approach).

systems analysis and systems design The process of discovering what users and stakeholders feel an information system should do and setting out a plan for a feasible development.

systems model A diagram which sets out the main components of the context as related systems and subsystems.

technical aspects The range of component aspects which combine to produce the total information system.

user/machine interface One view of the latest and fifth period of the computer age. The focus is the communication between the user and the machine.

UNIX A computer operating system originally designed by Bell Laboratories. Long thought of as the natural system for minicomputers it is also being adopted for microcomputers.

viruses Software, sometimes designed for fun, sometimes with malign intent, which will make a computer break down in a minor or major way. Viruses are usually brought into computers on pirated software or from email attachments. They can be a minor nuisance or can lead to total information systems collapse.

WAN – wide area network A system which links local computers with national and sometimes international computer systems and databanks.

website A unique address on the World Wide Web where organizations and/or individuals can produce multimedia information about themselves.

workspace The amount of store or memory or time or all three which is allotted to a user.

worldview The underlying assumptions about the world for any one individual, group of people or organization. Worldviews will vary with different perspectives of different stakeholders in any given context.

World Wide Web A growing element of functionality available on the internet providing users with multimedia images and information in a graphic format.

SUGGESTED READING

Chapter 1: Information Systems and Organizations

Disasters relating to IT
Bicknell 1993
Collins 1993; 1996a; 1996b; 1997a; 1997b; 1997c; 1997d; 1997e
Davies 1996
Drummond 1996
Lyytinen and Hirschheim 1987
Schneider 1997

The nature of organizations and their capacity to deal with change
Argyris 1960; 1982; 1985
Barlow 1991
Burrell and Morgan 1979
Calhoun and DeLargy 1992
Checkland 1984
Dykman and Robbins 1991
Gotsch 1985

Chapter 2: What is Systems Analysis and Systems Design?

Soft systems
Checkland 1984; 1988; 1994; 1997; 2001
Checkland and Holwell 1993; 1998a; 1998b
Checkland and Scholes 1990
Open University 1987; 2000

A technological focus
Lucas 1985; 1994
Maciaszek 2001
Weaver et al 1998

The human side of information systems
Ensworth 2001
Kozar 1989

The nature of action research
Heron 1990; 1996
Reason 1994
Reason and Heron 1995

Exploring complex contexts
Galliers 1987; 1990; 1992a; 1992b
Galliers and Land 1987

Multiview
Antill and Wood-Harper 1985
Avison and Fitzgerald 1995
Avison and Wood-Harper 1990; 1991
Bell 1996a; 1999
Bell and Wood-Harper 1998
Flew 1979
Warmington 1980
Wood-Harper 1988; 1989; 1990
Wood-Harper and Corder 1988

Chapter 3: The Role of the Systems Planner or Systems Analyst

Self analysis and reflective practice
Bell 1992; 1996b; 1997
Biggs 1995
Biggs and Smith 1995
Boud 1985
Burgoyne and Reynolds 1997
Checkland 1984
Dryden 1996
Flood et al 1997
Horney 1994
Long 1992
Marshall and Reason 1997
Moon 1999
Russell 1986
Stowell et al 1990
Weill 1997

Metaphors of the analyst
Bell 1997
Briggs Myers et al 1994
Harvey and Harvey 1994
Hirsh and Kummerow 1990
Morgan 1997
Myers and Kirby 1994

The internet
Naughton 2000
Panos 1995
Qureshi 1997
Wilsdon 2001

Chapter 4: Terms of Reference and Selecting our Planning/Development Tools

Developing participation in information systems work
Bjorn Andersen and Skousen 1984
Chambers 1997
Jarvenpaa and Ives 1991
Jones and King 1998
Koh and Heng 1996
Land 1982
Stowell et al 1997a; 1997b
Vowler 1997

The human activity system
Checkland and Scholes 1990
Davies 1989
Haynes 1995
Ison 1993
Macadam et al 1990

Chapter 5: What is the Problem? The Human Activity System: Making a Model

Interview techniques
Bell 2000
Gosling and Edwards 1995
IIED 1995
Kumar 1993
Patton 1980

Pickles 1995
Reason 1994

Chaper 6: Information Modelling: Making a Workable System

Extended development of information models
Bowers 1988
Dennis and Haley 2000
Maciaszek 2001
Weaver et al 1998

Object orientated programming
Cats-Baril and Thompson 1997
Moreton and Chester 1997
Tozer 1996

Chapter 7: Technical Needs, Social Needs: Getting the Right Balance

ETHICS approach
Mumford 1981; 1983; 1985; 1995; 1997
Mumford and Weir 1979

Future analysis and scenario planning
Chermack et al 2001
Godet et al 1999
Kaivo-oja 2001
Land 1982; 1987
Mack 2001
Martelli 2001
Mercer 2001

Chapter 8: The Human–Computer Interface
Andreu and Ciborra 1996
Avison and Fitzgerald 1995
Awad 1988
Bell 1996
Bell and Minghze 1995
Bush and Robbins 1991
Korth and Silberschantz 1986
Oz 1993
Smith 1996; 1997

Wainright-Martin et al 1994
Yeoman et al 1996

Prototyping
CCTA 1993b

Chapter 9: Technical Aspects

Projects and management
Bell 1987; 1996
Casley and Kumar 1988
Coleman 1987b
Eyben 1995
Hirschheim and Smithson 1987
Lavrijsen 1994
McPherson 1994
Mendelssohn 1989
Montgomery et al 1995
Murphy and Sprey 1982
Quan 1995
Rajakutty 1991
Richards undated
Rossi and Freeman 1985
Theis 1994

Project failure
Bicknell 1997
Collins 1997a; 1997b; 1997c; 1998a; 1998b; 1999
Computer Weekly 1998
Drummond 1998
Green-Armytage 1993
Heeks 1999
Hyde 2000
Kaye 1997
Lytle 1991
Lyytinen and Hirschheim 1987
Maslen 1997
Redmill 1999
Sauer 1993
Secure Computing 1997
Taylor 2000
Vowler 1997a; 1997b
White 1997

Logical framework
Bell 1996
Chambers 1996
Coleman 1987a
Commission of the European Communities Directorate General for Development Evaluation Unit 1993
Cordingley 1995
Cusworth and Franks 1993
Forster 1996
Gasper 1997
Goebel et al 1996
IIED 1995

Chapter 10: The Total Design, Training, Hardware, Software and Implementation

Learning with information systems
Andreu and Ciborra 1996
Bell 1996a; 1996b; 1998
Buckler 1998
Chambers 1997
Checkland 1985
Fellers 1996
Kakabadse and Kouzmin 1996
Linsheng 1998
Lousberg and Soler 1998
Mansell 1997
McConnell 1997
Mingers and Stowell 1997
Mumford 1997
Savage 1996
Smith 1998
Stowell et al 1997a; 1997b

General interest
Albert and Bradley 1997
Alexander 1998
Beeson 1997
Benjamin and Blunt 1992
Bennets et al 2000
Bjorn Andersen and Skousen 1984
Buckler 1998
Bush and Robbins 1991
Cats-Baril and Thompson 1997
Chambers 1997

Checkland and Holwell 1998b
Drobik 2000
Hughes and Cotterell 1999
Hyde 2000
Kaye 1997
Korac-Boisvert and Kouzmin 1995
Paucar-Caceres 1998
Redmill 1999
Saran 1998
Sauer 1993
Savage 1996
Stowell et al 1997a
Zhu 1998b; 1999b

Appendix 1

There is a wealth of material on the development and comparison of methodology. The references we provide here are not definitive or absolute. Rather they represent work which we feel has been influential and has raised questions of general interest.

Atkinson 1997
Bell 1994; 1999
Bell and Wood-Harper 1988
Callo and Packham 1997
CCTA 1993a
Checkland 1994; 1997
Checkland and Scholes 1990
Davies 1989
Dervin 1996
Foss 1989
Gold 2001
Gu and Zhu 2000
Haynes 1989
Holwell 2001
Macadam et al 1990
Midgely and Wilby 1996
Mingers 2001
Mingers and Brocklesby 1996
Munro and Mingers 2000
Orchard 1972
Probert 1997; 1998
Senoh 1990
Tagg and Brown 1989
Valle 1999
Zhu 1998a; 1999a; 1999b

REFERENCES

Albert, S, and Bradley, K (1997). *Managing Knowledge: Experts, Agencies and Organizations*. Cambridge University Press, Cambridge

Alexander, I (1998). 'Charting a path to project success.' *The Computer Bulletin*, July, pp26–27

Andreu, R, and Ciborra, C (1996). 'Organizational learning and core capabilities development: The role of IT.' *Strategic Information Systems*, Vol 5, pp111–127

Antill, L, and Wood-Harper, T (1985). *Systems Analysis*. Heinemann, London

Argyris, C (1960). *Understanding Organizational Behaviour*. Tavistock Publications, London

Argyris, C (1982). *Reasoning, Learning and Action*. Jossey Bass, San Francisco

Argyris, C (1985). 'Making knowledge more relevant to practice: Maps for action.' In E Lawler (ed) *Doing Research that is Useful for Theory and Practice*. Jossey Bass, San Francisco

Atkinson, C (1997). 'Soft information systems and technologies methodology, SISTeM: A case study on developing the electronic patient record.' *Requirements Engineering*, Vol 2, pp1–22

Avison, D E (1997). 'The discipline of information systems: Teaching, research and practice.' In J Mingers and F Stowell (eds) *Information Systems: An Emerging Discipline?* McGraw-Hill, London, pp113–136

Avison, D E, and Fitzgerald, G (1995). *Information Systems Development: Methodologies Techniques and Tools. Second Edition*. McGraw-Hill, London

Avison, D E, and Wood-Harper, A T (1990). *Multiview: An Exploration in Information Systems Development*. McGraw-Hill, Maidenhead

Avison, D E, and Wood-Harper, A T (1991). 'Information systems development research: An exploration of ideas in action.' *Computer Journal*, Vol 34, No 2

Awad, E M (1988). *Management Information Systems: Concepts, Structure and Applications*. Benjamin Cummings, Menlo Park

Barlow, J F (1991). 'Group decision-making in computer project justification.' *Journal of Systems Management*, June, pp13–16

Beeson, I (1997). 'The body in the information system.' In R L Winder, S K Probert and I A Beeson (eds) *Philosophical Aspects of Information Systems*. Taylor and Francis, London, pp215–223

Bell, S (1999) 'Rapid and participatory IS analysis and design: A means to defy the "Anatomy of Confusion"?' Paper presented at the Annual Conference of the UK Academy for Information Systems, 7–9 April, University of York, York

Bell, S (1987). 'A guide to computing systems evaluation and adoption for users in LDCs: Some problems encountered in applying standard techniques.' *Journal of Information Technology for Development*, Vol 3 (March)

Bell, S (1992). 'Self-analysis and pre-analysis: Lessons in the application of systems analysis in developing countries.' In G Cyranek and S C Bhatnagar (eds) *Technology Transfer for Development: The Prospects and Limits of Information Technology*. Tata McGraw-Hill, New Delhi

Bell, S (1994). 'Methods and mindsets: Towards an understanding of the tyranny of methodology.' School of Information Systems Research Seminar, 3 March, University of East Anglia, Norwich

Bell, S (1996). 'Approaches to participatory monitoring and evaluation in Dir District, North West Frontier Province, Pakistan.' *Systems Practice*, Vol 9, No 2, pp129–150

Bell, S (1996a). *Learning with Information Systems: Learning Cycles in Information Systems Development*. Routledge, London

Bell, S (1996b). 'Reflections on learning in information systems practice.' *The Systemist*, Vol 17, No 2, pp54–63

Bell, S (1997). 'IT training, personality type and Winnie-the-Pooh.' *The Systemist*, Vol 19, No 3, pp133–146

Bell, S (1998). 'Information systems projects in Africa: Reflections on learning.' *African Development Review*, Vol 10, No 1, pp173–189

Bell, S (1998). 'Managing and learning with logical frameworks: The case of an MIS project in China.' *Human Systems Management*, Vol 17, No 1, pp15–28

Bell, S (1999). 'Defying the anatomy of confusion in information systems development.' Paper presented at the Public Administration and Development Jubilee Conference, 'The Last Fifty Years and the Next Fifty Years: A Century of Public Administration and Development', 12–14 April, St Anne's College, University of Oxford

Bell, S (2000). 'Vulnerability and the aware IS practitioner: A reflective discourse on unfinished business.' In S Clarke and B Lehaney (eds) *Human Centered Methods in Information Systems: Current Research and Practice*. Idea Group Publishing, London

Bell, S, and Minghze, L (1995). 'MIS and systems analysis applications in China: A case study of the Research Institute for Standards and Norms.' In M Odedra-Straub (ed) *Global Information Technology and Socio-Economic Development*. Ivy League, Nashua, pp153–160

Bell, S, and Wood-Harper, A T (1988). 'Information technology adoption and less developed countries (LDCs): Towards a best fit appropriate methodology for information systems development.' Tata McGraw-Hill, Delhi

Bell, S, and Wood-Harper, A T (1998). *Rapid Information Systems Development: Systems Analysis and Systems Design in an Imperfect World. Second Edition*. McGraw-Hill, London

Benjamin, R, and Blunt, J (1992). 'Critical IT issues: The next ten years.' *Sloan Management Review*, Summer, pp7–19

Bennets, D, Wood-Harper, T, and Mills, S (2000). 'An holistic approach to the management of information systems development: A view using a soft systems approach and multiple viewpoints.' *Systemic Practice and Action Research*, Vol 13, No 2, pp189–206

Bicknell, D (1993). 'Any takers for a stretcher case?' *Computer Weekly*, London, 4 March, p14

Bicknell, D (1997). 'They're on the road to nowhere.' *Computer Weekly*, London, 3 April, p32

Biggs, S (1995). 'Contending coalitions in participatory technology development: Challenges to the new orthodoxy.' Paper presented at conference on 'The Limits of Participation', 23 March, Intermediate Technology, London

Biggs, S, and Smith, G (1995). 'Contending coalitions in agricultural research and development: Challenges for planning and management.' Paper presented at conference, 'Evaluation for a New Century', Vancouver

Bjorn Andersen, N, and Skousen, T (1984). 'User-driven systems design.' In *Participation in Change: Readings in the Introduction of New Technology*. Department of Employment and Industrial Relations, Canberra

Boud, D (1985). *Reflection: Turning Experience into Learning*. Kogan Page, London

Bowers, D (1988). *From Data to Database*. Van Nostrand Reinhold, London

Briggs Myers, I, Kirby, L, and Myers, K (1994). *Introduction to Type. Fifth Edition*. Oxford Psychologists Press, Oxford

Buckler, B (1998). *A Learning Model to Achieve Continuous Improvement and Innovation*. MCB University Press, Bradford, UK

Burgoyne, J, and Reynolds, M (1997). *Management Learning: Integrating Perspectives in Theory and Practice*. Sage, London

Burrell, G, and Morgan, G (1979). *Sociological Paradigms and Organizational Analysis*. Heinemann, London

Bush, C, and Robbins, S (1991). 'What does "MIS" really mean?' *Journal of Systems Management*, June, pp6–8

Calhoun, C, and DeLargy, P (1992). 'Computerization, aid-dependency and administrative capacity: A Sudanese case study.' In S Grant Lewis and J Samoff (eds) *Microcomputers in African Development*. Westview, Boulder

Callo, Y, and Packham, R (1997) 'Soft systems methodology: Its potential for emancipatory development.' Australia and New Zealand Systems Society Conference, Institute of Continuing and TESOL Education, University of Queensland, Brisbane, Australia

Casley, D, and Kumar, K (1988). *The Collection, Analysis and Use of Monitoring and Evaluation Data*. World Bank Publications, New York

Cats-Baril, W, and Thompson, R (1997). *Information Technology and Management*. Irwin, Chicago

CCTA (1993a). *Applying Soft Systems Methodology to an SSADM Feasibility Study*. HMSO, London

CCTA (1993b). *Prototyping in an SSADM Environment*. HMSO, London

Chambers, R (1996). 'ZOPP, PCM and PRA: Whose reality, needs and priorities count?' In R Forster (ed) *ZOPP Marries PRA? Participatory Learning and Action: A Challenge for our Services and Institutions*. Deutsche Gesellschaft für Technische Zusammenarbeit (GTZ), Eschborn, Germany

Chambers, R (1997). *Whose Reality Counts? Putting the First Last*. Intermediate Technology Publications, London

Checkland, P (1981). *Systems Thinking, Systems Practice*. Wiley, Chichester

Checkland, P (1984). 'Systems thinking in management: The development of soft systems methodology and its implications for social science.' In H Ulrich and G J B Probst (eds) *Self Organization and Management of Social Systems*. Springer-Verlag, Berlin

Checkland, P (1985). 'From optimization to learning: A development of systems thinking for the 1990s.' *Journal of the Operational Research Society*, Vol 36, No 9, pp757–767

Checkland, P (1988). 'Information systems and systems thinking: Time to unite?' *International Journal of Information Management*, Vol 8, pp239–248

Checkland, P (1994a). 'Systems theory and management thinking.' *American Behavioral Scientist*, Vol 38, No 1, pp75–83

Checkland, P (1994b). 'Varieties of systems thinking: The case of soft systems methodology.' *Systems Dynamics Review*, Vol 10, No 2–3, pp189–197

Checkland, P (1997). 'New maps of knowledge.' University of Lancaster, Lancaster

Checkland, P (2001). 'The emergent properties of SSM in use: A symposium by reflective practitioners.' *Systemic Practice and Action Research*, Vol 13, No 6, pp799–823

Checkland, P, and Holwell, S (1993). 'Information management and organizational processes: An approach through soft systems methodology.' *Journal of Information Systems*, Vol 3, pp3–16

Checkland, P, and Holwell, S (1998a). 'Action research: Its nature and validity.' *Systemic Practice and Action Research*, Vol 11, No 1, pp9–21

Checkland, P, and Holwell, S (1998b). *Information, Systems and Information Systems: Making Sense of the Field*. John Wiley & Sons, Chichester

Checkland, P, and Scholes, J (1990). *Soft Systems Methodology in Action*. John Wiley & Sons, Chichester

Chermack, T, Lynham, S, and Ruona, W (2001). 'A review of scenario planning literature.' *Futures Research Quarterly*, Vol 17, No2, pp7–31

Coleman, G (1987a). 'Logical framework approach to the monitoring and evaluation of agricultural and rural development projects.' *Project Appraisal*, Vol 2, No 4, pp251–259

Coleman, G (1987b). 'M&E and the Project Cycle.' Overseas Development Group, University of East Anglia, Norwich

Collins, T (1993). 'Lack of systems back-up causes hospital chaos.' *Computer Weekly*, London, 12 August, p2

Collins, T (1996a). 'Bank chief learns from computer failure.' *Computer Weekly*, London, 21 November, p24

Collins, T (1996b). 'GP's network buckles under huge workload.' *Computer Weekly*, London, 28 November, p1

Collins, T (1997a). 'Feast or famine?' *Computer Weekly*, London, 11 September, p18

Collins, T (1997b). 'Millions lost as DSS ends legal battle.' *Computer Weekly*, London, 12 June, p1

Collins, T (1997c). 'Systems bombs at nuclear lab.' *Computer Weekly*, Computer Weekly website

Collins, T (1997d). 'How British Gas took the blame and still managed to survive.' *Computer Weekly*, London, 20 March, p20

Collins, T (1997e). 'Why British Gas jumped out of the frying pan...' *Computer Weekly*, London, 13 March, p26

Collins, T (1998a). 'A £160 m disaster?' *Computer Weekly*, London, 2 July, p20

Collins, T (1998b). 'BBC acts on IT chaos.' *Computer Weekly*, London, 15 October, p1

Collins, T (1999). 'Lessons learnt from last passport disaster.' *Computer Weekly*, London, 8 July, p10

Commission of the European Communities Directorate General for Development Evaluation Unit (1993). *Project Cycle Management: Integrated Approach and Logical Framework*. European Community, Geneva

Computer Weekly (1998). 'Swanwick battles against IT logjam.' *Computer Weekly*, London, 25 June, p18

Cordingley, D (1995). 'Integrating the logical framework into the management of technical cooperation projects.' *Project Appraisal*, Vol 10, No 2, pp103–112

Cusworth, J, and Franks, T (1993). *Managing Projects in Developing Countries*. Longman Scientific and Technical, Harlow

Davies, L J (1989). 'Cultural aspects of intervention with soft systems methodology.' Unpublished MSc thesis, University of Lancaster, Lancaster

Davies, T (1996). 'GP link suffers network blockage.' *Computer Weekly*, London, 28 November, p4

Dennis, A, and Haley, B (2000). *Systems Analysis and Design in Action*. John Wiley & Sons, Chichester

Dervin, B (1996). 'Chaos, order and sense-making: A proposed theory for information design.' http://edfu.lis.uiuc.edu//allerton/95/s5/dervin.draft.html

Drobik, A (2000). 'E-business is not easy business.' *The Computer Bulletin*, January, pp27–29

Drummond, H (1996). 'The politics of risk: Trials and tribulations of the Taurus project.' *Journal of Information Technology*, Vol 11, pp347–357

Drummond, H (1998). '"It looked marvellous in the prospectus": Taurus, information and decision-making.' *Journal of General Management*, Vol 23, No 3, pp73–87

Dryden, W (1996). *Handbook of Individual Therapy*. Sage, London

Dykman, C, and Robbins, R (1991). 'Organizational success through effective systems analysis.' *Journal of Systems Management*, Vol 42, No 7, pp6–8

Ensworth, P (2001). *The Accidental Project Manager*. John Wiley & Sons, Chichester

Eyben, R (1995). *Reviewing Impact During Project Implementation*. ODA, London

Fellers, J (1996). 'Teaching teamwork: Exploring the use of cooperative learning teams in information systems education.' *The Database for advances in Information Systems*, Vol 27, No 2, pp44–59

Flew, A (1979). *A Dictionary of Philosophy*. Pan, London

Flood, B, Weil, S, and Romm, N (1997). 'Critical reflexivity: A multi-dimensional conversation.' Paper presented at 'Forum 2: Action Research and Critical Systems Thinking', 23–25 June, Hull

Forster, R (ed) (1996). *ZOPP Marries PRA? Participatory Learning and Action: A Challenge for Our Services and Institutions*. Deutsche Gesellschaft für Technische Zusammenarbeit (GTZ), Eschborn, Germany

Foss, R (1989). 'The organization of a fortress factory.' In R Espejo and R Harnden (eds) *The Viable Systems Model: Interpretations and Applications of Stafford Beer's VSM*. John Wiley & Sons, Chichester

Galliers, R (1987). 'An approach to information needs analysis.' In R Galliers (ed) *Information Analysis: Selected Readings*. Addison Wesley, Wokingham

Galliers, R (1990). *Choosing Appropriate Information Systems Research Approaches: A Revised Taxonomy*. North Holland, Amsterdam

Galliers, R (1992a). *Information Systems Research: Issues, Methods and Practical Guidelines*. McGraw-Hill, Maidenhead

Galliers, R (1992b). 'Choosing information systems research approaches.' In R D Galliers (ed) *Information Systems Research*. Blackwell Scientific Publications, London

Galliers, R, and Land, F (1987). 'Choosing appropriate information systems research methodologies.' *Communications of the ACM*, Vol 30, No 11

Gasper, D (1997) 'Logical frameworks: A critical look.' Development Studies Association, University of East Anglia, Norwich

Gasper, D (1999). 'Evaluating the "logical framework approach": Towards learning-orientated development evaluation.' *Public Administration and Development*, Vol 20, No 1, pp17–28

Godet, M, Monti, R, Meunier, F, and Roubelat, F (1999). 'Scenarios and strategies: A toolbox for scenario planning.' Laboratory for Investigation in Prospective and

Strategy: Toolbox, LIPS Working Papers, special issue, 2nd edition, April, available at www.cnam.fr/deg/lips/toolbox/toolbox2.html

Goebel, M, Seufert, C, and Forster, R (1996) 'Recent Developments in GTZ's Project Management Approach.' In R Forster (ed) *ZOPP Marries PRA? Participatory Learning and Action: A Challenge for Our Services and Institutions*. Deutsche Gesellschaft für Technische Zusammenarbeit (GTZ), Eschborn, Germany

Gold, J (2001). 'Storytelling systems: Managing everyday flux using mode 2 soft systems methodology.' *Systemic Practice and Action Research*, Vol 14, No 4, pp557–574

Gold, S (1997). 'Global piracy continues to skyrocket.' *Secure Computing*, June, pp5–6

Gosling, L, and Edwards, M (1995). *Assessment, Monitoring, Review and Evaluation Toolkit*, Save the Children Fund, London

Gotsch, C (1985). 'Application of microcomputers in Third World organizations'. Working Paper No 2, Food Research Institute, Standford University, USA

Green-Armytage, J (1993). 'Shake up at exchange to aid Taurus progress.' *Computer Weekly*, London

Gu, J, and Zhu, Z (2000). 'Knowing Wuli, sensing Shili, caring for Renli: Methodology of the WSR approach.' *Systemic Practice and Action Research*, Vol 13, No 1, pp11–20

Hall, R (1997). *The Cartoonist's Workbook*. A and C Black, London

Harvey, C and Harvey, S (1994). *Sun Sign, Moon Sign*. Thorsons, London

Haynes, M (1989). 'A participative application of soft systems methodology: An action research project concerned with formulating an outline design for a learning centre in ICI chemicals and polymers.' Unpublished MSc thesis, University of Lancaster

Haynes, M (1995). 'Soft systems methodology.' In K Ellis (ed) *Critical Issues in Systems Theory and Practice*. Plenum, New York, pp251–257

Heeks, R (1999). 'Information technology and the management of corruption.' *Development in Practice*, Vol 9, No 1&2, pp184–189

Heron, J (1990). *Helping the Client*. Sage, London

Heron, J (1996). *Cooperative Inquiry: Research into the Human Condition*. Sage, London

Hirschheim, R, and Smithson, S (1987). 'Information systems evaluation: Myth and reality.' In R Galliers (ed) *Information Analysis: Selected Readings*. Addison Wesley, Wokingham

Hirsh, K, and Kummerow, J (1990). *Introduction to Type in Organizations*. Oxford Psychologists Press, Oxford

Holwell, S (2001). 'Soft systems methodology: Other voices.' *Systemic Practice and Action Research*, Vol 13, No 6, pp773–798

Horney, K (1994). *Self-Analysis*. Norton, London

Hughes, B, and Cotterell, M (1999). *Software Project Management*. McGraw-Hill, Maidenhead

Hyde, A (2000). 'Failure? Who pays?' *Computer Bulletin*, July, pp26–29

IIED (1995). *A Trainers Guide for Participatory Approaches*. International Institute for Environment and Development, London

Ison, R (1993). 'Soft systems: A non-computer view of decision support.' In J Stuth and B Lyons (eds) *Decision Support Systems for the Management of Grazing Lands*. UNESCO, Paris, pp83–121

Jarvenpaa, S, and Ives, B (1991). 'Executive involvement and participation in the management of information technology.' *MIS Quarterly Review*, June

Jones, T, and King, S (1998). 'Flexible systems for changing organizations: Implementing RAD.' *European Journal of information Systems*, No 7, pp61–73

Kaivo-oja, J (2001). 'Scenario learning and potential sustainable development processes in spatial contexts: Towards risk society or ecological modernization scenarios?' *Futures Research Quarterly*, Vol 17, No 2, pp33–55

Kakabadse, N, and Kouzmin, A (1996). 'Innovation strategies for the adoption on new information technology in government: An Australian experience.' *Public Administration and Development*, No 16, pp317–330

Kaye, J (1997). 'Falling at the final hurdle.' *Computer Weekly*, London, 8 May, p44

Koh, I, and Heng, M (1996). 'Users and designers as partners: Design method and tools for user participation and design accountability within the design process.' *Information Systems Journal*, No 6, pp283–300

Kolb, D (1984). *Experiential Learning: Experience as the Source of Learning and Development*. Prentice-Hall, London

Korac-Boisvert, N, and Kouzmin, A (1995). 'Transcending soft-core IT disasters in public sector organizations.' *Information Infrastructure and Policy*, Vol 4, pp131–161

Korth, H, and Silberschantz, A (1986). *Database System Concepts*. McGraw-Hill International Editions, London

Kozar, K A (1989). *Humanized Information Systems Analysis and Design: People Building Systems For People*. McGraw-Hill, New York

Kumar, K (1993). *Rapid Appraisal Methods*. World Bank Publications, Washington DC

Land, F (1982). 'Adapting to changing user requirements.' *Information and Management*, Vol 5, pp59–75

Land, F (1987). 'Is an information theory enough?' In D E Avison (ed) *Information Systems in the 1990s: Book 1 – Concepts and Methodologies*. AFM Exploratory Series. University of New England, Armidale, New South Wales

Lavrijsen, J (1994). 'PROMES: An automated system for monitoring and evaluation.' WS Atkins Agriculture, Weijereind

Linsheng, H (1998). *Learning Organization and Computer Supported Management*. China International Engineering Consulting Corporation, Beijing

Long, N (1992). 'Research endeavours and actor struggles.' In N Long and A Long (eds) *Battlefields of Knowledge: The Interlocking of Theory and Practice in Social Research and Development*. Routledge, London

Lousberg, M, and Soler, J (1998). 'Action research and the evaluation of IT projects.' *Active Learning*, No 8, pp36–40

Lucas, A (1994). 'The impact of structural adjustment on training needs.' *International Labour Review*, Vol 133, No 5–6, pp677–694

Lucas, H C (1985). *The Analysis, Design and Implementation of Information Systems*. McGraw-Hill, New York

Lytle, R (1991). 'The PPS information system development disaster in the early 1980s'. In F Horton and D Lewis (eds) *Great Information Systems Disasters*. Aslib, London

Lyytinen, K, and Hirschheim, R (1987). 'Information systems failures: A survey and classification of the Empirical Literature.' *Oxford Surveys in Information Systems*, Vol 4, pp257–309

Macadam, R, Britton, I, and Russell, D (1990). 'The use of soft systems methodology to improve the adoption by Australian cotton growers of the Siratac computer-based crop management system.' *Agricultural Systems*, Vol 34, pp1–14

Maciaszek, L (2001). *Requirements Analysis and System Design*. Addison Wesley, London

Mack, T (2001). 'The subtle art of scenario building: An overview.' *Futures Research Quarterly*, Vol 17, No 2, pp5–6

Mansell, G (1997). 'Systems: An arcane discipline.' *Systemist*, Vol 19, No 4, pp289–293

Marshall, J, and Reason, P (1997). 'Collaborative and self-reflective forms of inquiry in management research.' In J Burgoyne and M Reynolds (eds) *Management Learning: Integrating Perspectives in Theory and Practice*. Sage, London

Martelli, A (2001). 'Scenario building and scenario planning: State of the art and prospects of evolution.' *Futures Research Quarterly*, Vol 17, No 2, pp57–74

Maslen, G (1997). 'Universities sue UK supplier.' *Times Higher Education Supplement*, London, 9 May, p33

McConnell, D (1997). 'Computer support for management learning.' In J Burgoyne and M Reynolds (eds) *Management Learning: Integrating Perspectives in Theory and Practice*. Sage, London

McPherson, S (1994). *Participatory Monitoring and Evaluation Abstracts*. Institute of Development Studies, Brighton

Mendelssohn, G (1989). 'The use of microcomputers for project planning, monitoring and evaluation.' ODI Network Papers, No 1. ODI, London

Mercer, D (2001). 'From scenarios to robust strategies: The links managers make.' *Futures Research Quarterly*, Vol 17, No 2, pp75–85

Midgely, G, and Wilby, J E (1996). 'Systems methodology: Possibilities for cross-cultural learning and integration.' In *Proceedings of a Conference held at the Institute of Systems Science, Beijing, China*. Hull

Mingers, J (2001). 'An idea ahead of its time: The history and development of soft systems methodology.' *Systemic Practice and Action Research*, Vol 13, No 6, pp733–756

Mingers, J, and Brocklesby, J (1996). 'Multimethodology: Towards a framework for critical pluralism.' *Systemist*, Vol 18, No 3, pp101–131

Mingers, J, and Stowell, F (1997). *Information Systems: an emerging discipline?* McGraw-Hill, Maidenhead

Montgomery, R, Davies, R, Saxena, N C, and Ashley, S (1995). *Guidance Materials for Improved Project Monitoring and Impact Review*. Overseas Development Administration, London

Moon, J (1999). *Reflection in Learning and Professional Development*. Kogan Page Ltd, London

Moreton, R, and Chester, M (1997). *Transforming the Business: The IT Contribution*. McGraw-Hill, London

Morgan, G (1997). *Images of Organization. New Edition*. Sage, London

Mumford, E (1981). 'Participative system design: Structure and method, systems, objectives.' *Solutions*, Vol 1, No 1, pp5–19

Mumford, E (1983). *Designing Human Systems*. Manchester Business School, Manchester

Mumford, E (1985). *Research Methods in Information Systems*. North Holland, Amsterdam

Mumford, E (1995). *Effective Requirements Analysis and Systems Design: The ETHICS Method*. Macmillan, Basingstoke

Mumford, E (1997). 'Requirements analysis for information systems: The QUICK ethics approach.' In A Stowell, R Ison and R Armson (eds) *Systems for Sustainability: People, Organizations and Environments*. Plenum, London, pp15–20

Mumford, E, and Weir, M (1979). *Computer Systems in Work Design: The ETHICS Method*. Associated Business Press, Manchester

Munro, I, and Mingers, J (2000). 'The use of multimethodology in practice: Results of a survey of practitioners.' University of Warwick, Warwick

Murphy, J, and Sprey, L (1982). 'Monitoring and evaluation of agricultural change.' ILRI Publication, No 32. University of Wageningen, Wageningen

Myers, K, and Kirby, L (1994). *Introduction to Type: Dynamics and Development*. Oxford Psychologists Press, Oxford

Naughton, J (2000). *A Brief History of the Future: From Radio Days to Internet Years in a Lifetime*. Overlook Press, New York

Open University (1987). *T301 – Complexity Management and Change: A Systems Approach*. Open University Systems Group (ed). The Open University Press, Milton Keynes

Open University (2000). *T306 – Managing Complexity: A Systems Approach*. Open University, Milton Keynes

Orchard, A (1972). 'The methodology of general systems theory.' *General Systems Theory Yearbook*

Orna, E (1999). *Practical Information Policies. Second Edition*. Gower, London

Orna, E, and Stevens, G (1995). *Managing Information for Research*. Open University Press, Buckingham

Oz, E (1993). *Ethics for the Information Age*. McGraw-Hill, London

Panos (1995). *The Internet and the South: Superhighway or Dirt Track?* Panos Institute, London

Patton, M (1980). *Qualitative Evaluation Methods*. Sage, San Francisco

Paucar-Caceres, A (1998). 'Systems thinking: East and West.' *Systemist*, Vol 20, No 2, pp98–105

Pickles, T (1995). *Tool Kit for Trainers*, Gower, London

Probert, S (1997). 'The metaphysical assumptions of the (main) soft systems methodology advocates.' In R L Winder, S K Probert and I A Beeson (eds) *Philosophical Aspects of Information Systems*. Taylor and Francis, London, pp131–151

Probert, S (1998). 'A critical analysis of soft systems methodology and its (theoretical and practical) relationship with phenomenology.' *Systemist*, No 21, pp187–207

Quan, J (1995). 'Process monitoring and documentation.' *The Potential for Process Monitoring in Project Management and Organizational Change*. ODI, London

Qureshi, Z (1997). 'Yes, we got the web. Now what, an internet strategy? Time for a long hard look at IT.' International Cooperative and Mutual Insurance Federation, Altrincham, p12

Rajakutty, S (1991). 'Peoples participation in monitoring and evaluation of rural development programs: concepts and approaches.' *Journal of Rural Development (India)*, Vol 10, No 1, pp35–53

Reason, P (1994). *Participation in Human Inquiry*, Sage, London

Reason, P, and Heron, J (1995). 'Cooperative inquiry.' In R Harre, J Smith, and L Van Langenhove (eds) *Rethinking Methods in Psychology*. Sage, London

Redmill, F (1999). 'Why systems go up in smoke.' *The Computer Bulletin*, September, pp26–28

Richards, H (undated). *The Evaluation of Cultural Action*. Macmillan, London

Rossi, P, and Freeman, H (1985). *Evaluation: a systematic approach*. Sage, San Francisco

Russell, D (1986). 'How we see the world determines what we do in the world: Preparing the ground for action research.' University of Western Sydney, Hawkesbury

Saran, C (1998). 'Getting your information to do all the hard work.' *Computer Weekly*, London, 25 June, p56

Sauer, C (1993). *Why Information Systems Fail: A Case Study Approach*. Alfred Waller, London

Savage, C (1996). *5th Generation Management*. Butterworth Heinemann, Boston

Schneider, K (1997). 'Bug delays £25m court case system.' *Computer Weekly*, London, 20 February, p1

Secure Computing (1997). 'Cyber terrorism.' *Secure Computing*, July, pp21–27

Senge, P, Ross, R, Smith, B, Roberts, C, and Kleiner, A (1994). *The Fifth Discipline Fieldbook: Strategies and Tools for Building a Learning Organization*. Nicholas Brealey, London

Senoh, K (1990). 'Information generating and editing methodologies: SSM and KJ methodology.' *Journal of Applied Systems Analysis*, Vol 17, pp53–61

Smith, A (1997). *Human Computer Factors: A Study of Users and Information Systems*. McGraw-Hill, Maidenhead

Smith, I (1998). 'A new mould for IT projects.' *The Computer Bulletin*, January, pp14–15

Smith, S (1996). 'Outsourcing: Better out than in?' *Computer Weekly*, London, 23 May

Stowell, F A, Holland, P, Muller, P, and Prior, R (1990). 'Applications of SSM in information system design: Some reflections.' *Journal of Applied Systems Analysis*, Vol 17, pp63–69

Stowell, F, Ison, R, Armson, R, Holloway, J, Jackson, S, and McRobb, S (eds) (1997a). *Systems for Sustainability: People, Organizations and Environments*. Plenum, New York

Stowell, F, West, D, and Stansfield, M (1997b). 'Action research as a framework for IS research.' In J Mingers and F Stowell (eds) *Information Systems: An Emerging Discipline?* McGraw-Hill, Maidenhead

Tagg, C, and Brown, J (1989). 'TBSD: Notes on an evolving methodology.' Hatfield Polytechnic, Hatfield

Taylor, A (2000). 'IT projects: Sink or swim.' *The Computer Bulletin*, pp24–26

Theis, J (1994). 'Review of monitoring systems.' London

Thompson, J (1995). 'User involvement in mental health services: The limits of consumerism, the risks of marginalization and the need for a critical approach.' Research Memorandum No 8. Centre for Systems Studies, University of Hull, Hull

Thompson, M, and Chudoba, R (1994). *Case Study Municipal and Regional Planning in Northern Bohemia, Czech Republic: A Participatory Approach.* World Bank Report. Washington DC

Tozer, E (1996). *Strategic IS/IT Planning*. Butterworth Heinemann, Boston

Valle, A (1999). 'Managing complexity through methodic participation: The case of air quality in Santiago, Chile.' *Systemic Practice and Action Research*, Vol 12, No 4, pp367–380

Vowler, J (1997). 'Guardian tracks data with guide.' *Computer Weekly*, London, p34

Vowler, J (1997a). 'The heart of the matter.' *Computer Weekly*, London, 8 May, p18

Vowler, J (1997b). 'How to avoid being a disaster area.' *Computer Weekly*, London, 27 March, p34

Wainright-Martin, E, Hoffer, J, DeHayes, D, and Perkins, W (1994). *Managing Information Technology: What Managers Need to Know*. Macmillan, New York

Warmington, A (1980). 'Action research: Its methods and its implications.' *Journal of Applied Systems Analysis*, Vol 7, pp23–39

Weaver, P, Lambrou, N, and Walkley, M (1998). *Practical SSADM Version 4+*. Prentice Hall, London

Weill, S (1997). 'Struggles with ourselves as researchers.' Paper presented at 'Forum 2: Action Research and Critical Systems Thinking', 23–25 June, Hull

White, L (1997). 'Going nowhere slowly.' *Computer Weekly*, Computer Weekly website

Willcocks, L, and Mason, D (1987). *Computerizing Work*. Paradigm, London

Wilsdon, J (ed) (2001). *Digital Futures: Living in a Dot-com World*. Earthscan, London

Wood-Harper, A T (1988). 'Characteristics of information systems definition approaches.' School of Information Systems, University of East Anglia, Norwich

Wood-Harper, A T (1989). 'Role of methodologies in information systems development.'

Wood-Harper, A T (1990). 'Comparison of information systems approaches: An action-research, Multiview perspective.' University of East Anglia, Norwich

Wood-Harper, A T and Corder, S W (1988). 'Information resource management: Towards a web based methodology for end user computing.' *Journal of Applied Systems Analysis*, Vol 15, pp83–99

Yeoman, I, Peters, S, Lehaney, B, and Clarke, S (1996). 'Effective group knowledge elicitation through problem structuring methodologies.' *Systemist*, Vol 17, No 2, pp79–91

Zhu, Z (1998). 'Confucius and Lao Tzu: Are their teachings relevant to information systems development?' *Systemist*, Vol 20, pp271–283

Zhu, Z (1998). 'Conscious mind, forgetting mind: Two approaches in multimethodology.' *Systemic Practice and Action Research*, Vol 11, No 6, pp669–690

Zhu, Z (1999a). 'Integrating ontology, epistemology and methodology in IS design: The WSR case.' Lincoln School of Management, Lincoln

Zhu, Z (1999b). 'Towards synergy in search for multi-perspective systems approaches.' In A Castell, A Gregory, G Hindle, M James and G Ragsdell (eds) *Synergy Matters: Working with Systems in the 21st Century*. Kluwer Academic/Plenum Publishers, Dordrecht, pp475–480

INDEX

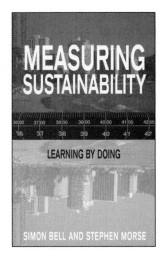

SUSTAINABILITY INDICATORS
Measuring the Immeasurable
Simon Bell and Stephen Morse

'Sustainability indicators, the barometer of sustainable development (a new doctrine for the new millennium) are explored from reductionist roots to a systemic approach. This book tells me, as an SI "practitioner", where I have been and why and, more importantly, how I should be thinking in order to effectively present to and empower the local community in the years ahead'

DAVID ELLIS, Principal Pollution Monitoring Officer, Norwich City Council

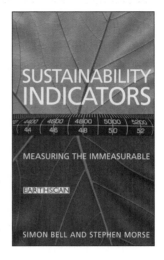

'A valuable contribution to the theory and practice of using indicators for sustainability. It introduces systems ideas and a range of tools and techniques that have the potential to broaden and deepen our understandings of a whole range of complex situations. Well worth a closer look'

CHRISTINE BLACKMORE, Systems Lecturer, Open University, Milton Keynes

Sustainability Indicators addresses the crucial issue of sustainability: how can it be measured. The authors review the development and value of such sustainability indicators. In contrast to the current trends in developing sustainability indicators, the authors discuss the advantages of taking a holistic and more qualitative approach, rather than focusing on strictly quantitative measures which may be inappropriate. Building on practices such as the sustainable cities initiative, they describe a systematic approach to sustainability indicator development, and conclude by developing a series of questions for future development.

Practical and concise, this is essential reading and excellent course material for students, researchers and practitioners in all the social and natural sciences contributing to sustainability.

Paperback £14.95 1-85383-498-X • Hardback £40.00 1-85383-497-1

To order
www.earthscan.co.uk
Earthscan Freepost • 120 Pentonville Rd, London, N1 9JN, UK
Fax +44 (0)20 7278 1142 • Email earthinfo@earthscan.co.uk

INSTALLING ENVIRONMENTAL MANAGEMENT SYSTEMS
A Step-by-Step Guide
Christopher Sheldon and Mark Yoxon

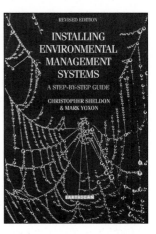

'Everything you could possibly want to know about corporate environmental management'

SUPPLY MANAGEMENT

'A comprehensive analysis of the role of business in safeguarding the environment'

INDUSTRY AND ENVIRONMENT

'A user-friendly, "teach yourself how" manual'

GREEN FUTURES

'A plain language, practical handbook for corporate executives and project managers'

INSTITUTE OF ENVIRONMENTAL MANAGEMENT AND ASSESSMENT (IEMA)

This authoritative guide to the implementation of effective environmental management systems describes how such a system can be used to prioritize actions and resources, increase efficiency, minimize costs and lead to better, more informed decision-making. In easy-to-follow steps, it divides the implementation process into setting up, planning, doing, checking and acting.

Drawing on extensive hands-on experience, the authors cover issues of commitment, effective communication, training and awareness, efficient documentation and improved operational controls. They explain the importance of carrying out an initial environmental review, identifying cause and effect, understanding legislative and regulatory issues, developing a policy and defining objectives and targets. They describe how to design an effective environmental management programme and implement a successful audit and review.

Full of practical examples and insider tips, *Installing Environmental Management Systems* is the standard manual for managers and consultants at all levels.

Paperback £29.95 1-85383-868-3

To order
www.earthscan.co.uk
Earthscan Freepost • 120 Pentonville Rd, London, N1 9JN, UK
Fax +44 (0)20 7278 1142 • Email earthinfo@earthscan.co.uk

THE GREEN OFFICE MANUAL
A Guide to Responsible Practice
Wastebusters Ltd

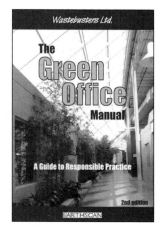

'The Manual will enable you to structure your own environmental office programme'

*INDUSTRIAL ENVIRONMENTAL MANAGEMENT*

'A business can't manage what it doesn't measure. This is a welcome update of The Green Office Manual, *with a comprehensive new chapter on environmental reporting. I recommend the advice it offers to all office based companies and encourage them to take advantage of the opportunities to make their office more resource efficient, more competitive and more sustainable in the long term'*

CAROLINE SMITH, Environment, Business and Consumers Division, Department of the Environment, Transport and the Regions

'A practical and common-sense approach to the environmental issues that face ordinary businesses in a service industry. This is a comprehensive point of reference covering the numerous environmental impacts, the applicable guidelines, those who can assist, the experience of those who have tried and solutions and templates for those who are still trying. I have found the book to be invaluable'

MARK RADCLIFFE, Company Secretary, Reed Elsevier Plc

'A cornucopia of great contacts and great ideas for ensuring that actions are practical and really work – as useful at home as at work'

SARA PARKIN, Programme Director, Forum for the Future

'A useful guide to establishing responsible practices that are both workable and cost effective. It clearly demonstrates that sound environmental practice makes good business sense'

PAUL DE JONG, Environmental Policy Officer, National Grid Company plc

This jargon-free guide to greener working practice highlights the opportunities for achieving cost savings with environmental improvements. It sets out effective, simple mechanisms to encourage participation and commitment from staff and suppliers. Suitable for businesses of all sizes, it offers clear and reliable independent information and provides details of useful organizations.

Paperback £40.00 1-85383-679-6

To order
www.earthscan.co.uk
Earthscan Freepost • 120 Pentonville Rd, London, N1 9JN, UK
Fax +44 (0)20 7278 1142 • Email earthinfo@earthscan.co.uk